Winning the Peace

The Regional Commissioner, Henry Vaughan Berry (left), shakes hands with the *Bürgermeister* (mayor) of Hamburg, Max Brauer, symbolizing post-war cooperation between British and German officials and administrators in occupied Germany. Brauer spent the war in exile in the United States. Photo courtesy of Kate Owen.

Winning the Peace

The British in Occupied Germany, 1945–1948

Christopher Knowles

BLOOMSBURY ACADEMIC
LONDON • NEW YORK • OXFORD • NEW DELHI • SYDNEY

BLOOMSBURY ACADEMIC
Bloomsbury Publishing Plc
50 Bedford Square, London, WC1B 3DP, UK
1385 Broadway, New York, NY 10018, USA

BLOOMSBURY, BLOOMSBURY ACADEMIC and the Diana logo are
trademarks of Bloomsbury Publishing Plc

First published in Great Britain 2017
Paperback edition first published 2018

A catalogue record for this book is available from the British Library.

ISBN: HB: 978-1-4742-6743-4
PB: 978-1-3501-0187-6
ePDF: 978-1-4742-6745-8
ePub: 978-1-4742-6744-1

Names: Knowles, Christopher (Historian), author.
Title: Winning the peace : the British in occupied Germany, 1945-1948 /
Christopher Knowles.
Description: London ; New York : Bloomsbury Academic, 2017. | Includes
bibliographical references and index.
Identifiers: LCCN 2016029665| ISBN 9781474267434 (hardback) | ISBN
9781474267441 (epub)Subjects: LCSH: Germany–History–1945-1955. |
British–Germany–History–20th century. | Reconstruction
(1939-1951)–Germany. | World War, 1939-1945–Peace. | Military
government–Germany–History–20th century. | Great Britain–Armed
Forces–Germany–History–20th century. | BISAC: HISTORY / Military /
World War II. | HISTORY / Europe / Great Britain.
Classification: LCC DD257 .K54 2017 | DDC 943.087/4–dc23 LC record available
at https://lccn.loc.gov/2016029665

Typeset by Integra Software Services Pvt. Ltd.

To my parents
Charles Ingram and Rose Marie Knowles

Contents

List of Illustrations

Acknowledgements

Many people, too numerous to mention all by name, have helped me at various stages of my research and writing the book. I would like to thank my fellow doctoral students at the Institute of Contemporary British History at Kings College London, especially Kath Sherit and Mary Salinsky, who read and commented on draft chapters. I would like to thank the late Sir Michael Palliser and Jan Thexton for agreeing to be interviewed, and Michael Howard for giving me a signed copy of his memoir *Otherwise Occupied* and for answering various questions on his life and work in occupied Germany. Renate Greenshields shared her memories of what it was like to be one of the first German war brides in Britain and introduced me to the family of Henry Vaughan Berry. Professor George Bain kindly gave me his permission to research the papers of Allan Flanders at the Modern Records Centre, Warwick. Sisters, sons, daughters, nephews, nieces and friends of other individuals I have researched have been generous in sharing family memories, including Martin and Mike Albu, Nick Chaloner, Joan Woodward, the late Leila Ingrams, Catharine Campbell, Jay Blumler, Rene Saran and Kate Owen, who lent me copies of personal letters from her uncle, Vaughan Berry, and kindly gave permission to use photos from a family album as illustrations in the book. Ray Partridge sent me copies of the photos Jan Thexton and his wife exchanged with each other in 1945. Librarians and archivists who have been especially helpful include Sarah Paterson at the Imperial War Museum, Andrew Riley at Churchill Archives Centre, Ed Weech at the Royal Asiatic Society and Heinz Egleder, Hauke Janssen and Sylvia Reiß at *Der Spiegel*. I owe a great debt of gratitude to my supervisors Professors Pat Thane and Bernd Weisbrod, who have encouraged me to think carefully about all aspects of my research. Lastly without the help and support of my wife, Mary Anne, and children, Emily and Jack, I could never have started on the project of studying for a PhD, completed the thesis or written this book.

List of Abbreviations

ALG	Administration and Local Government branch of CCG (BE)
CCG (BE)	Control Commission for Germany (British Element)
CIGS	Chief of the Imperial General Staff
COGA	Control Office for Germany and Austria
DP	Displaced Person(s)
FO	Foreign Office
IAC	Internal Affairs and Communication division of CCG (BE)
ISK	'Internationaler Sozialistischer Kampfbund' (An international socialist group)
IWM	Imperial War Museum
IWM SA	Imperial War Museum Sound Archive
PR/ISC	Public Relations and Information Services Control division of CCG (BE)
PID	Political Intelligence Department
PWD	Psychological Warfare Division of SHAEF
PWE	Political Warfare Executive
SHAEF	Supreme Headquarters Allied Expeditionary Force
SPD	Social Democratic Party of Germany

1

Introduction

In a personal message to his troops issued on Victory in Europe (VE) Day, 8 May 1945, Field Marshal Montgomery, the Commander-in-Chief of British forces in Germany, wrote: 'We have won the German war. Let us now win the peace.'[1] The same message was repeated many times in the months that followed,[2] but what Montgomery and his British colleagues meant by 'winning the peace' changed over time and was never entirely clear.[3] British policy towards Germany in the first three years after the war is full of apparent contradictions: limitations on industrial growth imposed at the same time as measures to promote economic reconstruction, pragmatism combined with idealism, occupiers and occupied living separate lives in parallel worlds coexisting with examples of intense personal engagement. Whether examining the economic, political, social or cultural aspects of the occupation, these contradictions make it difficult to identify coherent British policies in occupied Germany, compare British ruling strategies to those of the other Allies or assess the legacy of the British occupation.

At the end of the Second World War Germany was divided into four zones of occupation by the victorious Allies: the United States, Britain, the Soviet Union and France. This book is based on a detailed study of twelve people who worked in the British Zone during the first three years after the end of the Second World War. It explores what they aimed to achieve, and why, and how their aims and perceptions changed over time. Collectively these twelve individuals represent the British 'governing elite' in occupied Germany, including some of its internal differences. Through examining their motivation, aims and achievements, and also the limitations and constraints on their scope for action, the book explains why their understanding of what was required to 'win the peace' changed after the end of the war: from the 'Four D's' agreed by Britain, the United States and the Soviet Union at the Potsdam conference in July and August 1945 – De-militarization, De-nazification, De-industrialization and Democratization[4] – to a more positive policy that I have described as the 'Three R's' – physical and economic Reconstruction, political Renewal and personal Reconciliation.

The time period covered is from the end of the war in Europe in May 1945 to currency reform and the start of the Berlin airlift in May and June 1948. Allied troops first entered Germany at the end of 1944 and planning for the occupation started much earlier, so there is occasional reference to these earlier phases of the occupation. Some policies took time to play out and reference is also made to later events and outcomes where this appears relevant. The focus of the book, however, is on the first three years, when British military officers and civilian officials made a rapid adjustment from occupation policies devised during the war to those they considered appropriate for peace.

The book is divided into three parts, each addressing one of three groups of four individuals. Although there is considerable overlap, there is also a general chronological and thematic progression. The first part explains why those at the top of Military Government initiated a policy of reconstruction soon after the start of the occupation and how this developed over the first two years. The second part examines different approaches to achieving political renewal over the three years from May 1945 to May 1948. The third part assesses the motivation of a group of younger and more junior officers, examines whether they shared the aims of their seniors and discusses how personal relationships, between the British occupiers and German individuals they met through their work or leisure activities, contributed to reconciliation between former enemies. In the final chapter I have brought together common themes and drawn conclusions that apply to the book as a whole.

Scope and purpose

The brief period after the end of the war, when the British occupied and ruled a large part of north-western Germany, with a population of over 20 million,[5] lies at the intersection of the national histories of Britain and of Germany. It also forms a pivot point between two contrasting periods in European history, described by Eric Hobsbawm in *The Age of Extremes* as 'The Age of Catastrophe', before and during the Second World War, and 'The Golden Age' afterwards.[6] Historians of modern Germany have generally treated the period of Allied occupation as an 'interregnum' after the 'collapse' of the Nazi government, forming part of the pre-history of the Federal Republic (BRD) in the West and the German Democratic Republic (DDR) in the East, leading to liberalization, democratization and eventual reunification in 1990.[7] Alternatively, they have emphasized continuities with the Nazi past and the legacies of dictatorship, war, death, destruction and the Holocaust, which left their 'long shadows' over the subsequent history of Germany.[8] When considered from a British rather than a German, 'Allied' or 'Anglo-American' perspective, the occupation also forms part of the history of British engagement overseas, as a great power in Europe and as global empire builders and administrators.[9] This book contributes to all three approaches. It clarifies the motivation and intentions of the British governing elite in occupied Germany, while analysing their reactions to the Nazi past, the Holocaust, and the death and destruction they found when they first arrived in Germany. It challenges narratives of 'Westernization' or 'Americanization', which focus on the role of the United States to the virtual exclusion of the other Western Allies, and suggests that the British contribution to post-war reconstruction and political renewal in Germany, and to personal reconciliation between former enemies, was distinctive and needs to be reassessed.

The first histories of the British occupation were written by officers who were there at the time or with their close cooperation, notably Michael Balfour and John Mair, *Four Power Control in Germany and Austria 1945–1946*, published in 1956, and the relevant volume of the official history of the war by Frank Donnison, *Civil Affairs and Military Government. North-West Europe 1944–1946*, published in 1961.[10] Subsequent historical studies concentrated on the political context, international relations and the emergence of the Cold War.[11] Issues such as whether the division of Germany was inevitable and when the 'Turning Point' in British policy towards Germany occurred continued to be debated well into the 1990s.[12] Many generals and senior administrators in Germany published their memoirs or were the subject of biographies.[13] Most of the early studies shared a positive view of the occupation, the creation of a Western, anti-communist alliance, and the British contribution to the 'miracle' of a stable and prosperous West Germany.[14]

In contrast to self-congratulatory accounts by British generals and officials, many historians in the 1970s and 1980s portrayed the British as incompetent, as ineffective or as hindering German attempts to reform the structure of government and society, echoing earlier criticism in both the British and German press.[15] British planning for the occupation had been 'haunted by the past'.[16] The British Zone of occupation in 1945–6 was 'a badly managed disaster area'.[17] Radical German historians reflected contemporary left-wing concerns that West German society remained authoritarian and repressive and had never been properly democratized, liberalized or modernized. They argued, in a debate over *Neuanfang oder Restauration* (New Start or Restoration), that the end of the war and the 'collapse' of May 1945 were not a definitive break with the past, as suggested by the idea of *Stunde Null* (Zero Hour), but the precursor to a conservative restoration, aided and abetted by the Allies, in which many elements of Weimar and Nazi Germany reappeared in the Federal Republic of the Adenauer era.[18]

The role of the British occupiers in the immediate post-war period was further marginalized in the debate on whether the 'Americanization' of German industry, culture and society was to be welcomed, as helping to promote liberal democracy and the social market economy, or deplored, signifying a decline in quality and standards and the 'Coca-colonization' of German society.[19] When US and German historians referred to 'Allied' policies or attitudes, the British contribution was assumed to be identical to the American, or insignificant, in view of increasing US dominance throughout Europe in all spheres of human activity: political, economic, social and cultural.[20] As one historian commented, writing in 1997:

> Only recently has research begun to depart from the German perspective that focused on unsuccessful and destructive British policies and that characterized British policy as hypocritical and myopic, even though British policy was quite insignificant, given the dominant position of the United States.[21]

Following the trend towards social and cultural history, historians of post-war Germany found evidence of social and cultural continuities, which spanned the occupation period and the great political and economic divide of 1945.[22] Interest in identifying any distinctive legacy from the British occupation diminished further, as they discovered that, despite being subject to a political and economic settlement imposed upon them and to geopolitical forces outside their control, 'in the 1950s West Germans made their own history and created themselves'.[23]

In the 1980s and 1990s, after official British documents became available for study in accordance with the thirty-year rule, historians produced monographs and articles on various aspects of the British occupation, including economic development, industrial policy, de-nazification, re-education, food and rationing, and case studies of specific geographical areas.[24] British aims in occupied Germany were described as the restoration of peace and the preservation of Britain's status as a great power,[25] economic security and economic reconstruction,[26] the restoration of conditions of economic stability,[27] political re-education,[28] the promotion of British democracy,[29] and the propagation of the British 'way of life' or 'spreading our creed'.[30] Although these descriptions are valid as broad generalizations, there has been little attempt to explain how conflicting aims were reconciled, how they evolved over time, or the motivation of key individuals responsible for the formation and implementation of policy. Whereas consolidated histories of the United States, Soviet and French Zones are available,[31] there is still no single volume history of the British Zone which links these various threads together and places the activities of the British in Germany in the context of the post-war national histories of Germany and Britain.[32]

This book is not a history of the occupation; some significant aspects have been covered briefly or not at all, such as de-nazification, restitution and reparations, economic policies, education and religious affairs. It focuses on the transition from war to peace. Through examining the aims and intentions of a diverse group of individuals who were important and influential in different ways, it addresses questions of motivation and agency, to explain why many British officers and civilian administrators devoted so much time and energy to the reconstruction of their former enemy. In so doing, it aims to unravel some of the apparent contradictions in British policies and contribute to a re-evaluation of the part played by the British occupiers in the transition from twelve years of Nazi dictatorship to the formation of the Federal Republic of Germany in 1949, and post-war democracy, peace and prosperity in Germany, Britain and Western Europe.

A biographical approach

In my research, I adopted a biographical approach, following twelve individuals through the archives, to gather as much information as possible on each from a variety of sources.[33] A biographical approach enables us to examine subjective factors, such as how an individual's previous experience of the occupation of the Rhineland after the First World War or the administration of the British Empire influenced their later actions. I have termed these personal influences the 'mental baggage' the British occupiers brought with them to Germany, by which I mean their family background, education, social status, previous experience at work, networks of friends and colleagues and religious, political and moral beliefs. Implicit assumptions shared with colleagues and personal prejudices, values and beliefs do not emerge easily from studies based on official documents or from statistical surveys, but were an important factor influencing policy and actions at a time when official directives appeared to be out of date, or inappropriate for the circumstances they found on the ground.

'Following the people' offered a more effective research methodology for discovering patterns and trends over the course of the occupation than examining policies, which may not have been implemented, or institutional structures, which changed rapidly as responsibility for the various aspects of government was transferred from the occupation authorities to newly established German administrations. In addition to exploring subjective issues, a biographical approach can reveal aspects of the wider historical context, as individuals were affected by and responded to circumstances beyond their control. Biographical methods, modified to place the subjects firmly within their historical context, seemed appropriate for a book on what British people aimed to achieve in occupied Germany, and why, and how this changed over time, and preferable to a thematic or chronological approach to a relatively short period of occupation, when there were no established economic or political structures and the future appeared uncertain.

The twelve individuals discussed in the book were selected because they formed part of the British 'governing elite', with authority, power and influence at different levels in the hierarchy. They also reflected some of the diversity of background and opinion among British people in occupied Germany. All could be considered part of the British professional middle classes, by family background, education and employment, and all except one attended private rather than state-funded schools.[34] All were based in Germany and held an official position with officer status (or civilian equivalent) in the British armed services or Control Commission for at least one year during the period from May 1945 to May 1948.

The first group of four comprises those with the highest level of authority, power and influence: the three Military Governors of the British Zone, Field Marshal Bernard Montgomery, Marshal of the Royal Air Force Sholto Douglas and General Brian Robertson, together with one of their senior generals, Alec Bishop, who held a position at the top of Military Government for an extended period of five years and was also highly influential. Douglas was the exception among the three Military Governors. His more pragmatic approach is contrasted with the idealism of the other three and represents a second, subsidiary strand among those at the top of the military hierarchy.

The second group of individuals discussed in the book comprises four civilian diplomats and administrators who had responsibility, in different ways, for promoting democracy in Germany. Although the army generals remained highly influential throughout the occupation, civilians were appointed to senior positions as Regional Commissioners and departmental heads in the Control Commission, the body responsible for the administration of the British Zone.[35] The Control Commission was nominally a civilian body, performing a similar role to the civil service in Britain, but many of its staff had served in the armed forces during the war and continued to use their military titles and ranks. The Military Governor was head of the Control Commission and Commander-in-Chief of the armed services, and the term 'Military Government' was used to describe the British administration in occupied Germany generally, including both the armed services and the Control Commission.

Although there was therefore no clear distinction between military and civilian roles, civilians brought a different set of experiences, attitudes and preconceptions to their task in Germany. Harold Ingrams was a professional diplomat and colonial administrator with responsibility, as head of the Administration and Local Government branch of the Control Commission, for restoring democracy at local level within the British Zone. Austen Albu and Allan Flanders were committed international socialists, appointed by John Hynd, the minister for Germany, to senior positions in the Control Commission's Political Division. Vaughan Berry, a former businessman and active Labour Party supporter, was one of four Regional Commissioners who, in May 1946, replaced the army Corps Commanders as the most senior representatives of Military Government at regional level. Studying these four civilian administrators demonstrates some of the diversity of aims within one policy area, governmental organization and the promotion of democracy. Officials in other Control Commission divisions attempted, in similarly diverse ways and with mixed success, to revive the economy, reform the police, control print and broadcast media, or restore the education system, purged of its Nazi elements.

In order to assess whether younger officers, lower down the ranks, shared the aims of those at the top of the Military Government, the third group comprises four young officers responsible for the implementation of policy. They therefore represent the opposite end of the spectrum from the Military Governors on criteria of age and influence, and could be considered a younger 'generation' with no adult experience but war, in contrast with the older 'generation' of Military Governors and army generals and the very diverse group of civilian administrators. Two of the four 'young officers', John Chaloner and Michael Howard, held responsible positions with considerable freedom of action and were influential in their own right. This was not atypical. Many other junior officers were given positions of great responsibility, were given freedom to act on their own initiative and were highly influential in their own areas.[36]

The other two young officers were selected in order to explore the subjective experiences of British people in occupied Germany in more depth. Both were the subject of oral history interviews I conducted for this study. Jan Thexton approached the Centre for Contemporary British History at the University of London in September 2007, asking if it would be possible to record his life history. His role changed completely during the years he worked in Germany, from removing war plants and equipment as reparations in 1946–7, to assisting British manufacturers sell weapons to the newly formed West German armed services in the 1950s. He met and married his wife in Germany. Sir Michael Palliser agreed to be interviewed after I met him in September 2009 at a Witness Seminar organized by the Allied Museum of Berlin, at which he spoke of his experiences as a young officer in the city.[37] His role at the time was that of an ordinary and, by his own account, typical junior officer. He therefore acts as a counterweight to the more exceptional experiences of the other three in this group. Palliser subsequently had a distinguished career in the Foreign Office, where he played a significant role in negotiating British applications to join the European Community under both Conservative and Labour governments.

Sources used

A wide range of sources has been used including memoirs and autobiographies (some published, some unpublished), official documents in the public archives, contemporary publications such as the *British Zone Review*, the official journal of Military Government, personal papers and oral history interviews. Subjective accounts have been placed in their historical context in order to understand individuals' perceptions, motivations and personal interests, together with the limitations and constraints on their scope for action.

For the first two groups, the Military Governors and army generals, and civilian administrators, contemporary written materials in the National Archives and collections of personal papers comprise the principal sources used. Wherever possible, later personal accounts were validated through reference to contemporary sources. There is an abundance of contemporary written material in the archives. Although files are often fragmentary, poorly indexed and, in the case of personal papers, sometimes unsigned and undated, I was able to find many documents which provided direct evidence of individuals' aims and intentions, as expressed at the time in different contexts.

The post-war period and the occupation of Germany are now on the edge of living memory. In the case of the third group, four young men with no adult experience but war, relatively few contemporary written sources are available in the public archives. There is, however, a substantial body of oral history evidence to draw on. Interviews I conducted comprise the principal sources for Palliser and Thexton, both of whom have since, sadly, died.[38] Interviews conducted by others were used as sources for Howard and Chaloner, together with later written accounts and, in the case of Chaloner, documents from the private archive of the German news magazine *Der Spiegel*, in Hamburg.[39] The four selected young officers were not necessarily typical of a fairly large and diverse group so, to compensate for any bias arising from a relatively small sample, research findings were validated through reference to interviews with a further twenty young men and one woman who worked in occupied Germany, undertaken by the Imperial War Museum (IWM) Sound Archive.[40] The views expressed by the IWM interviewees were consistent with those of the four principal individuals in this group and have been cited as evidence where appropriate.

As Paul Thompson has noted, lapses in memory and confusion over specific events are not uncommon in personal memoirs and oral history interviews, especially among elderly people, whose memories are usually better at recalling recurrent events, atmosphere and characters than specific details of past events.[41] Nevertheless, despite well-documented concerns regarding the fallibility of memory,[42] by cross-referencing individual accounts with one another and with contemporary records, it was possible to form a judgement as to their accuracy and reliability. As expected in a study of twelve individuals with great differences of age, personal background, previous experience, official responsibilities and political views, attitudes were diverse, but there was little evidence of any significant distortion, concealment or gaps in the evidence collected.

Mary Fulbrook has argued that 'subjective perceptions and self-representations themselves form a crucial part of history'.[43] The overall impression I gained from reading many different personal accounts of the occupation and checking these against contemporary written sources, wherever possible, was that the individuals' interpretation of this period in their lives was created while they were in Germany or soon after they left, and remained largely unchanged since.[44] It was seen as an exceptional time, in some cases a formative influence on the rest of their lives, but also a neglected period, not well understood by those who were not there in person. Overshadowed by the war, their experiences 'winning the peace' deserve greater prominence. The immediate post-war period 'laid the foundations of the modern world'.[45]

Part One

Physical Reconstruction: The Military Governors and Army Generals

2

Creating Order Out of Chaos

In his memoirs, Field Marshal Bernard Montgomery described the situation in the British Zone of Germany after the unconditional surrender on VE Day, 8 May 1945, as follows:

> The immediate problem that now faced us was terrific. We had in our area nearly one and a half million German prisoners of war. There were a further one million German wounded, without medical supplies, and in particular with a shortage of bandages and no anaesthetics. In addition, there were about one million civilian refugees who had fled into our area from the advancing Russians; these and 'Displaced Persons' were roaming about the country, often looting as they went. Transportation and communication services had ceased to function. Agriculture and industry were largely at a standstill. Food was scarce and there was a serious risk of famine and disease during the coming months. And to crown it all there was no central government in being, and the machinery whereby a central government could function no longer existed.
>
> Here was a pretty pickle.
>
> I was a soldier and I had not been trained to handle anything of this nature. However, something had to be done, and done quickly.[1]

Montgomery flew to London on 14 May to meet the Prime Minister, Winston Churchill, and argue the case for urgent action. His appointment as Military Governor, Commander-in-Chief of the British armed forces in Germany and head of the Control Commission was confirmed on 22 May.[2] The next day he told Control Commission staff in London, who had been preparing over the past year for the occupation of Germany: 'Between us we have to re-establish civil control, and to govern, a country which we have conquered and which has become sadly battered in the process.'[3] His official biographer, Nigel Hamilton, commented: 'Monty's sympathy with the plight of Germany came as a shock to those in the auditorium who pictured him as a ruthless, Cromwellian commander, until two weeks ago waging implacable war upon the Nazis.'[4]

This chapter explores what Montgomery and two of his most senior colleagues, Brian Robertson and Alec Bishop, aimed to achieve in occupied Germany, and how they responded to the conditions they found when they first arrived. Historians have suggested different reasons for when and why British policy changed after the end of the Second World War from holding Germany down to 'putting Germany on its feet again',[5] such as 'a change of mood in Britain' in early 1947,[6] economic pressures in the winter of 1946,[7] or the emerging Cold War and the perceived threat from the Soviet Union, culminating in the Berlin blockade of 1948–9.[8] For Montgomery, Robertson and Bishop, the key 'turning point' was earlier than any of these: the transition from war to peace from May to September 1945.[9] Faced with the reality of conditions on the ground, plans for a harsh occupation prepared during the war appeared inadequate and were rapidly superseded. The policy of reconstruction was confirmed by Montgomery in a new directive on Military Government, issued by Robertson as his chief-of-staff on 10 September 1945.

Montgomery is probably the best-known British Second World War general. He attracted tremendous loyalty from those who served under him and was often greeted by cheering crowds in the streets of Britain in the years immediately

Figure 2.1 Bernard Law Montgomery, 1st Viscount Montgomery of Alamein, by Elliott & Fry, c. 1946. © National Portrait Gallery, London.

after the end of the war.[10] He was commissioned as an officer in 1908. He fought in the First World War and was wounded in France. He subsequently served in Germany for a year during the British occupation of the Rhineland, in Ireland during the fighting which led to the establishment of the Irish Free State in 1923, and in Egypt, India and Palestine, being promoted Major General in 1938. At the outbreak of the Second World War, he commanded a division of the British Expeditionary Force in France and took part in the retreat and evacuation at Dunkirk. In 1942 he was transferred to North Africa to command the 8th Army. After successfully holding the position at El Alamein, he counter-attacked in October 1942 and, in the first decisive Allied victory of the war, broke through the enemy lines. He returned to Britain and acted as Commander-in-Chief of over two million British, US and Canadian troops during Operation Overlord, the invasion of Normandy. He was replaced by General Eisenhower at the end of the campaign, due to the growing preponderance of American forces, but continued to command the Allied 21st Army Group in its advance through France, Belgium and the Netherlands and across the Rhine into Germany. On 4 May 1945 he accepted the unconditional surrender of all German forces in Northwest Europe at his field headquarters on Lüneburg Heath, shortly before the formal German surrender in Reims and Berlin on 8 and 9 May. He left Germany on 1 May 1946 to take up his appointment as Chief of the Imperial General Staff, the most senior position in the British armed forces.[11]

Brian Robertson, Montgomery's deputy and later successor as Military Governor, and Alec Bishop, appointed head of the Public Relations and Information Services Control branch of the Control Commission (PR/ISC) in July 1945, were nearly ten years younger than Montgomery.[12] Their background and experience were typical of the army generals who served under Montgomery during the war or as staff officers in London, and held the most senior positions in Military Government throughout the occupation. Both were professional career soldiers, from military families, and both fought as young officers in the First World War. Bishop wrote in his memoirs that while his father had not served in the army, 'most of my forbears on my Mother's side had been soldiers' dating back to the 'Parliamentary Wars of the seventeenth century' and it was assumed that he too 'would follow the profession of arms'.[13] Robertson's father, Sir William Robertson, had been Chief of the Imperial General Staff during the First World War and was the only British soldier to rise from the ranks to Field Marshal, the most senior rank in the army.[14] Both Robertson and Bishop served in India, and both were selected to attend the Army Staff College in 1926, where Montgomery was an instructor. During the Second World War Robertson served with the 8th

Figure 2.2 Brian Hubert Robertson, 1st Baron Robertson of Oakridge, 1948, by Walter Stoneman, bromide print, 1947. © National Portrait Gallery, London.

Army under Montgomery in North Africa and was then Chief Administrative Officer to General Alexander in Italy. Bishop spent most of the war as a staff officer in London, appointed Major General, Director of Quartering in 1944.[15] For the last three months of the war, he was Deputy Director of the Political Warfare Executive (PWE), the British government organization responsible for news and propaganda broadcasts to Germany.[16]

Montgomery and the army generals who held the most senior positions in the British Military Government had little if any experience of civilian administration and felt unprepared for their new role as the rulers of a defeated enemy country. Most had spent all their working lives in the army, had no knowledge of the German language, culture or society, and had played no part in British planning for the occupation. Bishop's selection as Head of PR/ISC was agreed between the director of PWE, Sir Robert Bruce Lockhart, and Sir William Strang, the senior Foreign Office official who acted as political adviser to Montgomery.[17] Robertson later described his unexpected recall from Italy, when his predecessor as Montgomery's deputy, General Weeks, retired due to ill health in July 1945, after two months in post:

> I was suddenly sent for. I was told to take over this job, and I went to Germany the next day. I didn't speak a word of German; I'd never been in the country before. I had been in South Africa for half a dozen years or more. I knew nothing

Figure 2.3 Sir (William Henry) Alexander Bishop, by Walter Stoneman, April 1945. © National Portrait Gallery, London.

> about the situation at all, nothing [*sic*], nor had I taken any part of the great preparatory work that had been carried forward in London.[18]

Nevertheless, their first impressions, when they arrived in Germany, of a devastated country and a demoralized people, led them to conclude that the wartime planners and the politicians at home knew even less than they did.[19] Plans prepared during the war had assumed, incorrectly, that a central German administration would remain in place. The main tasks of the occupation forces and the civilian Control Commission were expected to be to prevent armed resistance, which never materialized, and to supervise and control German authorities, rather than having to act as civilian administrators themselves, maintain law and order, and undertake reconstruction work such as building bridges and clearing rivers and canals to make them navigable.[20] Montgomery and his colleagues were in no doubt of the need for complete disarmament and de-nazification, to destroy any future German government's ability to make war in future, but they also assumed it was part of their duty and personal responsibility to rehabilitate Germany and, great as the task was, they believed they knew, or could learn, what had to be done to achieve this.[21]

'First things first'

Many contemporary accounts by British soldiers, administrators, diplomats and journalists included descriptions of the devastation they saw when they first arrived in Germany after the war, looking out of aeroplane or train windows, or driving through the streets of one of the cities.[22] US observers, including President Truman, General Clay and journalists Walter Mills and Joseph Barnes, wrote in similar terms.[23] Despite their experience of two world wars and various smaller conflicts, Montgomery, Robertson and Bishop were surprised and shocked at the extent of the physical destruction of Germany. Bishop, for example, wrote in his memoirs:

> It is very difficult for anyone who did not see the situation in Germany when the war came to an end to realise what it was like. The first impression was of the appalling destruction which had been caused by the Allies' bombing. Very few towns had escaped wide-spread destruction. In some of the Ruhr towns such as Duisburg, over eighty per cent of the buildings had been reduced to rubble, under which lay the bodies of thousands of casualties.[24]

General Templer, Director of Civil Affairs for 21st Army Group and later Deputy Chief of Staff to Montgomery, responsible for internal administration of the British Zone in the first year of the occupation, described his first impressions of 'The Early Days' in similar terms, in an article in the *British Zone Review*, the official journal of Military Government:[25]

> Military Government was met by chaos. A team of four officers and six other ranks would be confronted by an area of many square miles. There was no local authority whatever with whom to deal. Devastation was often on a prodigious scale. There were no communications, no power. Fields were deserted. Crops and cattle had been left unattended. Half the population had been evacuated eastwards. Those that remained were stunned and cowed. Everything was at a standstill.[26]

Montgomery, Robertson, Bishop and many other senior army officers such as Templer, worked after the war to restore the basic elements of what they perceived as civilized society: enforcement of law and order, provision of enough food to prevent starvation, control of disease and rebuilding the economic infrastructure. Brigadier Donnison, the author of the relevant volume of the British official history of the Second World War, ended the book with a 'personal impression'; although regular officers at first disliked a posting to 'Civil Affairs', many of those he met in the course of his work told him that by the time they left 'they had come to feel it was the most rewarding work they had ever undertaken'. One even said it was 'the only really worth while thing he ever did in his life'.[27]

Rather than working through the civilian Control Commission, which he believed was out of touch with the realities of the situation on the ground, did not move to Germany until July and August, and was not fully integrated with army Civil Affairs detachments before the end of the year, Montgomery decided to treat the work that needed to be done as if it were a military operation.[28] The battles he and his troops had fought to win the war were followed by another to win the peace, which he called 'The Battle of the Winter', the objectives of which were not to repel enemy attack or win territory, but to provide 'food, work and homes'.[29] Operations Overlord (the invasion of Normandy), Market Garden (the attack on Arnhem described in the film *A Bridge Too Far*) and Plunder (the final assault across the German border to the Rhine) were followed, after the end of the war, by Operations Barleycorn (the release of captured German POWs to work on the land and help bring in the harvest), Coalscuttle (a further release of POWs to work in the coalmines of the Ruhr) and Stork (the evacuation of young children from the British Zone in Berlin).[30]

Robertson described the role of British Military Government in the first months of the occupation, in an article in the *British Zone Review*, as similar to that of a policeman taking control at the scene of an accident, using his initiative and responding to the specific circumstances. He told the story of a horse and cart careering down a street, overturning and causing chaos, when:

> Into this crowd came a British Military Policeman who immediately took charge of the situation. He was not an expert in horses and carts, but he saw very clearly that certain essential things were to be done.
>
> This is a simple story. We have all seen things like this happen. It has a moral for us. The German apple-cart has been upset, the madmen who were in charge of it are dead or in prison, the German people lies bleeding and helpless. We represent the policeman destined to take charge of the proceedings.[31]

In a second article, published in January 1946, Robertson wrote again of the need for improvisation and the application of common sense in unexpected conditions:

> The directives were not many, and much was left to the initiative of individuals … The detachments entered into a land of desolation and bewilderment. Government above the level of the parish council had ceased. Everything was in disorder; people were stunned and helpless … 'First things first' was the motto when Military Government first raised its sign in Germany.[32]

Initial concerns that they might have to deal with resistance from units of the German army who refused to surrender, die-hard Nazis or German nationalists, turned out to be unfounded. Montgomery reported in a memorandum to Sir Arthur Street, Permanent Secretary of the Control Office in London, that: 'The British Zone has remained quiet. So far scarcely a spark has occurred. I do not think we shall have any trouble with the Germans this winter; they are fully occupied with their own immediate troubles.'[33]

The transition in the first few months after the end of the war, from taking steps to prevent resistance from the defeated Germans, to a policy of creating order out of chaos and giving the Germans 'hope for the future', was later described by Robertson and Bishop as having occurred 'almost overnight'.[34] The rapid change in policy was reflected at lower levels of the military hierarchy and can be traced in contemporary documents, such as a series of Information Control Policy Directives issued by British Army Headquarters in Germany. The first directive, dated 12 May 1945, a few days after VE Day, adopted a harsh tone, instructing staff to emphasize issues such as: 'The completeness of Germany's defeat in the field… The common responsibility of all Germans for Nazi crimes' and 'The power and determination of the Allies to enforce their will'.[35] In this respect the directive was similar to orders Montgomery issued before the end of the war, such as his first message on non-fraternization, in March 1945, instructing British troops to:

> Keep clear of Germans, man, woman, and child… You must not walk out with them, or shake hands, or visit their homes, or make them gifts, or take gifts from them. You must not play games with them or share any social event with them. In short you must not fraternise with Germans at all.[36]

There was no change in the second Information Control directive, but the third, issued only two weeks later, on 27 May, stated that while earlier themes remained valid, 'the emphasis should now be shifted to more positive aims':

> The immediate need, from both Allied and German points of view, is for a supreme effort by the Germans at all forms of reconstruction work… Use every opportunity that honest reporting allows to emphasise with good space and prominence reconstruction activities by both the Allies and the Germans.[37]

Montgomery returned to Germany as Military Governor on 26 May, the day before the third directive was issued. The fourth directive, issued on 8 June, one month after VE Day and the end of the war in Europe, stated that the 'predominantly negative attitude' specified in the first directive was now superseded.[38] Subsequent directives and memos issued by Montgomery as

Military Governor, such as his three 'Notes on the present situation' and his third 'personal message' to the German people,[39] all emphasized the need for a new policy of reconstruction and of giving Germans 'hope for the future'.[40]

'A Buchenwald in Germany' – the food crisis

In a telegram to Montgomery sent on 5 June 1945, the Prime Minister, Winston Churchill, wrote that:

> I am alarmed by the winter prospect in Germany. I expect they will do everything you tell them and hold you responsible that they are fed. I wonder myself whether anything but German responsibility can secure the full German effort. It would NOT be thought a good ending to the war if you had a Buchenwald in Germany this winter with millions instead of thousands dying.[41]

With hindsight, we know that Churchill's understanding of the numbers was wrong. Millions of people, rather than thousands, died in the Holocaust, and thousands, rather than millions, died of starvation and disease in the British Zone after the end of the war.[42] However, at the time, famine and mass starvation in Germany and Europe, as had occurred during and after the First World War,[43] seemed a very real possibility. Before he left London in March 1945, General Templer was told by P.J. Grigg, Secretary of State for War, that:

> You must resign yourself to the fact that two million are going to die of hunger in Europe this spring. You and the Army must do all you can to mitigate it, but you won't be able to cure it.[44]

For three years after the end of the war, food rations in the British Zone for the so-called normal consumer varied between around 1,000 and 1,500 calories per day, well below the League of Nations' estimate of 2,000 calories as the minimum required to support a working adult. In comparison, the normal British ration at the time was around 2,800 calories, and average consumption in the United States was well over 3,000 calories.[45]

For the first three years of the occupation, food was the single most important issue for the British authorities.[46] At its simplest, their policy could be reduced to the question of what actions had to be taken to prevent starvation. Attempts at democratic, political and social reform were pointless if all people could think about was their next meal. Economic reconstruction could not proceed unless workers were adequately fed. A cut in rations in early 1946 resulted in an immediate reduction in coal production from 181,000 to 160,000 tons per day.[47] Absenteeism was high as workers took time off on 'hamster' visits to the countryside to try to find food for themselves and their families.[48] During the cold winter of 1946–7 the entire economy ground to a halt and factories, such as the Volkswagen works, ceased production for three months.[49]

A series of short term measures alleviated the problem without solving it: the use of Allied stocks of food held in reserve following the invasion in 1944, the diversion of supplies from the United States, the reduction of stocks of wheat held in Britain and attempts to increase production within the British Zone. The fundamental problem was that food production within the western zones, and the British Zone in particular, was not sufficient to feed the population and, until and unless industry revived, there was no revenue from exports to pay for food imports. The British government was therefore faced with the choice of reducing rations further, paying for food imports with scarce foreign currency or, as eventually happened but not until 1948, persuading the United States to assume financial responsibility for maintaining the British as well as their own zone.[50]

During this period, but especially in the eight months from October 1945 to May 1946, Montgomery and Robertson fought a continual battle with government ministers in London to maintain supplies of food above what they considered to be starvation level. In October 1945 Robertson sent an urgent request to the War Office for additional wheat allocations. The existing 1,550-calorie ration was already inadequate, he wrote, as '2,000 calories is the minimum ration to prevent disease and unrest'. Only 27,000 tons per week were available from the German harvest against a requirement of 61,500 tons.[51] On 24 October Montgomery met the Foreign Secretary, Ernest Bevin, during a visit to London. On his return to Germany, he restated his position in a telegram, saying that he had learned that the government were considering delaying further supplies. The 'already inadequate' ration of 1,550 calories would have to be reduced by 40 per cent and this, he continued, would mean 'famine conditions to an extent which no civilized people should inflict upon their beaten enemies'.[52]

On 26 February the following year, the matter had still not been resolved. Montgomery wrote to John Hynd, the minister responsible for Germany in London, to say he would have to cut the ration, with dire consequences:

> I have just returned from Switzerland and am utterly shocked by the latest telegrams from the Control Office regarding food supplies to the British Zone…
>
> I have therefore ordered an immediate reduction of the ration by 33 1/3% for the normal consumer. This means a ration of 1000 calories for the normal consumer which is well below the hunger mark…

> In my opinion we must immediately have substantial imports of wheat or equivalent for Germany. If we do not do so we shall produce death and misery to an extent which will disgrace our administration in history and completely stultify every effort which we are making to produce a democratic Germany.[53]

On 5 May Robertson wrote again to the Control Office in London, enclosing a strongly worded paper on the food situation. The 1,000-calorie ration had been introduced in March but, he added: 'It is not possible for an adult human being to subsist on 1,000 calories'; if there were no further imports, food grains would run out by 27 May and rations would be reduced to 450 calories: 'Coal production will stop. The trains will stop. The lights will go out.'[54]

With the introduction of bread rationing in Britain on 21 July 1946, and agreement to allocate an additional 200,000 tons of US wheat to the British Zone, the situation eased, but the relationship between the British occupiers and the German civilian population deteriorated after the cut in rations in March 1946 and never fully recovered. The Germans had considered the British Zone to be the best organized and best governed of all four zones, but their perception changed to one of muddle and incompetence.[55] In October 1946 an American dockers' strike brought food shipments almost to a standstill. In the spring of 1947, after rations were reduced again, to 750 calories in the Ruhr, there was a string of hunger strikes and demonstrations. Conditions did not improve until 1948–9, following substantial increases in US aid and food imports.[56]

'Epidemics need no passports' – disease and the fear of communism

Despite food shortages and relatively high levels diseases such as TB, diphtheria and typhus, epidemics were successfully controlled by Allied and German administrators in all four zones, but the fear of disease spreading from Germany to the rest of Europe was associated with political and economic, as well as medical dangers.[57] Poor public health in Germany after the Second World War reinforced the perception of Nazism as a social disease, and was viewed by both British and Germans as symptomatic of a general decline in civilized standards, in a country that had been very similar to Britain in terms of economic development, material prosperity and artistic culture.[58] Montgomery and his colleagues in the higher echelons of British Military Government believed that the restoration of law and order, the provision of enough food to prevent starvation and economic reconstruction to provide a reasonable standard of living were necessary, not only to help the German people, but because it was in their own interest to prevent social unrest spreading from Germany to the rest of Western Europe.[59] The epidemic of influenza at the end of the First World War was widely believed to have killed more people than the war itself.[60] A starving population was more susceptible to infection and, as the Foreign Secretary, Ernest Bevin, told Parliament on 26 October 1945: 'While the Channel could be used to stop Germans, it cannot stop germs. You cannot limit the devastation of an epidemic by a frontier or a strategic post.'[61] 'Epidemics need no passports', as the author of an article in the *British Zone Review* wrote in September 1945.[62]

Similar language was used to describe political threats to the established order. In his memoirs, Bishop seamlessly linked poor living conditions and epidemics of disease, not to the Nazi threat, but to communism:

> Without vigorous help and support it was inevitable that epidemics would spread throughout the country, endangering the health of the Occupying Forces and of the whole of Western Europe.
>
> It was also clear that unless the German people were helped to transform the conditions then existing into a situation which would provide a bearable if modest standard of living it would be impossible to prevent the spread of communism throughout the whole country.[63]

The idea that communism was a 'disease of the mind' had been widespread among Conservative Party politicians and the popular press in Britain since the Bolshevik revolution of 1917. Before the wartime alliance with the Soviet Union, Churchill, for example, had made full use of medical imagery to describe the 'menace of Bolshevism' as 'the poisoned peril' or 'a plague bacillus' infecting civilization.[64] In the following passage, published in 1929 but based on a newspaper article written in 1920, he graphically linked the geographical country of Russia with the triple threat of war, disease and ideology:

> [To the east of Poland] lay the huge mass of Russia – not a wounded Russia only, but a poisoned Russia, an infected Russia, a plague-bearing Russia, a Russia of armed hordes not only smiting with bayonet and with cannon, but accompanied and preceded by swarms of typhus-bearing vermin which slew the bodies of men, and political doctrines which destroyed the health and even the souls of nations.[65]

The emotional connection between war, disease and political doctrines could appear equally relevant in 1945. Between 1918 and 1922 an estimated three million people died in Russia from epidemic typhus, a highly infectious and often fatal disease spread by the human body louse.[66] Outbreaks of typhus were widespread in Germany in 1945 and were controlled by British and American health officers creating a 'sanitary border' along the Rhine and routinely dusting with DDT anyone suspected of being a source of infection, regardless of their nationality or status.[67]

Lloyd George famously remarked of Churchill: 'His ducal blood revolted against the wholesale elimination of Grand Dukes in Russia.'[68] Similarly, as army officers and privileged members of the British professional establishment, Montgomery, Robertson and Bishop spent their working lives defending Britain's position in the world and any threat to it, whether from Nazi Germany, communist Russia or elsewhere, affected them personally. Montgomery said in June 1945 in a speech on receiving the freedom of the City of Antwerp, echoing Churchill in his reference to 'toil and sweat':

> Our first task is now ended. Together we have won the war, and have destroyed the Nazi tyranny of Europe. Our hardest task remains to be tackled. Out of the chaos and confusion which the war has inflicted on Europe we have to rebuild our European civilisation. In destroying the Nazi power, we have destroyed one great evil; much that was good and beautiful has also been destroyed, and the economic organisation of Europe lies in ruins. We can rebuild what has been destroyed only by toil and sweat, and there is no short cut back to prosperity.[69]

For all three in 1945, as for Churchill in 1919, starvation, disease, political agitation and social unrest were four symptoms of the same fundamental problem, which could be summarized as a breakdown of the established social order and the need to 'rebuild civilisation', as they understood it.

At the end of the Second World War, Nazi Germany may have been destroyed and epidemics of disease controlled, but economic, social and political threats remained that appeared disturbingly similar to the situation in 1919. In May 1945, concerned at the establishment of a communist government in Poland, Churchill asked his Chiefs of Staff to draw up secret plans, codenamed 'Operation Unthinkable', for a surprise Anglo-American attack on the Soviet Union, with the assistance of ten German divisions.[70] 'Operation Unthinkable' was rapidly dismissed as impracticable by military planners in the general staff, but Churchill and Montgomery were still concerned, as they had been in 1919 after the Bolshevik revolution and the end of the First World War, that the Soviet Union would achieve its goals through political means, by encouraging communist agitators within Germany and Western Europe. A communist Germany allied with the Soviet Union could still threaten British interests, at home and overseas. In an exchange of telegrams with Churchill on 5 June 1945, Montgomery wrote:

> I have increasing evidence every day of communist propaganda going on in the British Zone and agents are working in the Russian DP camps and these meetings are being attended by German agents. The DP camps are being evacuated to the Russian Zone but this is a slow business and in any case communist 'cells' will be left behind for certain. I am watching the situation very carefully.[71]

After the Potsdam Agreements between Britain, the United States and the Soviet Union in August 1945, Montgomery was reassured that there was no longer any direct military threat to Britain from the Soviet Union.[72] However, the ideological threat of communism continued to underlie his concerns, expressed for example in his valedictory memo of 1 May 1946, that they might 'fail in Germany' due to food shortages, economic conditions, the attitude of the local population and the need for a 'change of heart'. If conditions did not improve, he wrote, an increasingly hostile German population would 'begin to look EAST. When that happens we shall have failed, and there will exist a definite menace to the British Empire'.[73]

The creation of a new directive on Military Government

For at least the first year of the occupation Montgomery and his senior officers were able to act on their own initiative and received little direct instruction from the government in London. Neither the outgoing coalition government under Churchill nor the new Labour government under Clement Attlee, which took office in July 1945, could spare much time to consider the problems of governing Germany, as they were fully occupied with the war in the Far East, the general election, internal domestic policies, and many other urgent economic and international issues. Reporting lines were unclear. Responsibility for the internal administration of the British Zone was transferred from the Foreign Office to the War Office on 1 June 1945, though both had previously worked on various aspects of planning for the occupation.[74]

After lengthy discussions with Sir Edward Bridges, the Cabinet Secretary, Attlee decided that a new department should be created to handle matters relating to the administration of the British Zone.[75] The Control Office for Germany and Austria (COGA) was ultimately responsible to the Secretary of State for War, but in practice operated independently of both the Foreign Office and the War Office. COGA's principal function was to act as the liaison between Military Government in Germany and Civil Service departments in London.

The Foreign Office retained responsibility for international aspects of British policy towards Germany, such as negotiating peace treaties and preparing for meetings of the Allied Council of Foreign Ministers.[76] After various delays to allay Foreign Office concerns, COGA was established in October 1945 and John Hynd, Chancellor of the Duchy of Lancaster, appointed Minister for Germany.[77] Hynd was a new and inexperienced MP, with no power base and little influence within the government. Though entitled to attend Cabinet meetings when Germany was discussed, he was not a full Cabinet member and so had little influence on policy at the highest levels.[78] Hynd and COGA were based in London, which also made it difficult to exert any executive authority over the Control Commission and Military Government in Germany.[79] Montgomery had little respect for Hynd. A handwritten note on one file in his personal papers stated that it contained 'important memoranda' with copies of letters to Attlee, Bevin and Hynd 'who was utterly useless'.[80]

The Foreign Office adopted a watching brief, rather than attempting to direct and control Military Government activities. When Foreign Office officials did intervene, they did so cautiously. In August 1945, after receiving concerns from the Political Intelligence Department (PID) regarding Montgomery's practice of issuing personal messages to the German people, the Permanent Secretary, Alexander Cadogan, minuted that while the government in London should 'lay down the broad lines of policy', implementation should be 'left to those with immediate responsibility'.[81] Officials drafted a letter for the Foreign Secretary, Ernest Bevin, to send to Montgomery, suggesting that while he did not wish to 'interfere in the day to day administration of Germany', he was concerned that they should not promise more than could be effectively delivered.[82] After Montgomery left Germany in May 1946, the Foreign Office gradually reasserted control, but did not assume overall responsibility for the occupation until April 1947, when COGA was abolished and absorbed within the Foreign Office.[83] Until then, Montgomery and his generals were left to govern the British Zone as they thought best, holding supreme authority over an area half the size of the UK with a population of over twenty million.

Montgomery and his senior officers were expected to act in accordance with a set of directives issued by the War Office in October 1944.[84] The directives covered military, legal, diplomatic and some economic issues, including disbanding the German armed forces, the status of prisoners of war, the destruction of war materiel, the control of German industries, international treaties, relations with neutral countries and the reform of Nazi laws, but provided little guidance on many of the most challenging problems they faced once victory had been achieved: the maintenance of law and order, food and housing shortages, chronically low levels of industrial production, massive population movements and, above all, the absence of any central German authority. In order to take action quickly, Montgomery and his colleagues adopted procedures they knew and understood from their experience in the army. The overall direction of policy was determined by Montgomery as Commander-in-Chief, in a series of notes, memos and conferences with his senior staff. Responsibility for translating these into detailed directives lay with his Chief of Staff, after consulting with the army Corps Commanders and various Control Commission heads of division.

Following two months of discussions within Military Government, initiated by Montgomery's second 'Note on the Present Situation', the policy of reconstruction was elaborated and confirmed in a new directive issued by Robertson in September 1945. In his Note, issued on 6 July, Montgomery wrote in general terms. He stated that over the past two months the 'full extent of the debacle' had become apparent and they now knew the 'magnitude of the problem that confronts us in the rebuilding of Germany'.[85] Part of the problem, he continued, was 'a tendency to adhere rigidly' to instructions issued earlier by SHAEF, the joint US and British Supreme Headquarters of the Allied Expeditionary Force, which were now out of date, and a new directive was required.[86] A week later in his third Note, Montgomery wrote:

> Our present attitude towards the German people is negative, it must be replaced by one that is positive and holds out hope for the future.[87]

Montgomery did not elaborate further in his 'Notes', but the actions now required from the armed services and Control Commission were specified in a 'rough draft' of a new directive sent on 21 July by his Chief of Staff, General Weeks, to army commanders and Control Commission heads of division.[88]

The 'rough draft' comprised twenty pages of detailed instructions on steps to be taken to reconstruct Germany, under thirty headings which had not been covered in previous directives including: 'Shortage of Food', 'Shortage of Coal', 'Inadequate Transportation Facilities', 'Re-Starting of Vital Industries', 'Housing Shortage', 'Freedom from Disease', 'Reopening of Schools', 'Trade Unions', 'Churches', 'German Youth', 'Freedom of Assembly', 'Freedom of Speech', 'Political Parties' and 'Elections'. Recipients were given only four days to consider the document and submit comments, rewriting paragraphs if necessary.[89] Unsurprisingly, given the scale of the task, finalizing the directive took a little longer. Over the next month Robertson, who arrived in Germany on 25 July, after his appointment as Deputy Military Governor and Chief of Staff had been confirmed by Churchill on 21 July, took over responsibility from Weeks.[90] The draft was revised, a few aspects toned down,[91] and the final directive issued on 10 September 1945.[92] When the Foreign Office received a copy, for information, a few days later, a senior official, Con O'Neill, minuted: 'It gives me, in general, the impression that British Military Govt. has now embarked on a policy of Full Speed Ahead for German rehabilitation.'[93]

The creation of the new directive demonstrates that Montgomery and his colleagues in Military Government were able to act on their own initiative, without input or approval from the government in London or from the United States or other Allies acting jointly. The many documents created by British and US occupation planners in London or Washington during the war are not necessarily a reliable guide to British policy as implemented once victory had been achieved. The first 'rough draft' of the new directive was issued on 21 July, after the general election in Britain on 5 July, but before the announcement of the results on 26 July and the formation of a new Labour government. The draft was issued while Truman, Stalin and Churchill, later Attlee, were meeting at Potsdam to decide the future of Germany, but before agreement was reached and the conference closed on 2 August. It appears as if Montgomery was trying to establish a new policy for the British Zone and pre-empt the outcome of both the election in Britain and decisions reached at Potsdam, while he had the freedom to act on his own initiative.

Britain and the United States did not agree on a common occupation policy before their two zones merged to form the 'Bizone' in January 1947. The often-quoted US directive, JCS 1067, which generally advocated a harsh occupation, did not apply to the British Zone.[94] JCS 1067 remained in force until July 1947, when it was superseded by a new directive (JCS 1779) for the US Zone.[95] Montgomery's September 1945 directive on Military Government for the British Zone did not conflict directly with previous instructions. It created new policies for circumstances that had not been predicted by the wartime planners, such as food, fuel and housing shortages; the need to revive, rather than control, the economy; and the need to establish new political systems and institutions. Taken as a whole, however, it represented a clear change in British occupation policy from prevention, control and restrictions on German economic and political activities, to reconstruction of the physical infrastructure, economic revival and the renewal of social and political life.

3

The Occupation as a Moral Crusade

In an 'Introductory Message from the Commander-in-Chief, British Zone' in September 1945, printed on the first page of the first issue of the *British Zone Review*, Montgomery wrote:

> Before launching my troops into battle it has always been my custom to issue to them a Personal Message. This is intended to define the common objective and thereby foster unity of purpose.

Their post-war task, he continued, 'may be summarised as the permanent eradication of Nazism, and the administration of Germany according to the principles which we hold to be right'. Twelve years of Nazi rule had resulted in 'more than material destruction'. For the past five months they had been 'clearing the ground'. There was more to do, but they were now approaching 'the second stage, the stage of reconstruction':

> Much of the responsibility for guiding and supervising this reconstruction rests with you. The defeated enemy must be made to put his house in order … At present he cannot sustain himself, far less repay what he owes. First he must be raised to his feet, and then made to work in such a way that he will not only be able to liquidate his debts but finally find his own salvation. We shall try to be wise conquerors. As we were strong in battle so we shall be just in peace.[1]

British policy in Germany has been described as pragmatic, lacking the missionary spirit attributed to their US counterparts.[2] Yet Montgomery, Robertson and Bishop justified the need for reconstruction in idealistic rather than practical terms, using phrases such as 'spiritual regeneration',[3] 'fighting a battle over the soul of Germany',[4] 'a change of heart',[5] 'the acceptance of the principles of Christian humanism and democracy'[6] and the 're-birth of moral and intellectual enlightenment'.[7] This chapter examines in more detail how their understanding of their task in Germany was influenced by the 'mental baggage' they brought with them: their memories of the First World War and the occupation of the Rhineland, their understanding of the British Empire, their family backgrounds and their personal, moral and religious beliefs. They had tremendous confidence in the strength of their own traditions and sought to apply these to the situation they found in Germany.

Disarmament and de-nazification, to prevent another war, appeared self-evident and did not need to be explained. Reconstruction was more difficult, both to define and to justify. In subsequent years, Montgomery, Robertson and Bishop looked back with pride on their achievements in Germany. The policies of physical and economic reconstruction, political renewal and personal reconciliation, which they started to implement in 1945, continued to apply throughout the occupation, despite changes in personnel, changes in emphasis and increased involvement by politicians in London.

Memories of the First World War

After the end of the First World War, British, French, US and Belgian armies occupied the Rhineland – a large part of western Germany including the cities of Aachen, Trier, Cologne, Mainz and Wiesbaden – but failed to prevent German re-armament. Two contrasting, but not mutually exclusive, sets of conclusions were drawn after the Second World War from British experiences during the Rhineland occupation. On the one hand there was a view, widely held among politicians in London, that the occupation forces had to guard against being deceived again by a duplicitous German civilian population, who had courted sympathy from well-meaning Allied soldiers, claiming they were victims of an unjust peace settlement, while planning their revenge and preparing for war. On the other hand, many of those with personal experience of the Rhineland occupation believed that while disarmament was necessary, restrictive measures alone, however strictly enforced, were insufficient to avoid mistakes made previously. The Allies had failed to offer sufficient support to democratic politicians in Germany; hunger, despair and unemployment had provided a fertile recruiting ground for the Nazis after the First World War; and if similar conditions were repeated after the Second World War, the eventual outcome might be a Nazi revival, and perhaps even a third world war. Mixed messages derived from memories of the Rhineland occupation were compounded by a fear of communism that dated back to the Bolshevik revolution of 1917. Nazism may have been destroyed, but the threat from communism remained.[8]

Throughout most of 1945, Montgomery and many of his colleagues assumed that the occupation would have to continue for twenty years or more, to prevent earlier mistakes being repeated.[9] Montgomery's first letter to his troops on non-fraternization, issued in March 1945, warned that:

> Twenty-seven years ago the Allies occupied Germany: but Germany has been at war ever since. Our Army took no revenge in 1918; it was more than considerate, and before a few weeks had passed many soldiers were adopted into German households. The enemy worked hard at being amiable…

Meanwhile the German general staff prepared for war, and

> 'Organising sympathy' became a German industry…So accommodating were the occupying forces that the Germans came to believe we would never fight them again in any cause.[10]

Similar cautionary messages were contained in a series of three articles, in early issues of the *British Zone Review*, written by the British Control Commission's Research Branch. According to the articles, the occupation was used by the Germans to divide the Allies, by courting sympathy from the British while complaining to them about the French. Meanwhile Germany was 'only shamming dead financially and economically'. Readers were encouraged to draw the 'lessons from history', that this time the Allies had to remain united, and a long occupation was needed to prevent German rearmament and another world war.[11]

Robertson recalled later that, following his appointment as Deputy Military Governor in July 1945, he had been given a copy of Brigadier Morgan's book *Assize of Arms* as 'our guide in preventing clandestine re-armament by the Germans'.[12] Morgan had been a member of the Inter-Allied Control Commission from 1919 to 1923. During the Second World War, he worked closely with a post-war policy group of members of both Houses of Parliament, which produced two reports on German disarmament and advocated a harsh post-war policy towards Germany.[13] But although 800 copies of *Assize of Arms* were printed by the War Office for distribution to British members of the Control Commission,[14] the book reflects the wartime attitudes of many MPs and politicians in London, rather than policy as implemented in Germany after the war was won.

Montgomery and Robertson could draw on a second strand of memory, popular in Britain in the 1920s and 1930s, which came to a different conclusion, blaming the Allies for the rise of extreme political parties on both sides of the political spectrum, Nazis and Communists, by imposing a harsh peace after the First World War and not doing more as occupiers to support democratic forces within Germany.[15] Numerous contemporary accounts, written in the 1920s, described how British troops generally got on well with the local population and in many cases returned home 'definitely pro-German'.[16] Violet Markham, for example, wrote in *A Woman's Watch on the Rhine* that 'Life in Cologne is very pleasant for the occupying army' and 'surely no Army of Occupation was ever so well housed or so comfortable as we are'. Although she had no doubts as to the 'noble ideal' for which the British had fought the war and was irritated at Germany's 'refusal to say she is sorry', she was critical of Allied post-war policy, especially the continuation of the economic blockade and the Treaty of Versailles which, she said, had 'scrapped the fundamental ideals for which we fought the war'. In her view, the democratic government which emerged in Germany in 1918 had an impossible task, 'confronted by hunger, defeat, despair, and the miseries which resulted from the blockade', and the Allies were partly to blame for the rise of the extreme parties and the decline in the vote for the Social Democrats in the elections of 1920.[17]

Robertson's father, Sir William Robertson, had commanded the British Army of the Rhine from 1919 to 1920, while Montgomery, as a relatively junior officer, was in command of a battalion. Robertson wrote later that, at first, *Assize of Arms* 'all seemed to make good sense', but he then referred to his own experience as a member of the British delegation at the League of Nations in Geneva in 1932–3 and how this had made him 'a first-hand witness of the failure to deal properly with Germany after World War 1'. He continued:

> My father had been Military Governor for a period then. He often talked to me about the mistakes and problems of those years. 'The idea that you can hold down a country like Germany with her face in the dust indefinitely is a foolish one' he used to say.[18]

If it was not possible to 'hold Germany down' for ever, they had to find an alternative to the purely negative policies of disarmament, demilitarization and economic controls, implemented at the end of the First World War.

A third set of memories of the First World War and its aftermath were centred on the impact of the Russian Revolution, the economic consequences of the war, and the threat to the established political and social order. A group of British intelligence officers, given the task of observing conditions in Germany in 1919, were concerned that economic deprivation would lead to social collapse and revolution, extending from Russia to Germany, and possibly the rest of Europe. One of the officers wrote in his report that 'Bolshevism' was a dangerous doctrine spread by agitators, who were either 'Adventurers' receiving financial support from

Russia or 'Idealists' who came 'from the "modern" intellectual and artistic classes'. In normal times, when people were contented and prosperous, the 'ordinary German' would pay no attention to the 'doctrines of the revolutionary', but:

> Under the increasing stress of famine and unemployment, there is no question but that the whole country will be consumed by the flame of Bolshevism which will spread with such rapidity that the waters of the Rhine will be incapable of checking its advance.[19]

A Foreign Office memo summarizing the reports concluded that it was in British and Allied interests to relax the blockade, permit food supplies to enter the country and so assist the Germans to resume a normal economic life.[20] Montgomery's telegrams to Churchill in June 1945, reporting that he had received evidence of communist propaganda and agents in the British Zone and was 'watching the situation very carefully',[21] reflected concerns among British army and intelligence officers that had changed little since 1919.

Montgomery, Robertson and Bishop were born and spent their formative years at a time of relative political stability, when the British Empire was at its height, and Britain was unquestionably a great power in the world. The lessons they drew from their family background, their education, their memories of the First World War, the Bolshevik Revolution of 1917, the occupation of the Rhineland, the German inflation of the 1920s, the general strike in Britain in 1926 and the global economic depression of the 1930s were that poverty and unemployment were a prime cause of social unrest, which contributed to the rise of extreme political parties and threatened their privileged position as members of the British professional establishment. After the Second World War, they did not question the need for the disarmament and demilitarization of Germany, but they also came to believe that measures to limit industrial production and military re-armament, such as those implemented after the First World War in the Treaty of Versailles, would fail to ensure a lasting peace, unless they were accompanied by the restoration of law and order, economic reconstruction and active support for democratic political parties.

Echoes of Empire

Many of the ruling strategies used by the British during the occupation can be traced back to techniques used at different times in different parts of the Empire, such as collaboration with local elites, the appointment of district commissioners and the appointment of a British Military Governor, followed by the formation of representative local assemblies, at first nominated and then elected.[22] Although the Empire was diverse and there was no imperial model or template that could be taken off the shelf and applied in its entirety, a defining characteristic of British imperial rule, which also dominated British occupation policy in Germany, was an overriding concern to pursue their interests at the lowest possible cost, and a willingness to work with traditional elites and other social groups that benefitted from British rule. Many Germans, on the other hand, resented what they considered to be British arrogance, treating them, so they believed, as if they were ignorant and uncivilized natives in some remote British colony.[23]

For Montgomery and the generals at the top of Military Government, the rhetoric of empire was as important as the practice. They and other senior army officers of their generation had spent most of their working lives in India, Africa or the Middle East, and their outlook on the world was permeated with the ideals, values and prejudices of the British Empire. Their descriptions of creating order out of chaos in post-war Germany echoed Thomas Babington Macaulay claiming in 1833 that, under the Mughal emperors, 'Indian Society was a chaos', and John Stuart Mill advocating enlightened British rule in 1861 as the means to achieve progress and good government.[24] An ideal vision of the Empire as a civilizing influence and force for good in the world was promoted and widely accepted in Britain, from the abolition of slavery in the early nineteenth century through to the rebranding of Empire as a 'Commonwealth of Nations' in the 1940s and 1950s.[25] This vision could be adapted to justify, at least in their own minds, their role and self-image as benevolent occupiers in Germany, acting in the best interests of the local population.

Although Montgomery was born in London, his family moved to Tasmania when he was two years old and he lived there for twelve years. After returning to London, he spent his teenage summer holidays at Moville, a country estate owned by his family for generations, twenty miles from Londonderry. In two speeches in September 1945, on being made Honorary Burgess of the City of Belfast and awarded the Freedom of the City of Londonderry, he referred to himself as an Irishman, and to Londonderry as 'almost my home town'. Moville is in County Donegal, across the border with the Irish Republic, but at the time, the Republic of Ireland was still technically part of the British Commonwealth, and the views Montgomery expressed were typical of many in Britain:

> Before the war, the Empire was everywhere weak ... A weak Empire is a danger to ourselves and to the whole world. But a strong and united Empire, united in a common belief in freedom and justice, is one of the greatest forces for good in the world today.

> This ancient city of ours can well understand these things, since it has itself been through difficult times and suffered great tribulations: the ancient city of Derry being finally reduced to ashes early in the seventeenth century. But the people of London assisted in the work of reconstruction, and a new city arose on the ruins of the old: and was called Londonderry, on account of its connection with the capital of the Empire.
>
> We of Londonderry thus have a link with the Empire that can never be broken: a link that binds us strongly to the very heart of the Empire.[26]

His theme of the people of London helping to rebuild the city of Derry, after it had been 'reduced to ashes' in the seventeenth century, though anathema to Irish republicans then as now, would have been part of the collective memory of his audience of Protestant Ulster Unionists, and emotionally significant for Montgomery, the younger son of a family of Irish Protestant landowners, with an estate that was now on the wrong side of the border, in the Irish Republic. It could also be understood as an allusion to the more recent destruction of cities in Britain and Germany, the threats he and his audience faced from many different directions, and their dependence on the unifying and stabilizing power of the British Empire.

If Montgomery's family background gave him a personal interest in the future of the British Empire, Bishop's five years in occupied Germany could appear as part of a lifetime of service. In the preface to his memoirs, one-third of which were devoted to Germany, he wrote that:

> This book is about a life mostly spent in the service of the British Empire. Although it is fashionable at the present time to decry this period of our history, the author hopes that his story may make some contribution towards a better understanding of our successes and failures and of the joys and sorrows which came our way.[27]

The British Empire gave his life as a professional soldier greater meaning and significance, as well as providing experiences and opportunities for advancement that would have been impossible had he stayed at home. After fighting in the First World War in Mesopotamia (now Iraq), he was stationed in India for six years from 1919 to 1925, where he enjoyed a privileged existence, big game shooting for 'tiger, bison, wild boar, sambhur, cheetah and spotted deer', recalling in his memoirs that: 'Life was very pleasant in those days for young officers serving in India.'[28] In 1931 he joined the Colonial Office in London and travelled extensively in Africa on tours of inspection of the Colonial Forces. After leaving Germany in 1950 he was appointed Assistant Secretary at the Commonwealth Relations Office and, from 1957 to 1962, British Deputy High Commissioner in Calcutta. His final posting before he retired was as High Commissioner in Cyprus.[29]

Robertson served as an officer in India at the same time as Bishop, but left the army in 1933 to take up a position as a civilian, managing a tyre factory for Dunlop in South Africa. He looked forward to a future that encompassed free trade between nations, rather than viewing the Empire as an exclusive club, bolstered by tariff barriers and Imperial Preference.[30] In 1939 he campaigned, as President of the Natal Chamber of Commerce, for South Africa to join the war on the British side. He volunteered to re-enlist and joined the South African Union Defence Force, serving in Kenya and then with the British 8th Army in North Africa and Italy.[31] He was still nominally employed by the South African Defence Force in 1945, when he was appointed Deputy Military Governor in Germany.[32]

In a speech to Control Commission staff in July 1947, Robertson compared their role in Germany with that of imperial pioneers in Africa, emphasizing the virtues of character and determination, by referring to the statue of Cecil Rhodes in Cape Town:

> We here are the empire builders ... The Empire whose boundaries we seek to extend is the Empire of true democracy, of peace and decency.
>
> In Cape Town there is a statue of a man who made a very great contribution towards building the British Empire ... and he sits there now looking over the sea towards the north, and on his statue are written his dying words, 'so much to do, so little done.'[33]

Invoking Rhodes and his expansionist ambitions in southern Africa to justify an imaginary British Empire of 'democracy, peace and decency' in Germany, may now seem inappropriate, even perverse, but at the time, critiques of Empire as racist, exploitative and based on the application of brute force were limited to the margins of British society.[34] Rhodes was still an iconic figure, endorsed by royal visits to his grave near Bulawayo in Southern Rhodesia (now Zimbabwe) before the war by the Prince of Wales and the future King George VI, and by the Queen Mother and Princess Margaret as late as 1953, the centenary of his birth.[35]

For Montgomery, Robertson and Bishop, the Empire was a force for good in the world. It was only by drawing on the strength, manpower and resources of the Empire that Britain had succeeded in defeating the continental powers of Germany and Italy. British rule was also, so they believed, in the best interests of the local population. As Bishop wrote in his memoirs:

> Many of the people in Britain and in other countries who take a delight in condemning the period of British Colonial rule in Africa and Asia had no part in its creation and administration, nor did they experience the devotion and idealism of the British administrators. I feel no doubt that when an authoritative

history of our Colonial Empire comes to be written, the part played by the British officials who administered it in establishing and maintaining law and order, in holding the interests of the people above all else and in educating and preparing them to run their own affairs in due course will become fully evident.[36]

Bishop's ideas reflected those of the Colonial Secretary in the Labour Government, Arthur Creech Jones and the Fabian Colonial Bureau, which advocated the concept of Imperial Trusteeship, whereby the British would administer a country until the 'natives' could be trusted to do it themselves.[37] The idea of imperial trusteeship could be translated into a similar view of the British role in occupied Germany. Legally and administratively the British Zone was never part of the Empire, but in the absence of any other framework, the British Empire was a model Montgomery and other officers, born before 1900, believed they knew and understood and could apply, with modifications, to the problems they faced in the chaos of post-war Germany.

'Saving the soul of Germany'

Montgomery, Robertson and Bishop held strong moral and religious beliefs. On occasions they referred to their work, helping Germans to 'find their own salvation',[38] as if they were missionaries trying to convert the heathen, rather than victors in war, administering a defeated enemy country. They were not alone in this. General Eisenhower started his personal D-Day message to all 'soldiers, sailors and airmen of the Allied Expeditionary Force': 'You are about to embark on the Great Crusade'.[39] His memoirs of the period are called *Crusade in Europe*. For many British as well as American soldiers, the crusade did not end when the war was won. A British colonel wrote that:

The re-birth of Germany is fundamentally a moral and not a material issue. It is in fact a moral Crusade ... Too much talk about 'democracy' (that overworked word) and not enough about Christianity will tend to place the whole of the vast undertaking to which we are committed on too low a plane.[40]

Robert Birley, Education Adviser to the Military Governor in Germany, expressed similar sentiments in a lecture on 'The German Problem and the responsibility of Britain', subsequently published by the Student Christian Movement. The experience of the First World War, he wrote, had 'taught us that military victory was not enough ... Above all we were faced with what was pre-eminently a spiritual problem'.[41]

Birley's views mirrored those of *Moot,* an informal group of liberal, mainly Anglican, theologians and writers who argued that the war had a religious and spiritual dimension. It was a battle of good against evil. Members of the group included the poet T.S. Eliot, the ecumenical Scottish missionary J.H. Oldham, who convened the group, the German-Jewish sociologist Karl Mannheim and Walter Moberly, Vice Chancellor of Manchester University, Chairman of the University Grants Committee and Chairman of the Central Advisory Council to the War Office on army education.[42] The rise of the Nazi Party within Germany, in their view, had been due to spiritual factors, or more accurately, to the growing secularization of society, a lack of spirituality and a lack of religious faith.[43] Similar views were expressed in Amy Buller's *Darkness over Germany* published in 1943, in which she referred to the 'fundamentally religious appeal to the Nazi youth in much of the teaching given to them'.[44] Buller was secretary of the Student Christian Movement from 1921 to 1931, and had close links with Archbishop Temple and other Anglican Church leaders. In 1947 she secured royal patronage from King George VI and Queen Elizabeth, who donated the premises for a new Christian college and foundation at Cumberland Lodge, in Windsor Great Park. Moberly was its first principal.[45]

In Buller's view, the growing secularization of society, in Germany and elsewhere, meant that young people were all too easily attracted to an *ersatz* religion, with the ceremonies and the sense of belonging that the Nazi party provided. After suffering hardship and unemployment during the economic depression, she wrote, the experience of fellowship and the ceremonies of the party gave them a 'new life and energy [which] transcended as well as transformed their immediate tasks and gave their own little existence a cosmic significance and eternal destiny'.[46] According to Birley, arguing similarly in December 1947, the 'moral collapse', which had occurred in Nazi Germany, was a symptom of 'a diseased condition in Western civilization as a whole', but although Britain, in his view, suffered from many of the same social and economic problems, 'the traditional foundations of public morality' remained secure. 'Material resources' would have to be provided from the United States, but the British had to provide a 'spiritual example' and it was their duty to 'offer the strength of our own traditions to Germany'.[47]

Views such as these were not typical of British public opinion generally, but were received sympathetically by men such as Montgomery, Robertson and Bishop, whose extended family included soldiers, country landowners and Anglican clergy. The twelve years of Nazi rule in Germany appeared to be a terrible warning of what might happen in Britain, but this could, they hoped, be avoided if traditional values, morality, social order and the authority of the churches were reinforced, in both Britain and Germany. Although such nostalgic attitudes may have done little to help Germans come to terms with the brutal realities of the Nazi past, they provided the context within which the crusading spirit and 'missionary idealism' of Montgomery and his colleagues in Germany is best understood. A belief in the restorative power of British traditions, many of which were shared with Germany, contributed to a focus on reconstruction and the need for a joint effort by both occupiers and occupied, which reinforced what they had in common, rather than dividing them.

Benevolent occupiers?

One of Montgomery's greatest strengths as a general was his ability to improve and maintain morale among his troops. In two pamphlets, 'High Command in War' and 'Morale in Battle', written while he was in Germany in June 1945 and April 1946, he wrote that morale was 'the most important single factor in war'. Most men fought because they were ordered to do so, not for a cause, but the more intelligent leaders fought 'because they believe in what they fight for' and nothing should minimize 'the influence of Cause on those officers and men who are moved by it'.[48] When the war was over, he tried to apply the same principles that had brought him success in battle, to the task of reconstruction in Germany.

Goronwy Rees, who acted as Montgomery's liaison officer in 1941, described him as having 'an air ... of extraordinary quietness and calm', more like a priest than a general.[49] Montgomery's father was an Anglican clergyman and missionary, vicar of the London parish of St Mark's Kennington, Bishop of Tasmania, and for the last eighteen years of his working life before retiring to his country estate in Ireland, secretary of the Society for the Propagation of the Gospel in Foreign Parts. In a eulogy written after his father died in 1933, Montgomery's mother (who was also a devout evangelical Christian, and the daughter of Dean Farrar, a noted Anglican preacher, writer and schoolteacher), described how her husband had imbued their family life with a sense of mission that combined duty to the Almighty with service to the British Empire. She recalled him preaching to his five oldest sons, including the future Field Marshal, in his chapel in Tasmania one evening, advising them in whatever profession they chose, 'to put God first and to strive to serve the Empire'. She added proudly that all five of their sons were now serving the Empire, four abroad and one in the Church at home.[50]

In later years after his father died, Montgomery's relationship with his mother was strained, but the influence of his early upbringing persisted.[51] Bishop recalled him saying that a shared belief in Christianity could form a common bond with the defeated enemy:

> All the bridges are down between ourselves and the Germans except one, we both share a common Christianity. Let us see how we can build on that.[52]

Over a quarter of the German Protestant clergy joined the Nazi Party before 1933,[53] and despite notable individual examples of resistance, such as pastors Dietrich Bonhöffer and Martin Niemöller, many prominent individuals in the German churches were sympathetic to at least some elements of Nazi ideology or, at best, failed to condemn evident crimes and atrocities.[54] But for men such as Montgomery, Robertson and Bishop, faced at the end of the war with problems that appeared all but insoluble, it was important to seek out common ground with Germans who shared their Christian values.[55]

As with the British Empire, the idealistic rhetoric of a benevolent occupation was not always consistent with the practice. Despite emphasizing the need to give Germans 'hope for the future' and to build on their 'common Christianity', Montgomery showed no hesitation in telling his Corps Commanders that they should use 'ruthless means' to deal with any disturbances and 'soldiers must shoot to kill'.[56] Nevertheless, the rhetoric of those at the top of the Military Government hierarchy is important. Montgomery's, Robertson's and Bishop's memories of the First World War, their experience serving the British Empire and their 'missionary idealism' provide a frame of reference within which their sometimes contradictory aims in occupied Germany can be understood.

Robertson went to school at Charterhouse, where a fellow pupil was the author and classical scholar Robert Graves.[57] Graves later quoted a friend saying, in their final year at school: 'Do you realize that we have spent fourteen years of our lives principally at Latin and Greek?' At least one in three of their generation at school died during the war.[58] Perhaps reflecting the classical training he received at Charterhouse, at the end of an article in the *British Zone Review,* titled 'The Year of Genesis', Robertson quoted a Latin verse from Horace to summarize what he believed should be their attitude in Germany: *Justum et tenacem propositi virum* (The wise man firm of purpose).[59] Two years later, at a press conference for journalists in 1947, he quoted the same line again, adding:

> If you want to know what I think should be our attitude in Germany then I recommend to you to read those lines yourselves.[60]

The full quotation from Horace is: *Justum et tenacem propositi virum / Non civium ardor prava iubentium / Non vultus instantis tyranni / Mente quatit solida* (The just man, firm of purpose cannot be shaken in his rocklike soul, by the heat of fellow citizens clamouring for what is wrong, nor by the presence of a threatening tyrant).[61] Robertson added that if his readers knew the poem, they would 'find that Horace wrote that Ode specially for the Control Commission in Germany'.[62] His reference to a Latin verse, in an article headed with a biblical reference, 'The Year of Genesis', illustrates his belief that the principles he had learnt at school should apply throughout his life, and furthermore, that his British colleagues in Military Government would understand and share his principles and beliefs.

Bishop stayed in Germany for five and a half years, longer than either Montgomery or Robertson and his work spanned three important areas of administration: Head of Information Services and Public Relations, Deputy Chief of Staff to Robertson and Regional Commissioner for North Rhine-Westphalia, the largest and most industrialized *Land*,[63] or region, in the British Zone. An article Bishop wrote in the *British Zone Review* entitled *'Ave Atque Vale'* (Hail and Farewell), on Montgomery's retirement as Military Governor in May 1946, perhaps best typifies the self-image of these three most senior British army officers as benevolent occupiers.[64] Bishop described their practical achievements in the first year of occupation under 'Field Marshal Montgomery's guidance and inspiration': disarming and disbanding the *Wehrmacht*, destroying quantities of ammunition, repatriating two million Displaced Persons, restoring road, rail and canal systems, the internment of 50,000 Nazi leaders and officials, the encouragement of new political parties, licensing of newspapers, and opening of schools and universities. But this was only part of their task as:

> The war unleashed by Nazism on the world has left Germany not only shattered materially but faced with grave spiritual difficulties ... None of these efforts can ... succeed unless they are accompanied by a spiritual regeneration of the German people.[65]

The 'greatest task facing the British authorities', he continued, was to 'hold out some measure of hope to the German people' that an acceptance of the Christian principles of 'humanism and democracy' would eventually produce the economic benefits of 'a reasonable standard of living', and their ability to re-enter 'the international economic life of Europe'.[66]

People, Bishop believed, were more important than organizational structures. The principles that meant most to him and his colleagues, Montgomery and

Robertson, were those of fairness, individual responsibility and personal character. Karl Arnold, a leading German politician, Christian socialist and Minister-President for North Rhine-Westphalia from 1947 to 1956, paid Bishop the following tribute in a personal letter written shortly before Christmas 1949:

> I am an honest admirer of your ability, not to lose sight of the human angle [*Das Menschliche niemals aus dem Auge zu verlieren*] in the most difficult situations, which is the decisive factor in the relationship between victor and vanquished, if our great and common peace interests are not to suffer.[67]

On 4 May 1950, shortly before he left Germany, Bishop's faith appeared to have been rewarded, when he was able to speak with confidence, at the opening of the 'British Centre', *Die Brücke* (The Bridge), in Cologne, and say to his German audience:

> You and I may hear, at times, the remarks of pessimistic people who say that we have so little in common, and that we can, therefore, learn so little from one another. That is not true. We have much in common, and much to learn from one another. The most important thing that we have in common is, of course, this.
>
> We both believe that there was once a man who, although he never went to a university, or wrote a book, or travelled more than 200 miles from where he was born, yet became the centre-piece of the human race, and the leader of the column of progress.
>
> I hope and pray that Almighty God may guide and bless our joint work in this house.[68]

Exactly five years after Montgomery received the unconditional surrender of all German armed forces in North-West Europe, Bishop was able to refer to their common belief in Christianity, the great 'kindness and hospitality' he had received in Cologne; to the 'one overriding wish' shared by 'ordinary peoples of all countries' that their children would live a better and more peaceful life than he or his generation had experienced; and to his understanding that the British and Germans had 'much in common and much to learn from one another'.[69]

4

Criticism at Home and Allegations of Corruption

Montgomery's successor as Military Governor, Marshal of the Royal Air Force Sholto Douglas, was the exception among the three British Military Governors. His pragmatic approach to a different set of challenges highlights the complexity and some of the contradictions of the occupation. Whereas Montgomery enjoyed his time in Germany[1] and Robertson looked back with satisfaction at having contributed to the 'miracle' of a prosperous and contented West Germany,[2] Douglas recalled it as 'the unhappiest period in my entire official life' and wondered why he, an air force officer, was asked to solve problems 'which should have been in the hands of the politicians'.[3] Though nominally in charge, he acted as a figurehead, with Robertson taking an increasingly important role in all aspects of administration.[4]

Douglas was born in Oxford in 1893, to a junior branch of an old-established aristocratic family distantly related to the Marquess of Queensbury. His grandfather was a clergyman and his father, who also trained as a clergyman, was Assistant Chaplain at Merton College, Oxford. Soon after Douglas and his two brothers were born, his father moved to Siena, in Italy, and left the Church to become a successful art critic and dealer. He emigrated to the United States in 1940, converted to Roman Catholicism and died in 1951 in Italy.[5] Douglas obtained a classical scholarship to Lincoln College, Oxford, and, with support from his father, attended university for one year before the outbreak of war in 1914. He was commissioned in the artillery, volunteered as an air observer for the Royal Flying Corps and qualified as a pilot in July 1915. He wrote later that obtaining his wings was 'one of the proudest moments that I have ever known in my life'.[6] He was promoted to command a squadron and awarded the Military Cross and Distinguished Flying Cross. Casualties were high, pilots flew without parachutes and mechanical breakdowns were frequent, but in later years he regretted the passing of this 'time of comparative innocence',[7] when pilots fought each other

Figure 4.1 (William) Sholto Douglas, 1st Baron Douglas of Kirtleside, by Walter Stoneman, February 1945. © National Portrait Gallery, London.

above and apparently a stage removed from the mass slaughter of troops on the ground. He ended the war, still only twenty-four years old, a lieutenant colonel and one of the most experienced pilots in the newly formed RAF.[8]

After a short break as a pilot in the embryonic civil aviation industry, Douglas rejoined the RAF in 1920. His only overseas posting was from 1929 to 1932, in Egypt, and as area commander in the Sudan. From 1936 he occupied senior administrative positions in the Air Ministry and succeeded Hugh Dowding as head of Fighter Command in November 1940. Other positions followed, as head of Middle East Command in December 1942 and Coastal Command in January 1944.[9] Despite his experience and seniority, success at the highest level eluded him. Military historians have argued that he was on the wrong side in debates over strategy, such as his advocacy of offensive sweeps over enemy territory in 1941, which resulted in casualties higher than those incurred during the Battle of Britain for little strategic benefit, and his support for Churchill's unsuccessful

Aegean campaign in 1943.[10] He was promoted in January 1946 to the rank of Marshal of the Royal Air Force, the highest in the RAF, but was disappointed not to have been appointed Chief of the Air Staff, losing out to Arthur Tedder when Charles Portal retired at the end of 1945.[11]

From August 1945 to January 1946 Douglas served in Germany as Commander-in-Chief of the British Air Forces of Occupation (BAFO).[12] He claimed later that he did not want the post, writing that 'I felt less like going to Germany than to anywhere else', but he accepted it because the position required an officer 'of the most senior rank', he had previously worked well with Montgomery and he was curious about the fate of the German air force.[13] He was nominally responsible for the disarmament of the *Luftwaffe* but left this to his deputy, Philip Wigglesworth, to manage.[14] He was thankful that his responsibilities did not extend beyond those of an air force commander, disliked the working environment and resented being increasingly 'drawn in to the web of international politics'.[15] In January 1946 he heard that he would be appointed Military Governor and Commander-in-Chief of all British forces in Germany, when Montgomery left Germany to take up his post as Chief of the Imperial General Staff on 1 May.[16]

Douglas's appointment as Military Governor is surprising, given his limited overseas experience, his intense dislike of working in Germany and his stated desire not to become involved in issues outside his personal competence, such as international politics. He claimed later that he did not want to return to Germany, but Montgomery recommended him and Arthur Tedder, the Chief of the Air Staff, persuaded him to accept the post. Douglas added that after returning to London in January 1946, he had second thoughts and only finally agreed after a personal meeting with Attlee.[17] I have not found any record of this meeting or other official documents relating to his appointment, apart from a letter in which Montgomery told Robertson it was 'fairly certain' that Douglas would succeed him as Military Governor.[18] This tends to confirm Douglas's account that Montgomery recommended him for the position, but does not explain why the government thought him a suitable candidate. His political allegiance may have been one factor. He claimed to have become a socialist at Tonbridge and Oxford, influenced by an 'aversion to snobbery' and sympathy for the underdog, but, as a serving RAF officer, he was not active in politics until after his retirement from Germany in 1947, when he accepted a peerage and supported the Labour Party in the House of Lords.[19] General Joseph McNarney, who replaced Eisenhower as Governor of the US Zone in November 1945, had served as an airman on the Western Front in the First World War[20] and it may have been thought advisable to follow the US lead by appointing an air officer rather than an army general to succeed Montgomery. Douglas's appointment may also have been intended to improve relations between the London and German arms of the administration, as Sir Arthur Street, Permanent Secretary of the newly created Control Office for Germany and Austria (COGA), had previously worked with him at the Air Ministry.[21] Overall, it would appear he was a safe choice, acceptable to the Labour government and to all three armed services in Germany, and able to maintain good working relations with his US, French and Soviet counterparts and with the Civil Service administrators in London.

Douglas's tenure as Military Governor from May 1946 to November 1947 coincided with the most difficult period of the occupation, and contrasts with the idealized image of benevolent British rule portrayed by Montgomery, Robertson and Bishop, discussed in the previous chapter. Many Germans blamed the British for the deterioration in their living standards after the food ration was cut in March 1946 from 1,550 to a near-starvation level of 1,014 calories per day.[22] Initial goodwill and relief that the war was over were succeeded by hunger strikes and protests.[23] Despite significant imports, the ration in the British Zone continued at low levels and did not improve significantly until the Spring of 1948, six months after Douglas had left Germany.[24]

Douglas wrote in similar terms to Bishop, Templer and other British army officers of his impressions of destruction in 1945 when he first visited Berlin,[25] but showed no signs of being motivated by Montgomery's 'missionary idealism' or by Robertson's belief that they were 'fighting a battle over the soul of Germany'.[26] In his later memoirs, he described the situation and his own role in personal terms, rather than expressing his opinions on geopolitical matters such as the reconstruction of Germany, the future of the British Empire or the need to 'rebuild civilisation'. This chapter contrasts his personal background and aims in Germany with those of the more idealistically motivated army generals.

Changing aims

Shortly after his appointment as Military Governor, Douglas spoke publicly for the first time, at the opening of an exhibition in London on 'Germany under Control', of his understanding of British aims:

> What are the objects of our occupation of Germany? In the first place we aim to destroy the military power of Germany and to eradicate Nazi-ism. We must not forget that these objects rank first in priority. Next we want to see Germany develop a sound sense of democratic government and social justice, to rebuild her peaceful industries and raise her standard of living to a reasonable level.[27]

These aims were uncontroversial and entirely consistent with British policy as formulated over the previous year by Montgomery and his generals, in combining the 'negative' aspects of demilitarization and de-nazification with the more 'positive' policies of economic reconstruction and democratization. As discussed in the previous chapters, the physical reconstruction of Germany was a British objective from the start of the occupation, to help create order out of chaos and prevent starvation and disease. From early 1946, however, despite Douglas stating that demilitarization and de-nazification were their highest priorities, the need to reduce costs led to an increased emphasis on economic reconstruction for another reason, the hope that German exports would offset the cost of food imports paid by the British taxpayer. Douglas provided a third, political, reason for economic reconstruction in his speech, when he said that the positive and negative aims of the occupation were 'completely interdependent: you cannot re-educate a starving and unemployed people'.[28] By accepting this argument, he implied that instead of imposing restrictions on the future level of German industry, as agreed by the Allies at the Potsdam conference in July and August 1945, it was more important, at least in the short term, to revive the economy. Reconstruction was justified as an essential precondition to make Germans more receptive to democratic ideas, and therefore less likely to be attracted to alternative political systems, such as National Socialism or communism.

At first, the government provided conflicting directions. John Hynd, the minister with responsibility for Germany, was one of the strongest advocates of the view, agreed in principle by all, that their primary aim was to make another war impossible, through fundamentally changing the structure of German politics and society. He spoke on the same occasion as Douglas, in June 1946, in idealistic terms of the importance of their task of creating a free and democratic Germany. Hynd acknowledged that the occupation would be costly and justified this by referring to the sacrifices of the previous six years and the need to secure peace, security and prosperity for their children, arguing that 'investment for peace is better, and infinitely cheaper than investment for war'.[29]

Hynd's views were not shared by the government as a whole. Hugh Dalton, Chancellor of the Exchequer, objected strongly to the cost of supporting the British Zone, estimated at £80 million for the 1946–7 financial year.[30] Around £70 million was required to pay for imports, mainly food,[31] which could only be recovered by a higher level of German exports. Eighty million pounds was a large amount, 2 per cent of the £3,837 million total government expenditure for the year, but still significantly less than the 'Defence and Supply' budget of £1,667 million, or the

£335 million budgeted for food subsidies in Britain.[32] Bevin, the Foreign Secretary, agreed with Dalton rather than Hynd, emphasizing at the Paris Council of Foreign Ministers on 10 July 1946 that unless the other Allies were willing to increase economic cooperation across the zones, 'my Government will be compelled to organise the British Zone of occupation in Germany in such a way that no further liability shall fall on the British taxpayer'.[33] The following day James Byrnes, the US Secretary of State, offered to cooperate economically with the other zones, an offer accepted by Bevin, but not by France or the Soviet Union. The eventual outcome was the creation in January 1947 of the 'Bizone', a jointly managed economic unit comprising the British and US zones.[34] Politically the two zones remained distinct until the creation in 1949 of an independent Federal Republic of Germany, now including the French in addition to the British and US zones.

Douglas used similar arguments when he explained, in a lecture at the Imperial Defence College in June 1947, why it was in Britain's interest to promote economic reconstruction in Germany. He started by referring to Germans telling him and his British colleagues: 'it's no use talking to us about democratic ideals unless you first fill our bellies', adding that 'leading thoughtful Germans' were very insistent upon the need to give them, echoing a phrase that had been used frequently by Montgomery, 'hope for the future'.[35] Without sufficient food, he continued, Germans were unable to work and there would be no economic revival. Douglas and his audience may have agreed with Dalton that paying to feed their former enemy was an unwelcome necessity, but by agreeing with the views of 'thoughtful Germans', he indicated that they shared a common interest. Food was the key to the situation. 'Short of letting Germans starve to death', he concluded, 'the only remedy for the British tax payer is to build up German industry to the point where Germans can pay for their own food by their own exports'.[36]

Douglas presented a second, political reason for reconstruction in his lecture, claiming that the Soviet Union wished to 'convert Germany into a Communist state'.

> They undoubtedly hope that the wretched conditions and low standard of living in the Western Zones will turn the eyes of the people towards communism, and that when a united Germany eventually appears it will be a Communist Germany.[37]

He added that the Russians wished to extract as much as they could in reparations from Germany, as 'a cow fed from the west and milked from the East', adopting the same phrase used earlier in the year by Bevin, in a conversation with the US Secretary of State, Marshall.[38] Helping the Soviet Union in this way, according to Douglas, was unacceptable to the British 'in view of the financial strain in which we find ourselves today'. He ended his speech by predicting that the division of Germany would persist, despite British attempts to work for unification.

Douglas did not initiate policy in this case, which was led by Dalton and Bevin, but he understood the economic logic of the situation. The driving force behind British policy was the perceived need to reduce the cost of the occupation. The British Zone was not self-sufficient in food, even at the low levels of rations imposed during the occupation. Agricultural production could not be increased sufficiently to cover the deficit, so to reduce the cost to the British taxpayer, German industry would have to be expanded to generate sufficient exports of manufactured goods to pay for the cost of food imports. But although a united Germany would be economically stronger than the British Zone on its own, and more likely to become economically self-sufficient more quickly, the Soviet Union was unlikely to agree to unification without continued reparations payments, which would hinder economic reconstruction and reduce the amount available to pay for food imports. Unless they were willing to let the Germans starve, and thereby run the risk of social unrest and greater support for the communists within Germany, the only way to reduce the occupation costs was to abandon any attempt to run Germany as a single economic unit, collaborate with the US and promote economic revival in the West. For financial as well as political reasons, British and US support for economic reconstruction had to be on their terms and therefore limited to the western zones.

Illicit gains

A few days after Douglas arrived in Germany, the Conservative MP Godfrey Nicholson expressed grave concerns in Parliament over 'alarming allegations of corruption' among Military Government staff.[39] The Prime Minister asked the Chiefs of Staff to investigate and they in turn referred the matter to Hynd at the Control Office in London (COGA) and to Robertson.[40] It emerged that Nicholson's source was a certain Captain R.C. Tarlton, a junior Military Government officer whom Nicholson knew personally. When asked for a written statement, Tarlton could only provide vague and imprecise allegations, such as unnamed Control Commission officers obtaining 'luxury goods' from German manufacturers in exchange for coal allocations, and others who used pre-war connections with German businesses to make 'gains unheard of in the normal business'.[41] Public Safety Branch, the Control Commission internal police force, investigated further and produced a report in October 1946 which dismissed most of the allegations.[42] Robertson wrote that: 'It is quite clear to me that the majority of the allegations made by Tarlton are based on chatter and groundless rumour.'[43] At the end of December Hynd minuted the Prime Minister, a little more circumspectly, that there was 'little substance in the charges' but he was setting up a new organization under a 'senior detective officer from Scotland Yard' to continue investigations into 'alleged malpractices by the staff of the Control Commission in Germany'.[44]

This was the first of many allegations that extended to the highest levels of Military Government, including some of Douglas's closest colleagues in the RAF.[45] The evidence which has survived in the archives is not sufficient to judge with any degree of certainty whether they were exaggerated, or if they represented the tip of an iceberg, with extensive corruption hidden from public view. Despite official denials, there appears to have been widespread corruption, but not to the extent claimed by reports in the popular press or by the Conservative opposition in Parliament, who used the issue as a convenient stick to beat the government. A senior official at COGA was probably correct when he minuted on the official report into Tarlton's claims that:

> The upshot has been to reveal a number of things which, to use General Robertson's words, 'are not as they should be'. The matters revealed are very different from the sensational happenings at which Mr. Godfrey Nicholson seemed to be hinting in his speech to the House on 10th May. Even so, however, there is little in the report ... to inspire any great confidence.[46]

Allegations included the theft of jewels and cash in May 1945 from *Schloss Glücksburg*,[47] thefts of paintings and antiques from *Villa Hügel*, the former home of the Krupp family, which had been converted into the headquarters of the British-run North German Coal Control,[48] and a twelve page internal report into illegal trading by British and US officers, produced in July 1946 by the Economics Information section of the Control Commission.[49]

The report alleged that investigations into the whereabouts of precious stones and metals with an estimated value of £250 million, formerly owned by the Nazi government, had revealed large scale black market activities in stolen works of art, looted museum pieces from across Europe, drugs and narcotics.[50] Two senior officers from the Metropolitan Police were sent to Germany to investigate and recommended that:

> There is a real need for an organisation to deal with serious crime committed by British Civil and Military personnel. Such crimes include serious 'Black Market' offences and the unlawful disposal and removal of very valuable property from Germany.[51]

A joint British and US exercise codenamed Operation Sparkler had some success in finding a small proportion of the missing precious stones and metals, to the value of £435,642.[52] The final report compiled in April 1947 showed a small increase in the value of materials traced in the British Zone. Results were better in the US Zone, locating property to the value of over $7 million.[53]

While it is difficult to judge the true extent of major black market activities, there is no doubt that small-scale illegal trading was widespread among British military and Control Commission personnel. Paul Chambers, Head of the Control Commission Finance Department, estimated this cost the Exchequer £41 million, half the estimated net cost of the occupation to the taxpayer in 1946–7.[54] British personnel bought goods in staff canteens and NAAFI shops, and sold them for much higher prices on the black market for German Reichsmarks (RM), which were accepted in British canteens and shops and could be used to buy more goods, or converted into sterling at the official exchange rate of 40 RM to £1 and sent home as money orders. For example, a packet of cigarettes, which cost 2–4 RM or 1–2 shillings (5–10p) in a British staff canteen, could be sold for 160 RM on the black market, worth £4 at the official rate of exchange.[55] The practice was partially stopped by issuing British staff with army forces vouchers for use in NAAFI shops, instead of allowing them to use German Reichsmarks, but until currency reform in May 1948 and the introduction of the new Deutsche Mark (DM), British soldiers and Control Commission staff could live well, by buying goods and services from Germans on the black market and paying for them with cigarettes sent from home or bought from the NAAFI with vouchers.[56]

Allegations of corrupt practices among military and Control Commission staff were linked in House of Commons debates with more general criticisms of mismanagement, muddle, deteriorating conditions in Germany and, above all, the cost to the British taxpayer. The Conservative opposition leapt on ill-judged remarks by Hugh Dalton in his budget speech in April 1946, which they took as an open invitation to criticize his Labour Party colleague and Minister for Germany, John Hynd. Dalton announced that the government estimated net expenditure on Germany and Austria in the coming year would be £80 million. This was a 'large figure', he said, and

> So far, we are getting disappointingly little in return, and that is a matter which may have to be probed in the House one of these days. I am quite sure that the British taxpayer cannot, and should not, much longer be expected to go on paying, on this scale, what are, in effect, reparations to Germany. Speaking as Chancellor of the Exchequer, I grudge the money.[57]

Responding to the Chancellor, Anthony Eden picked up immediately on the idea of 'paying reparations to Germany', adding that he wished to know more and the situation had to be remedied.[58] In two debates called by the Opposition, on 10 May and 29 July 1946, Conservative front bench spokesmen quoted Dalton's budget speech and launched personal attacks on Hynd.[59] One called him a 'minnow floating about amongst the whales', referring to the difference in size and stature between Hynd and the rather larger Foreign Secretary, Ernest Bevin.[60] Hynd received some support from Labour backbenchers,[61] but little from his party leaders. Attacks on the Control Commission in Parliament continued throughout 1946 and 1947, while Douglas was Military Governor.[62]

In the meantime, the press latched on to the story and sent reporters to Germany to investigate. On 8 July 1946 a full-page article appeared in the *Daily Mirror* under the headline '£160 million a Year – to teach the Germans to despise us'.[63] It purported to be the result of a seven-week investigation into 'widespread racketeering in the British zone of Germany' based on discussions with a large number of army and Control Commission officers. The article was written in a sensationalist style, with the tone set in the first paragraph:

> Lavish supplies of inexpensive drinks and easy, but dirty, money are causing widespread demoralisation and corruption among British personnel in Germany today at the expense of the British taxpayer's pocket and Britain's prestige.[64]

Articles later in the week placed the issue of the cost of the occupation in the wider context of the Allied Council of Foreign Ministers meeting in Paris to discuss the future of Germany, reporting Bevin's 'warning' that if no agreement was reached, 'Britain would be obliged so to organise her own zone economically that no continued burden would fall on the British taxpayer'.[65] The two issues were linked. The perception that occupation costs were too high justified Bevin's stance at Paris, and encouraged the press and politicians to seek out examples of lavish expenditure by Control Commission staff in Germany.

Press criticism of the Control Commission continued throughout 1946 and 1947, in up-market liberal journals and newspapers such as the *Manchester Guardian* and *New Statesman* as well as in the popular press.[66] On 8 July 1947 the lead article on the front page of the *Daily Mail* raised the allegations of corruption to a new level, by naming Douglas and three of the most senior RAF officers in Germany as 'assisting inquiries' into the disappearance of old master paintings, Gobelin tapestries, antique furniture, gold and silver plate and cutlery, carpets, china and glassware from the home of the aristocratic Schaumburg-Lippe family, *Schloss Bückeburg*, which had been requisitioned at the end of the war to serve as headquarters of the British Air Forces of Occupation (BAFO).[67] The allegations affected Douglas directly, as he was the senior officer commanding BAFO from July 1945 to January 1946 and had been based at Bückeburg.[68]

'Souvenir hunting'

In his memoirs, Douglas wrote that: 'vindictive suggestions and personal allegations about looting [were] levelled against even those of us who were in the most senior appointments'.[69] He commissioned a report by 'an officer from Scotland Yard' which, he claimed, 'proved conclusively the falsity of the newspaper attacks'.[70] The report, by Inspector Hayward, who conducted the earlier 'Operation Sparkler' investigations, has survived in the archives. It confirmed there was not 'a shred of evidence' Douglas 'ever removed a single article' from Germany.[71] According to the report and related documents, he and other senior British officials received items from *Schloss Bückeburg* which they used to furnish their official residences, but 'with the exception of very minor losses of small articles which can be safely attributed to normal domestic wastage or petty pilfering by staff, all was intact and could be accounted for'.[72] The report, however, stated that a large quantity of material was still missing. Although an RAF investigator attributed this to petty theft and 'souvenir hunting', in Hayward's view it had probably been subject to large-scale removals.[73]

The most serious allegation related to Douglas's predecessor as Commander of British Air Forces in Germany, Sir Arthur Coningham. According to the report, Coningham had arranged for an 'unknown quantity' of silver, porcelain and carpets from *Schloss Bückeburg* to be flown to his villa in Cannes, in July 1945, some of which was returned to Germany in August 1945 and some late in 1947, but, Hayward added: 'we have no means of ascertaining whether all that was originally taken was in fact returned'.[74] An earlier interim report by Hayward alleged that thirty-eight chests of silver had been removed from the *Schloss* to a 'farmhouse' on the estate that Coningham used as his living quarters. Sixteen chests of silver were given to the RAF Welfare branch and made available for use by senior officers. A further quantity of silver and other valuables was packed and 'accompanied' Coningham in his Dakota aeroplane when he left Germany for Cannes. When he arrived he found he had more than he needed, so the silver was re-packed and driven in his Rolls-Royce car to his house in Brussels, from where another officer collected it and returned it to the collection held by Welfare at Bückeburg. At no point, Hayward added, was any inventory made or record kept of the material.[75]

Hayward reported that Douglas told him in July 1947, when he started his investigation, that while neither he nor two other senior RAF officers had received any property other than that 'lawfully requisitioned' for use in their official residences, Coningham was 'open to criticism' for taking material to his house in Cannes.[76] Douglas added he was sure this had been done 'in good faith' and all would be returned in due course,[77] but his comment could be interpreted as an indication to Hayward of the line his inquiry should take. A few days later, Douglas received a letter from Coningham in which he acknowledged that he still had material from Bückeburg in his house, 'Villa Rosalie in the South of France', and now wished to 'return sundry articles of German furniture and equipment which were sent down there at the end of the war'.[78]

The matter ended tragically. In January 1948, before Hayward completed his final report, Coningham vanished without trace when his aircraft, including all crew and passengers, crashed into the sea near Bermuda.[79] Robertson was approached by the chief of the RAF Police, who asked if he could inform Lady Coningham, who was naturally distressed at her husband's sudden death, that 'as far as Sir Arthur is concerned, the allegations are without foundation'.[80] Robertson declined the request, replying that while he hoped this would be the case, it would be wrong to prejudge the outcome of the report.[81]

The files show that there had been disagreements dating back to 1945 between the RAF and local Control Commission branches nominally responsible for the property. It was possibly unfortunate for the RAF officers that Prince Wolrad, the owner of the estate, had been a member of the paramilitary *Stahlhelm* organization which merged with the Nazi SA after Hitler came to power in 1933.[82] He was therefore subject to automatic arrest at the start of the occupation and management of his property was transferred to the Control Commission's Property Control Branch, pending de-nazification proceedings. According to Hayward, the branch 'did in fact take charge of his financial affairs but were prevented from exercising control of the personal property by the attitude of the R.A.F. who claimed that it had been properly requisitioned for their use'.[83] A report by a Property Control Officer dated 7 July 1947, the day before the *Daily Mail* article appeared, was highly critical of the RAF, naming several senior officers including Douglas and Coningham.[84]

Files on the refurbishment of Douglas's official residence, *Schloss Ostenwalde*, formerly used by Montgomery, include a receipt for seventy-two items of silver and furniture from Bückeburg and for a small number of items requisitioned from other stately homes.[85] There is no evidence that any material was taken for his personal use, but Douglas and his wife appeared to have a taste for grand living that was in contrast with the dislike for pomp and ceremony he later claimed in his memoirs.[86] A letter from the brigadier responsible stated that redecoration had to be of the highest standard as 'visiting royalty will be entertained at the schloss'.[87] A swimming pool was required and provided by army engineers.[88] A large quantity of furniture was also ordered, to the designs of a Mr Dohler in Berlin, who had worked for other British officials. Wildfowling was arranged on a nearby lake and two guns reserved for Douglas and 'visiting VIPs'; roads to the residence were repaired, but arrangements to construct a new chimney and open a fireplace in the library had to be postponed due to other building priorities.[89]

The evidence available is far from complete, but suggests that, while there is no reason to believe that Douglas exploited the situation for his personal gain or removed any items of value from Germany, he had little regard for official procedures in his own dealings. When he complained that Dohler had not been paid for furniture ordered from him, Paul Chambers, head of Finance Division, wrote a terse reply suggesting he should have followed 'normal channels':

> There is in this country, as at home, a regular procedure for the authorisation and payment of work, the cost of which has to be borne by the public purse and where that procedure is not followed delay and irregularity is likely to occur.[90]

More generally, it would appear that corruption, petty theft and, in some cases, large-scale illegal activities were widespread in parts of the military forces of occupation and the Control Commission.[91] On the other hand, from 1946 onwards, the Control Commission branches responsible for establishing and enforcing controls appear to have become reasonably effective and were prepared to investigate cases at the highest levels. Inspector Hayward's report was shown to Lord Henderson, Parliamentary Under-Secretary at the Foreign Office, who commented that:

> Mr Hayward's report makes very disturbing reading. R.A.F. administration is shewn to be casual and negligent and to say the least, there is an atmosphere of irresponsibility about the whole business. It is a pity the enquiry could not be carried to a successful conclusion.[92]

The worst abuses occurred in the chaotic conditions of 1945, before the Control Commission was fully established in Germany. By 1946, issuing receipts and compiling inventories of items requisitioned appeared to have become standard practice.[93] Property Control Branch continued to compile inventories of material from *Schloss Bückeburg* and attempted to trace missing items until 1949.[94] In

January 1948, Robertson, now Military Governor, refused a request from the Chief of RAF Police to suspend Hayward's enquiry 'until every effort has been made to trace the bulk of this property and to bring to book any who may be responsible for the disappearances of large quantities of it'.[95] It proved impossible to recover material stolen more than two years earlier, but the corruption issue, which had tainted Douglas's Military Governorship, appeared to have been brought under control.

'A matter of conscience'

Douglas was generally pragmatic in the decisions he took, following policy agreed by his predecessor and delegating implementation to his deputies. It could be argued that his unhappiness as Military Governor was mainly due to his facing greater difficulties than Montgomery before and Robertson after him, but in his memoirs he advanced another explanation, which he described as 'a matter of conscience': his concerns over the use of the death penalty by the Nuremberg Tribunal and British Military Courts.[96]

Once economic reconstruction came to be seen as an essential prerequisite for political renewal, de-nazification assumed a lower priority, especially if former Nazis possessed skills or knowledge that were useful in rebuilding the economy.[97] Douglas later justified a pragmatic approach towards those who had supported a criminal regime by writing that 'cries for vengeance' had to be discouraged, in order to reduce the cost of the occupation:

> I had no particular liking for the Germans as a people, but I felt that it was imperative, in the position in which I was placed, that I should approach this problem with as broad and as fair a frame of mind as possible. There was more than enough vindictiveness in the air, and I felt that there was a very great need for caution over what could all too easily become vengeance. What we had suffered at the hands of the Germans during the war, and what we had discovered when we occupied Germany, were enough to encourage the cries for vengeance, but they had to be stilled if we were to achieve at least the relief of the very great burden on the shoulders of our own people of propping up the Germans.[98]

Douglas's relatively tolerant attitude towards former members of the Nazi party may have been influenced by his self-image as a professional airman and his identification with the German fighter pilots he had fought against in the First World War, believing that they shared similar values, such as individual bravery and a 'swashbuckling attitude to life'. He wrote favourably about the exploits of both British and German fighter pilots during the war[99] and of his admiration for 'the famous German ace Ernst Udet'.[100] They met in the Sudan when Udet had to make a forced landing after filming wild animals in Kenya, and compared experiences as fighter pilots on the Western Front. Douglas wrote later that he 'came to appreciate [Udet's] honesty and sincerity'[101] and Udet's death in November 1941 gave him 'cause for feelings of a distinct personal sadness'.[102] Together with Hermann Goering and Edward Milch, Udet was one of three former German First World War pilots responsible for rebuilding the *Luftwaffe* in the 1930s.[103]

As the British member of the Allied Control Council, Douglas had to hear appeals for clemency and mitigation of the death sentences imposed by the Nuremberg War Crimes Tribunal, including that on Goering, for whom he felt some personal sympathy, believing that their lives had run on curiously parallel lines. Both were born in 1893 and had been fighter pilots during the First World War. In 1915, Douglas wrote, Goering was 'doing exactly the same kind of work I was from across the other side of the lines'.[104] He speculated what might have happened had he shot him down in one of their encounters in the air:

> Whatever his subsequent crimes, Goering as a young man was undoubtedly a brave and good fighter pilot. I have wondered many times about the extent to which the course of history might have been changed if, in one of our encounters in the air at this time, I had managed to draw a bead on him long enough to finish him off. It would later have saved the world, and me, a lot of trouble many years later.[105]

His remarks about Goering and Udet did not imply that Douglas sympathized with the Nazis, or with Goering's conduct of the war in the air, but the fate of someone who had performed a similar role to his was, as he wrote later, 'almost of personal concern to me'.[106] Other British military commanders showed similar concerns for German generals they had fought against. General Horrocks, for example, visited Rundsted in prison after the war 'to fight some of the battles over again with him'[107] and Bishop took steps to improve living conditions in Werl prison where Kesselring and other German generals were held.[108]

Douglas took 'the strongest exception' to being told by Bevin that he could not use his discretion when confirming death sentences imposed at Nuremberg, but had to follow instructions from the government in London.[109] In particular he objected to being prevented from following his conscience, when German generals were sentenced to death on the basis that they had accepted orders, instead of following their conscience. The dilemma he faced was especially acute in the case of Goering. He justified his decision on the basis that Goering had almost certainly known of one atrocity which, as a former pilot, affected him personally – the shooting of British airmen after their escape from the POW camp, Stalag Luft III – but he still felt uneasy, writing that:

> Twenty-eight years before, Goering and I, as young fighter pilots, had fought each other in the cleaner atmosphere of the air. As I spoke the words that meant for Goering an inevitable death sentence, I could not help feeling, for all my loathing of what he had become, the strongest revulsion that I should have to be one of those so directly concerned with it.[110]

When he heard that Goering had committed suicide by taking poison, his reaction was not that Goering had evaded punishment, but some 'slight relief' at the news. Commenting on the decision of the Allied Control Council not to investigate further, he added: 'I was only too glad to be finished with the whole sordid business.'[111]

In addition to war criminals tried at Nuremberg, Douglas had to make the final decision in 'hundreds of cases' tried by British Military Courts, where those sentenced to death included not only concentration camp guards and other war criminals, but Polish Displaced Persons who had shot and killed Germans in revenge attacks or armed robbery after the war, a 'German peasant' ordered by his senior officer to shoot a British parachutist, and a British soldier who had strangled his German girlfriend.[112] In these cases he was allowed to use his discretion and commuted most of the sentences to life imprisonment. He claimed later that his experiences in Germany led to his conviction that the death penalty should be abolished, writing that:

> It is one thing to kill a fellow human being in the heat of battle, but these cold, judicial executions were, so far as I was concerned, an entirely different matter.[113]

Colleagues who worked with him in Germany confirmed his account. Bishop wrote later that Douglas found the use of the death penalty 'particularly repugnant',[114] and Frank Pakenham, Lord Longford, who succeeded Hynd as Minister for Germany in April 1947, wrote that 'many features of occupation life caused him [Douglas] distress', including 'the number of death warrants he had to sign'.[115]

Like many others at the time, Douglas did not fully comprehend the true nature and extent of the crimes committed during twelve years of Nazi dictatorship in Germany and Europe. As a result, he focussed on what he believed he understood:

his formative experiences as a pilot over the Western Front, his knowledge as a 'professional airman', his conscience and understanding of individual morality, and a concern for the fate of those with whom he could identify, such as British POWs shot after escaping from Stalag Luft III, or a former German fighter pilot such as Hermann Goering. He confirmed all the sentences passed by the Nuremberg Tribunal,[116] despite his personal reservations, but felt unprepared and unqualified for a role as Military Governor that included the power of life or death over individuals who had performed a similar role to his in wartime, or for whom he felt some personal sympathy.

'The unhappiest period in my entire official life'

Sholto Douglas illustrates some of the contrasts in the British occupation. He hated his time in Germany and later referred to it as 'the unhappiest period in my entire official life'.[117] Yet despite his evident dislike of the job and intense personal criticism, he tried to improve living conditions for the German population and fulfilled his responsibilities as Military Governor to the best of his abilities.[118] He did not share the 'missionary idealism' of Montgomery and the army generals, nor their idealistic vision of the British Empire as a force for good in the world, but pursued pragmatic policies to reduce the cost of the occupation to the British taxpayer and, so far as he could, promote economic revival.

Douglas left Germany on 1 November 1947. Earlier in the year in May, following press reports that he was going to resign, he wrote to Bevin that, rather than going when times were tough, 'as a rat leaving a supposedly sinking ship', he was prepared to stay as long as Bevin wished.[119] In June, however, Attlee and Bevin agreed he should go and be replaced by Robertson, who had turned down an earlier offer from Montgomery of an appointment as Quartermaster General, on a tacit understanding that in due course he would be promoted to Military Governor.[120]

There was no suggestion in the files that the decision was influenced by the *Schloss Bückeburg*, or other allegations. Pakenham, who replaced Hynd as Minister for Germany in April 1947, had a high regard for Douglas and recommended he be given a peerage. The recommendation was endorsed by Bevin, on the grounds that it would provide a clear demonstration of the government's support for the Control Commission and so improve staff morale. Moreover, as a Labour Party supporter, Douglas could be useful in the House of Lords.[121] He was enobled, as Lord Kirtleside, in the 1948 New Year Honours.

In March 1949, following the nationalization of civil aviation, he was appointed Chairman of BEA (British European Airways), where he remained for fifteen years and was considered one of the most successful chairmen of a nationalized industry, overseeing the airline's growth from 750,000 passengers in 1949 to 5.6 million in 1964.[122]

The issue of corruption among British military and Control Commission personnel has been covered at some length in this chapter, but this should not imply that theft and looting by the British in Germany was comparable to earlier wartime looting by Germans in Nazi-occupied Europe, or to the theft and looting of Jewish property within Germany. However, the issue of corruption during the British occupation is important for two reasons. Firstly, the debates in the House of Commons in May 1946 marked the start of a period of transition, in which the British in Germany lost the moral high ground, not in their own eyes, but in the eyes of many of those at home, and in the eyes of Germans who read the articles in British newspapers which criticized the occupation. It was difficult to ask Germans to emulate the British democratic 'way of life' when some prominent Britons appeared so obviously not to practise what they preached. Secondly, it provides a contrast to the idealized image of benevolent British army officers, represented by Montgomery, Robertson and Bishop, motivated by sincerely held Christian principles, who contributed to the creation of a democratic and prosperous West Germany. That may have been the outcome when viewed from the 1960s, 1970s and 1980s but, to many observers in Britain in 1946 and 1947, the occupation appeared corrupt, muddled and poorly managed.[123] The history of the occupation is complex and open to different interpretations. Both perspectives are correct to some degree, and one does not necessarily exclude the other.

Although much of the criticism in the press and House of Commons debates was unreasonable or exaggerated, some was justified and the occupation came to be perceived by many in Britain as part of the problem, not the solution. Robertson continued to issue the occasional exhortation to his staff, such as his speech on 31 July 1947 reminding them that they were 'the Empire builders … the Empire of true democracy',[124] but from the Spring of 1946 onwards, the primary concern of the government in London was to reduce the cost of the occupation. This limited the scope for the British Military Government in Germany to pursue further grandiose ambitions to achieve the 'spiritual regeneration'[125] of the German people or 'the rebirth of moral and intellectual enlightenment'.[126] Aims such as these were in any case vague and ill defined; aspirations rather than practical goals that could realistically be achieved by a relatively small number of

British soldiers and administrators.[127] Military Government policy remained the same, but the emphasis changed, from staying in Germany as long as necessary to change German culture and society, to reducing costs, provided this could be done without chaos, communism or a Nazi revival. Despite this change in emphasis, many idealistic individuals, including the four civilian administrators discussed in Part Two of this book, did what they could to further the original aims for which they believed Britain had fought the war and established the occupation.

Part Two

Political Renewal: Civilian Diplomats and Administrators

5

'Trying to Beat the Swastika into the Parish Pump'

Harold Ingrams was a former colonial official who was appointed head of the Administration and Local Government (ALG) branch of the Control Commission for Germany. He decided that, as far as possible, a British model of local government should be introduced in Germany. His attempt to impose structural administrative reforms was not typical of British policy in other areas of administration and has been considered a failure by historians,[1] but the arguments he used provide a clear example of how idealistic notions of the British Empire as a force for good in the world and a belief in the intrinsic superiority of the British 'way of life' influenced occupation practice in at least one important area – local government and the promotion of democracy – as well as permeating the rhetoric of the army generals at the top of the administration.

Ingrams had spent most of his working life in Arabia. In a new edition of *Arabia and the Isles*, an account of his earlier life and work first published in 1942, he provided a brief explanation why he had come to Germany, believing that he could help the country recover from twelve years of Nazi misrule. Writing in February 1946, in a 'small Westphalian town', he remembered discussions with his brother Leonard, sitting on the veranda of his house in Arabia some years earlier.[2]

> I mention these veranda memories because amongst them is a part explanation of my presence in Germany to-day. For it was in this room [the veranda in Arabia] that often of a night I used to think of the problem of the eradication of the ghastly doctrine of the Nazis and the redemption and regeneration of Germany. From these thoughts sprang the wish to help in the great task in which we are now engaged, to assist in the eventual peaceful co-operation by Germany in international life in Europe.[3]

Ingrams' personal background was similar to that of Field Marshal Montgomery and Generals Robertson and Bishop. He was born in 1897, the same year as

Bishop and one year later than Robertson. His father was a clergyman and teacher at Shrewsbury School, a leading English public school. He fought and was wounded in France in the First World War. He joined the Colonial Service in 1919 and was posted to Zanzibar, Mauritius and Arabia, where he served with great distinction.[4] In 1936 he brokered a peace agreement between warring Bedouin tribes in Southern Yemen, which is still known as the 'Ingrams Peace'.[5] During the war he served in various senior diplomatic posts in the Middle East, in Aden and the southern Arabian Peninsula.[6] He was seconded by the Colonial Office in July 1945 to the Administration and Local Government branch of the Control Commission for Germany and in December that year was made head of branch.[7] He stayed for just over a year, leaving in August 1946.[8]

Figure 5.1 Harold Ingrams. Reproduced with permission from the *Journal of the Royal Asiatic Society*.

Ingrams was an influential member of the Control Commission, chairing working parties on local government and electoral procedure.[9] He was also the British member of the Allied Control Council subcommittee on governmental structure and participated in bilateral meetings with his US counterpart in July 1946 to consider greater coordination between the British and US zones.[10] In an early study published in 1968,[11] Wolfgang Rudzio claimed that British local government policy was largely determined by Professor William A. Robson, an expert in public administration at the London School of Economics (LSE),[12] who advised Control Commission staff while they were based in London. Robson was a highly respected figure and his ideas were undoubtedly influential,[13] but Rudzio underestimated the contribution made by Ingrams and his colleagues in the ALG branch in Germany.[14] Robson played no part in the work of the Control Commission after they left Britain for Germany in July 1945.

Robson, Ingrams and his colleagues in ALG branch all agreed that local government in Germany had to be reformed before it could be re-established on a democratic basis. In the US Zone, decentralization was achieved by devolving power to three self-governing regions (*Länder*), while re-establishing lower levels of local government in cities, towns and rural districts on much the same basis as had existed during the Weimar Republic, before the Nazis seized power in 1933. The British believed the United States was acting prematurely in giving away too much power, too quickly, to local German authorities. General Philip Balfour, head of the Control Commission Internal Affairs and Communications (IAC) division, which included ALG branch, wrote in February 1946:

> The US aims at a restoration (with certain modifications) of the pre-1933 structure of local government, and the other Allies appear to agree with this. The British, on the other hand, consider that this form of government proved its weakness by its failure to withstand both Prussian militarism and the Nazis, and therefore do not propose to restore it without radical alterations.[15]

Robson saw the problem in organizational and structural terms, claiming that local government in Weimar Germany was fundamentally undemocratic, due to the privileged position of the bureaucracy, executive power vested in senior elected local officials such as town and city mayors (*Bürgermeister*), and local authorities acting as an arm of the state with accompanying police and regulatory powers.[16] While not disagreeing with the need for structural reforms and a complete break with the past, Ingrams drew on his family background, education and experience of Empire, to argue that democracy was essentially a matter of individual behaviour based on Christian morality. As he said in a lecture to Control Commission staff in February 1946: 'We are trying to beat the swastika into the parish pump and the parish council does not go to war.'[17]

'The most robust in the world' – promoting a British model of democracy

Not content with repealing Nazi laws and restoring the German local and regional administrative system as it had been in 1933 before Hitler came to power, Ingrams acted as if he were a missionary for democracy, as he understood it, attempting to convert the Germans to the British 'way of life' which, in his view, represented the essence of democracy and was the 'antithesis' of the German system.[18] The Weimar system of democracy had 'proved an easy prey for the Nazis' and 'to restore the pre-1933 system could be nothing more than ineffectual patch-work.'[19] He later elaborated on the idea of the colonial administrator as a secular missionary, not specifically in Germany, but throughout the Empire. British colonial administrators, he wrote, now went to Africa and Asia as Julius Caesar and St Augustine had come to England two thousand years earlier, to bring 'the civilisation of Rome and Christian faith to these lands.'[20] The colonial administrator's role was not to convert the heathen, but to bring peace, prosperity and democracy to the inhabitants of other nations and so 'help in achieving that peace, and happiness too, which is promised to men of goodwill of whatever faith they be.'[21]

Soon after he arrived in Germany, Ingrams recorded his thoughts on the implications of the October 1944 policy directives issued by the War Office to senior British officials in Germany.[22] Apart from a general requirement to promote decentralization and the development of local responsibility, the directives provided no guidance on local government and administration.[23] Ingrams wrote that true democracy was based on Christian principles, and the biblical 'thou shalt not' of the Old Testament must be replaced by, in his words, 'the principle of duty towards one's neighbour', adding that 'if we are to change German methods our only yardstick is our own system.'[24] This sentence embodied three principles he stuck to throughout his time in Germany: the need for a fundamental change to the former German system; his belief that the essence of democracy lay not in collective social or political structures or institutions, but in personal relations between individuals conducted in a spirit of Christian morality; and a conviction, based on his imperial experience, that the only practicable way forward was to introduce as much of the British model of democracy into Germany as possible, as this was not only 'the most robust in the world', but the kind of democracy he and his British colleagues knew and understood best.

The same fundamental principles were expressed in different ways in many other documents. In February 1946 Ingrams prepared a one-page paper with the title 'On Promoting Democracy in Germany' which he showed to General Robertson, the Deputy Military Governor. According to Ingrams, Robertson 'read it through carefully and then passed it back saying, with some emphasis "I agree with every word if it."'[25] British democracy, Ingrams wrote in the paper, was based on the superior character of the British people and on Christianity. It was their duty to set an example to the Germans (who if not British were at least Christian) by practising it themselves and, in so doing, encouraging the Germans to adopt the same beliefs, values and standards of behaviour:

> Our democracy, the most robust in the world, is the product of our character and our country. It is on British soil that it flourishes best but we do export it and tended carefully it grows and flourishes in diverse lands, even if it takes a long time to acclimatise itself.
>
> The democracy we seek to establish is based on Christianity, the fulfilment of our duty towards our neighbours. The welfare of everyone of us is the concern of each of us and this is the idea which we have to practise ourselves and help the Germans to practice in each other and to us.[26]

The paper was printed as the Foreword to a revised edition of a directive on local government issued the same month and circulated widely to Control Commission staff.[27]

Although Ingrams' ideal view of British democracy based on Christian principles was endorsed at the highest level by the Deputy Military Governor and can be considered typical of many of the older generation of British officers, diplomats and senior administrators in Germany, it represented a highly selective interpretation of history. In his emphasis on the role of the individual and an accompanying distrust of political parties, Ingrams ignored the widespread corruption in British politics before the 1832 Reform Act and the inequalities in British society. He evoked an imagined English rural past, in which the Anglican village parish church was the focus of community life. As he explained in a series of lectures to British Military Government detachment commanders across the zone:

> The real strength of local government in England, which is very constantly described as the home of local government, resides ... in the parish; and

> the strength of the parish was originally in that Christian life of collective organisation for mutual help which centred round, and was often directed by, the Church.[28]

His perception of a robust English parish democracy was similar in some respects to that of Sidney and Beatrice Webb and their successors at the LSE, who believed that an 'extra-legal democracy' had been established in some localities in Britain by the early nineteenth century. The Webbs regretted that this model had not been extended more widely in the 1830s, when municipal boroughs were reformed and rural parishes ceased to be an effective unit of local government, but the most common form of parish government in rural districts, they wrote, was not a democratic meeting of equals but a 'parish oligarchy' in which:

> Official relationships between the parties were inextricably woven into the economic relationships that existed between the same individuals in their private capacities … Even the clergyman, who was in many respects the most independent person in the village, often owed his position to the squire, let his glebe to the Churchwarden, bargained with the Overseer as to the rates on his tithes, and drew these tithes from every occupier of land in the parish.[29]

In Anglican churches in rural Britain in the eighteenth century, attendance at Sunday service reflected an authoritarian and hierarchical social order, rather than robust self-government.[30] Callum Brown has argued in *The Death of Christian Britain,* that the established clergy regretted their reduced social and economic status after they lost much of their formal responsibility at the start of the nineteenth century, in matters such as poor relief, education and the moral welfare of their parishioners.[31] Before his posting to Germany, Ingrams had spent the whole of his working life overseas. His idyllic view of a 'golden age' of British parish democracy probably owed as much to what he had been taught at school or learned from his clergyman father, as to any genuine understanding of past or contemporary British society.

A 'benevolent despotism'

In June and July 1945, Montgomery and his senior officers took steps to initiate the process of political renewal in the British Zone. The new Directive on Military Government issued on 10 September (see Chapter 2) covered broad principles only and the formulation of detailed policies was undertaken by the

Control Commission divisions. Ingrams was responsible for implementing the directive in his area of responsibility: local government and administration. Because British policy was to build from the bottom up, his responsibilities included the renewal of political life generally including public meetings and political parties, as well as the establishment of local and regional councils and preparations for elections. General Philip Balfour, head of the Internal Affairs and Communication Division, wrote to his immediate subordinates on 2 August, telling them that a working party was to be established under the chairmanship of Ingrams to 'prepare clear and concise directions' on the issues of freedom of assembly, liberty of discussion and the formation of political parties.[32] The first meeting of the newly constituted 'Working Party on Democratic Development' took place the following Monday, 6 August and met daily until its eighth and final meeting.[33] Ingrams was the driving force in these meetings, preparing drafts of papers, ordinances, instructions and directives, which were generally accepted by the other participants, with only minor amendments.[34]

To assist the Working Party with their discussions, Ingrams circulated a thirteen-page paper which outlined the background to their task and the reasons why he believed political reform was necessary.[35] He explained that the paper was concerned with 'the permanent decentralisation of administration in Germany', and their aim was 'to give the ordinary German man and women [*sic*] the maximum amount of say in the government of the country at all levels and to make it as difficult as possible for any one to establish the *Führer* principle again'.[36] He argued that the ban on all forms of political activity, imposed at the start of the occupation, must be relaxed before they could change German political culture. Freedom of speech was to be permitted and 'indeed encouraged' as 'the German, who is entirely unused to such a luxury must gradually be brought to realise that it is not a luxury but a vital necessity which he or she must never surrender again'.[37] Every adult German man and woman would be given the right to vote and although, as in England, many would be apathetic, 'the Englishman would certainly resist if his right to vote was taken away from him and ideally the German must be taught to think likewise'.[38] The formation of political parties would be allowed, but in the Weimar Republic constituencies had been too large for voters to know the individuals they were voting for, and 'a vote should be cast for a candidate not a party'.[39] If ordinary men and women were given responsibility for government, this 'should also make it impossible for the Germans to say again with any shadow of truth "It wasn't our fault but our leaders"'.[40]

Most of the paper covered the detailed principles to be adopted for the establishment of indirect rule through local and regional Nominated Representative Councils.[41] Ingrams wrote with great confidence on the subject, based on his colonial training and experience. British policy in Germany, he wrote, was that of indirect rule, which he defined as 'rule through indigenous authorities' and 'one of the methods of teaching people to take responsibility in governing themselves'.[42] He provided detailed advice on how to establish nominated councils, their recommended size, functions and responsibilities, the role of the chairman and the creation of standing orders to govern procedure. British detachment commanders were advised to select members to ensure adequate representation of all the 'party or sectional' interests in an area. This was defined widely, including religious groups, trade unions, political parties, farmers and industrialists, or geographically by residential areas.[43]

The task Ingrams envisaged Military Government commanders performing in Germany was analogous to that undertaken by District Officers in a British colony or dependent territory. A few weeks earlier, on 17 July, he wrote to a former colleague in the Personnel Department of the Colonial Office in London asking for his help with recruitment, saying he expected they would need around 600 officers before long, adding that 'it does seem to me that the jobs are very much what any D.O. [District Officer] or A.D.O. [Assistant District Officer] has to cope with especially in indirectly ruled territories'.[44] Revealing something of his personal circumstances, he added that those attracted to the job might include 'officers in the same position as myself, who have about 18 months leave due to them who would like to spend a year doing a useful job in a decent [i.e. temperate] climate'.[45]

In addition to re-drafting the relevant sections of the general directive,[46] the Working Party prepared five Military Government Ordinances, numbers 8–12,[47] and a new supplementary directive on 'Administrative, Local and Regional Government', which provided guidance for Military Government detachment commanders on actions to be taken within their own areas.[48] An explanatory section started by discussing the 'Nature of the Problem – The Individual German':

> The German people have had National Socialism and Nazi doctrine pumped into them for many years. There are few ordinary Germans alive who are used to thinking for themselves.[49]

Until democratically elected Councils could be established, the directive continued, British Military Government had to function as a 'benevolent despotism' which should act impartially and ensure that the 'legitimate needs' of all sections of the population were met 'as far as is proper and reasonable'.[50] Similar sentiments were expressed at the end of the section on 'Political Parties', which contrasted a constructive and impartial Military Government with unscrupulous Nazi 'gangsters', and ended with an analogy which embodied the theme of a new birth for Germany, aided by the British:

> Finally, it should be emphasised here as elsewhere that the aim of Mil. Gov. is constructive rather than repressive. Political parties should be the natural expression of political consciousness, in Germany as in England... Mil. Gov., in fact, should aim to be regarded as the midwife of German political thought rather than as its repressor.[51]

This passage in the directive echoed similar comments by Robertson, telling his staff in an article in the *British Zone Review* that their task in Germany was not just a matter of physical or economic reconstruction, but more like educating a child, as the German nation was 'being reborn in the present stage of its history'.[52] Despite the obvious paternalism and the persistence of negative stereotypes of Germans as ignorant and incapable of thinking for themselves, the wartime discourse of death and destruction was being superseded by a more positive one of new birth and renewal.

Ingrams was not successful in recruiting 600 former colonial officials to implement the directive but, by May 1946, Military Government officials had successfully established Nominated Representative Councils in 7,738 of 7,969 communities (*Gemeinde*), the lowest level of administration, and in 189 of 193 urban districts (*Stadtkreise*). The official in ALG branch who reported the figures commented:

> On the whole it can definitely be said that the meaning of British democracy is beginning to penetrate the dormant, apathetic minds of the average German citizen.[53]

It may seem ironic that his comment, on the meaning of democracy, accompanied a progress report on the establishment of non-elected bodies, appointed by the British Military Government. It indicates that Ingrams and his colleagues did not consider true democracy to be unqualified rule by the people or their elected representatives; this was how Hitler had come to power. It was rather the responsible exercise of power, by independent, public-spirited individuals. How they were elected or appointed was the means to the end, not the end in itself; what mattered was that the 'right' people ended up in charge.

Achieving a compromise on electoral reform

Whereas the establishment of Nominated Representative Councils proceeded smoothly, Ingrams and his colleagues in ALG branch encountered opposition among both British and Germans to their proposed changes to the German voting system. The most contentious issue was Ingrams' proposal to replace the system of proportional representation used in the Weimar Republic (in which electors voted for a party and multiple candidates were selected from a party list, in proportion to the number of votes each party received), with the British 'first past the post' or 'single majority' system, in which electors voted for a person, not a party, and the one individual who received the most votes was elected in each constituency. The eventual outcome after several months of discussions was a compromise: the introduction of a new hybrid electoral procedure, which combined elements of both the British and German electoral systems.

Ingrams started work on arranging elections in November 1945, soon after he had completed the Directive on Administrative, Local and Regional Government. He was asked to convene a 'British Working Party to supervise a German Working Party on Electoral Procedure'.[54] The original intention was to give a selected group of German politicians and local government officials the ability to provide input on points of detail, but not allow them to determine the key elements of the system to be adopted. At the first meeting of the (British) Working Party on 20 November, Ingrams reported that decisions on the most important policy issues had already been taken, but they wished to consult the Germans on matters of detail, such as the size of constituencies, qualifications for inclusion in the electoral roll and the design of the ballot boxes.[55] However, German politicians opposed to the changes were able to bypass Ingrams and the British Working Party, and enlist support from John Hynd, the Minister for Germany. As Hynd's agreement was required before a new electoral system was implemented and elections held, Ingrams found he could no longer restrict discussions with the Germans to matters of detail or impose changes without consultation, as he had done in the September 1945 directive on local government, establishing nominated representative councils.

Ingrams introduced the second meeting of the German Working Party, at the end of January 1946, by making a speech on the benefits of the British single majority system. He argued that it worked well in the Empire, and should therefore also work in Germany. He continued by describing the benefits of the British system in similar fashion to his earlier lectures to Control Commission staff, emphasizing that democracy was a matter of individual behaviour, rather than a contest between political parties; proportional representation did not lead to a 'democratic way of life'; it was impersonal and led to 'one strong man with a weak following'; the individual was especially important in local government which was the concern of everyone. Political parties should be interested in the day-to-day issues that most concerned constituents in their areas, such as: 'Are the streets muddy? We would like to know why.'[56] Some of the German delegates were either persuaded by Ingrams' arguments, or believed that the British system would work to their benefit. At the end of the meeting, the delegates voted – eight in favour of the British single majority system and seven for proportional representation – but, unfortunately for Ingrams, this was not the end of the matter.[57]

It emerged during the meeting that Ingrams had received specific instructions from Hynd on a visit to London a few days earlier, that if the German delegates rejected the British single majority system, he should offer them the alternative vote instead.[58] This was a more proportional system, but preserved the principle of electors voting for an individual, not a party. As a former railway official, Hynd was familiar with the alternative vote from its use by the National Union of Railwaymen (NUR) in their internal elections. Hynd was also sympathetic to the German Social Democratic Party (SPD), some of whose leading members he had known while they were in exile in London during the war. The SPD was more dependent on a strong party organization than their rivals on the centre and right of politics, and therefore had most to gain from proportional representation, but all the German political parties opposed the British 'single majority' system. Although eight of the Working Party delegates had voted in favour of the British system, the seven delegates voting against included all the representatives of the political parties. Hynd was not prepared to proceed without their agreement.[59]

The issue was resolved when Austen Albu arrived in Germany in early February 1946, to take up a position in the Political Division of the Control Commission. Albu was an active socialist, personally appointed by Hynd. Robertson, who until then had supported Ingrams, told Albu at their first meeting that he had decided to go ahead with the British single majority system rather than proportional representation and, if Hynd wished to change this, he should say so sooner rather than later.[60] At a divisional meeting a few days later, Albu put forward Hynd's objections to Ingrams' proposed reforms. He told the meeting that Hynd was 'averse to imposing on the Germans a system of which they were not wholly in favour'; the fact that it worked in Britain did not necessarily mean it would work in Germany; proportional representation was 'well established in Europe … had considerable support in England' and 'could not be lightly dismissed'. After a long discussion it was agreed that the best solution would be a compromise: proportional representation but without the party list. Albu and Ingrams wrote a brief for Robertson, who was due to speak to the German Working Party at its next meeting on 14 February.[61]

The brief still outlined the advantages of the British majority system, but represented a change in tone from Ingrams' earlier assertions that the British system was the best in the world and there was no reason why it should not be adopted in Germany.[62] In his address, Robertson was conciliatory. He re-emphasized that the Working Party should 'choose a system under which the voter declares himself for an individual and not merely a party' and that the existing electoral system in Germany was unsound and had contributed to the downfall of democracy in the Weimar Republic. However he concluded, somewhat ambiguously, by saying that:

> What is good for England is not necessarily good for Germany. That is why we will not impose our system on you unless we are convinced that it will give general satisfaction to your people.[63]

The process of democratization had now become a dialogue, not the forced imposition of one particular system by the British on the Germans.

The German Working Party considered Robertson's arguments, but was not able to reach a consensus either to adopt the British system or propose an acceptable alternative. Faced with an impasse, the final decision was taken by the British, taking account of German views, but not yet prepared to allow the Germans to make the decision for themselves. At a meeting in London, Hynd, Robertson, Albu and Ingrams agreed that a compromise system should be adopted, which combined the form of the British system – electors voting for an individual in their constituency – with the substance of the former German proportional representation system.[64] Results of individual ballots were supplemented by the selection of additional candidates from a party list, to increase the total elected to reflect the proportion of votes cast for each party.[65] Albu later claimed that the introduction of the compromise system was his idea, writing that, when studying the papers for the meeting, he 'suddenly remembered' Jim Middleton, secretary of the Labour Party, telling him about a similar system in France.[66] The new hybrid system was implemented and, despite its rather convoluted origins, has stood the test of time remarkably well. With some slight modifications, it continues to be used in Germany today. Very similar systems have been adopted in Britain, in more recent times, for elections to the Scottish, Welsh and London Assemblies.

Dialogue and debate

A second dispute with leading German politicians arose over Ingrams' proposed abolition of the post of *Bürgermeister*, an elected mayor with executive responsibilities, and its replacement by two positions following the British model of local government in city, county and district councils: an elected and unpaid 'Chairman of the Council', and a professional salaried chief executive or 'Town Clerk'. In practice this meant that the executive functions of the *Bürgermeister* would transfer to an unelected official, and the *Bürgermeister* would no longer receive a salary. The measure was part of a package of reforms designed to establish a politically neutral civil service, on the principle that senior paid government officials (*Beamten*) should be 'servants of the people', not of the state, and should not be active members of any political party.[67] The proposed reforms were strongly criticized by German officials and politicians, who saw them as an attempt to impose an alien system that conflicted with long-established and effective German administrative traditions.[68]

Opposition to the reforms generally, and to the proposed changes in status of the *Bürgermeister* in particular, first emerged at a consultative body, comprising the German leaders of the regional governments in the British Zone.[69] Michael Thomas, a half-Jewish German refugee who fled Germany in 1939 and returned in 1945 as an officer in the British army, acted as the British liaison officer for early meetings of the group.[70] He reported in October 1945 that:

> The main objection the Germans raise against our [draft] directive is the transfer of the executive functions of the political head of an administration to a paid public servant. They argue that such a system might work well in England, but in present day Germany there would not be anybody who could afford to hold the political office without pay. To pay him although he has no executive functions would defeat the object of the scheme, quite apart from the financial burden to the administration.[71]

The next meeting of the group was attended by General Templer, Deputy Chief of Staff to Robertson, who defended the reforms in a speech based largely on a brief prepared by J.M. Cobban, a close colleague of Ingrams, with the usual arguments that British democratic models were used in many countries and the pre-war German system 'was not good enough to prevent the seizure of power by anti-democratic forces'.[72]

The German politicians were not impressed. Thomas reported that they approached him many times, claiming that British authorities on the subject considered 'the German local government code preferable to the English system in many ways'.[73] Thomas did not specify which authorities they were referring to, but the German Civil Service was regarded favourably and admired for its independence, professionalism and lack of corruption in British and US local government studies written before 1945, such as William Harbutt Dawson's *Municipal Life and Government in Germany* (1914).[74] Harold Laski, the radical Labour Party politician and Professor of Political Science at the LSE, writing early in his career in 1917 when he was working in the United States, had contrasted the German tradition of self-government favourably with 'an over-centralized unitary sovereign state' in Britain, claiming that: 'there was in normal times a far more vigorous and autonomous culture of local and civic self-government in Germany than in Britain, where local authorities were merely an "anaemic reflex of the central power"'.[75]

The issue illustrates some of the difficulties Ingrams and his colleagues faced when they attempted to apply the principle of a politically neutral civil service to Germany. Despite its reputation for independence and integrity, the established bureaucracy in Germany had been one of the four pillars of Nazi rule, the others being the Party, the Army and the large industrialists.[76] The great majority of German professional administrators still in post in 1945, if not themselves party members, had survived the Nazi seizure of power in 1933 and had supported the government throughout the war. Those who opposed the Nazis had generally resigned, been forced into exile or imprisoned. But German politicians from across the political spectrum had personal reasons for opposing changes to the existing system. The Social Democratic Party had been the ruling party in many regional, city and district authorities before 1933. While many of the SPD's leading figures were appointed to positions of responsibility by the British in 1945 and 1946, replacing former Nazis, they were financially dependent on their salaries and strongly opposed any moves towards the British model, which would have prevented active party members from receiving a salary if they were employed as government officials.[77] All the German parties benefitted from a system that gave leading members the opportunity to earn a salary from their positions in local and regional government.

Ingrams left Germany in August 1946, after completing a year's secondment from the Colonial Office. In November 1946, Military Government Ordinance no. 57 transferred responsibility for local government and elections from the British to the German authorities.[78] Ingrams' plans to introduce major changes to the German system of local government were shelved and apparently forgotten. Most of the civil service reforms which he had been able to implement previously were rolled back in later years.[79] His colleagues in ALG Branch adopted an advisory role, running training courses and setting up a local government school of administration where invited British lecturers and German participants exchanged views and debated best practice.[80]

Shortly before he left Germany, in July 1946, Ingrams complained in a personal memo, written to his immediate superior, about the lack of support he received from his British colleagues and from the government in London.[81] He wrote that he retained his sense of mission as 'one that needs to be carried through in the interests of humanity and our nation', but was increasingly discouraged by difficulties placed in his way internally by the British Control Commission. He was disappointed at the failure to authorize increases in staff, to advance the status of his branch to that of a division and the refusal by the Treasury to increase his pay following his promotion the previous December to head of branch. He no longer wished to remain in Germany and had asked the Colonial Office to find him another post adding: 'They know well that my main experience and interests lie in the Middle East.'[82] Soon after, he left Germany for a period of leave in England, before being offered a post, not in the Middle East, but in Africa. In an article in the April 1947 issue of the *Quarterly Review*, however, summarizing his work and achievements in Germany, he concluded more positively that: 'contact and cooperation' with the Germans were 'necessary to bring the task to a successful conclusion'.[83]

Ingrams, like many of his contemporaries, displayed an arrogant belief in the superiority of the British character and way of life.[84] He treated Germans as ignorant natives, doubting their ability to think for themselves or understand complex issues such as proportional systems of voting in democratic elections.[85] At the same time he possessed a sincere belief that his actions were in the Germans' best interests. The British, he wrote, had 'a great record in helping other nations and races along the path to true democracy' and the best British administrators were 'guided by the three principles of honesty of purpose, just dealing and humanity'.[86] Such views could appear plausible in the 1940s, before decolonization led to bitter conflict and government by dictatorship in many newly independent countries in the British Empire, rather than liberal democracy.

The limited nature of Ingrams' electoral and administrative reforms was in stark contrast to the scale of his ambition to fundamentally reform Weimar democracy. Even so, he met significant resistance. As the occupation progressed, the British authorities at the highest level were increasingly unwilling to impose structural reforms without the support of a clear majority of leading German politicians, arguing, as Hynd did in July 1946, that it 'would be wrong to impose a British system arbitrarily on the Germans'.[87] Ingrams' proposals were heavily criticized by contemporaries and never fully implemented, but we should not conclude from this that his attempt to reform local government in Germany should be ignored or judged to have been a failure. The most important contribution of the British during the occupation, in this as in other fields, was not that they succeeded or failed in imposing their particular conception of democracy, but that they proposed an alternative model for the future that was different from both the former Nazi and Weimar models. They discussed fundamental political and constitutional issues with leading German politicians, at a time when both sides looked back to Nazi dictatorship and the horrors of war, and believed that the solutions they eventually adopted would be critical to achieving a stable and peaceful future for them and their children. They argued and debated with each other what kind of system was most appropriate, initially at local and regional level and then for the Federal Republic, and in so doing discovered shared democratic values as well as differences.

Despite disagreements over electoral procedure, proportional representation and the status and responsibilities of elected city mayors, German politicians agreed with Ingrams and his British colleagues on many fundamental democratic principles. They agreed that the electoral system should promote stable government with an effective but loyal opposition, and that it should discourage extreme or 'freak' parties, as Ingrams called them.[88] They agreed on the need to protect individual rights and safeguard the individual against excessive demands from an authoritarian government.[89] They were sympathetic to the principles of decentralization and the development of local responsibility. The dialogue continued during the occupation. German politicians and administrators attending British-run local government schools pointed out inconsistencies between the principles they were taught and increased centralization in Britain, such as the nationalization of locally managed hospitals within the newly created National Health Service. As Raymond Ebsworth, a former British official working for ALG branch later related, such inconsistencies 'genuinely shocked the German audience'.[90] When viewed in this way, Ingrams' and his British colleagues' early attempts to impose democratic reform in Germany did not comprise 'forced re-orientation' dictated by the Allies (as proposed by some historians),[91] but heralded a period of dialogue and debate, which continued through the following decades with the creation of the German Basic Law (*Grundgesetz*) in 1949, the liberalization of West German society in the 1960s, and the fall of communism in the East in the 1980s and 1990s, to the present.[92]

6

International Socialist Visions of Political Renewal

Austen Albu and Allan Flanders were appointed to positions in the Political Division of the Control Commission by John Hynd, the Chancellor of the Duchy of Lancaster and minister responsible for Germany.[1] All three had been active in socialist organizations before and during the war, in the Fabian Society, the Labour Party and various fringe groups that attempted to influence Labour Party policy.[2] They were also closely associated with German socialist refugees who fled to Britain from Nazi Germany. According to a former official at his department, Hynd owed his appointment to his contacts with German exiles.[3] Albu had close links with a small but influential socialist splinter group, *Neu Beginnen* (New Beginning), originally formed by dissident members of the German Social Democratic Party (SPD) and the German communist party (KPD).[4] Flanders was the leading member of the Socialist Vanguard Group, the British arm of another small radical socialist group founded in Germany, the *Internationaler Sozialistischer Kampfbund*, translated into English as Militant Socialist International, but usually referred to by its initials, ISK.[5]

Albu's and Flanders' socialist views and contacts with comrades from different national, social and cultural backgrounds gave them a different perspective from Montgomery, Robertson, Bishop, Ingrams and other high ranking British soldiers and administrators considered in previous chapters. They wanted to change the world for the better, not preserve the established social order and their own privileged position within it. They had an international outlook and believed that inequalities in society, between rich and poor, capitalists and workers, the strong and the weak, were more important than national differences.[6] German socialists, especially those in exile, expected to take power after the Nazi State had been defeated, and they believed that a Labour government in Britain would help them to achieve this.[7] Albu and Flanders tried to support their German comrades but found they had limited scope to implement policies they considered necessary to achieve constructive change. They returned to Britain at the end of 1947 disappointed with their achievements and with a pessimistic outlook for the future.

Albu was born in 1903 into a moderately prosperous British Jewish family. His paternal grandfather had immigrated to London from Berlin. After training as an engineer at the City and Guilds College in London,[8] he moved to Newcastle where he met his future wife and became a socialist, appalled at the living conditions in some of the Tyneside boroughs and, as he later wrote in his memoirs, 'dissatisfied with the hypocrisy of the middle-class ethos in which I had been brought up and with the military nationalism which had

Figure 6.1 Austen Harry Albu, by Bassano Ltd, 1950. © National Portrait Gallery, London.

inevitably accompanied the [first world] war'.[9] After a brief flirtation with the theatre, he settled down, married and obtained a well-paid job as works manager for Aladdin Lamps, who were planning to build a factory in West London. He spent a year in the United States to learn the business, returned to London and opened the factory in 1931. He continued with his political activities, joining the Socialist League when it was formed in 1932. He was also active in the Fabian Society and in 1933 was elected chairman of his local constituency Labour Party in Uxbridge.[10]

Albu first met representatives of the *Neu Beginnen* group in London in the 1930s. He and his wife, Rose, visited members in Prague and later in Paris.[11] They also assisted members who left Germany as refugees when they arrived in Britain. The historian Francis Carsten, for example, stayed with them after leaving Amsterdam in 1939, before being offered a fellowship at Wadham College, Oxford.[12] Patrick Gordon-Walker, a friend of the Albus and a don at Oxford, had made contact with *Neu Beginnen* on visits to Germany in the early 1930s.[13] In 1937, he and Albu founded a new organization, the Socialist Clarity Group. Members included William Warbey, later a left-wing Labour MP, Michael Chance, an ethologist who later attempted to explain the rise of Nazism in terms of social pathology,[14] and Jon Kimche, a journalist and co-author with his brother David of *Secret Roads,* a history of Jewish migration to Palestine,[15] together with two or three of their German *Neu Beginnen* comrades, now in exile in London.[16]

In 1939, shortly after the outbreak of war, Albu prepared a draft 'manifesto' for his comrades in the Socialist Clarity Group, in which he wrote that:

> A federation of free, democratic Socialist states of Europe is the only peace settlement which can ensure that the tragic history of the last twenty years is never again repeated.[17]

His views reflected those of his German friends in *Neu Beginnen* and many others on the political left in Britain and Germany. They argued that the war had been caused by the 'ruling classes' of all countries. In Germany, the industrialists, the 'militarists' in the army and the landowning Prussian Junkers were to blame, not the workers who, they believed, opposed the war and would eventually understand that their true interests lay in supporting a socialist revolution. The logical consequence of these views was that an Allied victory would not in itself prevent a third world war, as competition among the ruling classes of different nationalities would continue unchecked. The only way to achieve a lasting peace was through the creation of a new socialist world order.[18]

There is no evidence that Albu had any particular interest in post-war planning for Germany. He was more concerned with Britain. He was interested in industrial psychology and production planning and control. He wrote a Fabian pamphlet on management and was active in the Society, joining the executive committee in 1943.[19] He tried to further his political ambitions through being adopted as a Labour Party prospective parliamentary candidate. He was shortlisted for two constituencies but not selected.[20] He wrote in his memoirs that, though excited by the Labour victory in 1945, he was disappointed to have played no part in it. He 'hoped and half expected' that the new Labour government would find some use for his services but, when Hynd telephoned him in early 1946 suggesting he should go to Germany, 'the idea of taking part in what seemed the impossible task of restoring democracy to Germany and deciding its future was not one I would have chosen myself'. Nevertheless, he accepted the position on a temporary contract for three months, with no clear brief from Hynd as to what the job entailed.[21]

Figure 6.2 Allan Flanders. Photo courtesy Rene Saran.

Flanders and the ISK had a different vision for the post-war future of Germany from *Neu Beginnen*. They were equally committed to the defeat of fascism, but did not share *Neu Beginnen*'s belief in the opposition of the working class to Hitler. Flanders was first persuaded to join the ISK in 1928, when he was 18 years old and still at school in London.[22] He decided to attend a three-year course for young adults aged 17–20 at the ISK's training school in Germany, the *Walkemühle*, in preference to going to a British university and pursuing a career in scientific research. In addition to academic study, the curriculum included practical subjects, such as woodwork and metalwork, and political education in the form of attending local Nazi rallies and speaking out in opposition.[23] Flanders joined the ISK in 1930 after completing an application form that included a declaration that he was a vegetarian and did not belong to any church. The form has been preserved in the archives. His answer to the question 'why I am a socialist' illustrates his and the ISK's understanding of socialism as a personal and political fight against injustice:

> I am a socialist because of what I have seen and heard. I have seen how the workers live; I know that many have not even the possibility to earn their living at all; I am convinced it is unjust, that the majority of the people have no opportunity to develop their lives at all, and others are enabled because of stolen wealth to satisfy any desire they may have ... I am convinced it is my duty to help in the abolition of all this injustice. That is what I mean when I say I am a socialist.[24]

The ISK was unusual among socialist groups at the time in taking its ideology not from Marxist economics, but from the ethical principles of Kant, as interpreted by the founder of the group, Leonard Nelson, a professor of philosophy at Göttingen University. The overwhelming ethos of the group was rationalist, anti-religious and anti-clerical. In keeping with Kant's 'categorical imperative', their brand of ethical socialism included a belief in the equal moral value of all men and women, the need for individuals to act not in their own selfish interest but in accordance with rationally derived universal principles, and opposition to exploitation of all kinds: of peasants by landowners, of workers by capitalists, of the poor by the rich or, more generally, of the weak by the powerful, which they considered to be irrational, unjust and immoral.[25]

Flanders returned to Britain in 1932, shortly before the *Walkemühle* was closed by the Nazis. Over the next ten years he worked as a door-to-door salesman and technical draughtsman in Sheffield. He lived in communal houses with other members and helped to organize the Socialist Vanguard Group, the tiny English branch of the ISK, which never comprised more than twenty-six members.[26] At first, the English group sold copies of the German ISK journal translated into English, but after the ISK was banned by the Nazis in 1933 and most of its members had to leave Germany, they published their own paper, *The Vanguard*, renamed *Socialist Vanguard* from 1936, re-launched in September 1940 as *Commentary* and renamed from 1941 until it closed in 1979 *Socialist Commentary.*[27] In 1933 Flanders underwent a 'marriage of convenience' with a leading German ISK member, Mary Saran, so that she could enter Britain as a refugee from Nazi Germany. Other German ISK members entered marriages of convenience in order to acquire British citizenship, including the leader of the London group in exile, Grete Herrmann (Margaret Henry), a distinguished quantum physicist.[28]

In 1943, the ISK leadership, then in exile in London, decided that the English branch should operate independently.[29] Flanders wrote a long paper for his colleagues on 'The Future of British Socialism' in which he argued that a new social order should be based not on the theoretical doctrine of the class struggle, but on the ethical principles of freedom and equality.[30] He joined the local Sheffield Fabian Society and in 1942 became branch secretary. He wrote a pamphlet, *Wage Policy in Wartime,* which helped him succeed in his application in 1943 for a post in London as one of three Research Assistants at the Trade Union Congress (TUC), from 310 applicants.[31] In keeping with his ISK principles, which opposed all forms of exploitation, he argued that cartels, monopolies and vested interests were the problem, not private ownership of the means of production. Ethical principles, in his view, formed the basis of socialism, not nationalization which was at best only a means for securing their aims, not an end in itself.[32]

While Flanders and the Socialist Vanguard Group discussed the future of British socialism, their German ISK comrades in exile in London debated the social and political order they wished to see established in Germany after an Allied victory. In early 1941, German socialist groups in exile in London, including the SPD, *Neu Beginnen* and the ISK decided to forget their differences and form an umbrella organization, the Union of German Socialist Organisations in Great Britain. German exiles worked on information and propaganda broadcasts to Germany and for the Foreign Office research department. A few ISK members were trained by US and British special operations forces to parachute behind enemy lines and act as guides for advancing Allied troops. Very little came of this, but the leader of the ISK, Willi Eichler, was able to travel to Switzerland at the end of 1944 to meet former comrades in exile there, and re-establish contacts with some who had remained in Germany. In August and September 1945 he was permitted by the British authorities to travel to Germany. He and three ISK colleagues met with leaders of the newly re-formed SPD in the British Zone, at a time when political parties were still officially banned, and they agreed to collaborate on re-establishing the SPD in Germany.[33]

At the end of 1945, Flanders was uncertain whether to continue at the TUC, as he considered the job had 'lost most of its political importance', but he had no alternative position in mind.[34] In April 1946 he was shortlisted by Hynd for a senior appointment as one of five Regional Commissioners in Germany, but rejected by Attlee for not possessing the necessary experience.[35] The rejection did not deter Hynd from finding him another position. Flanders moved to Germany in May 1946, when Albu was promoted by Robertson to the influential position of Deputy Chairman of the newly formed 'Governmental Sub-Commission', a body intended to determine the British Control Commission's policy for the Zone. Flanders succeeded Albu as head of the 'German Political Department' in the Control Commission's Political Division, responsible for liaison with German political parties.[36]

Albu and Flanders had much in common and shared similar views. They knew each other personally, worked together and shared the same house in Berlin for a time.[37] As Albu was the more senior and influential of the two, this chapter discusses his work to a greater extent than that of Flanders. The conclusions, however, relate to both as committed international socialists. Differences between them are discussed in the text.

The Fusion campaign in Berlin

The first issue to engage Albu's attention on his arrival in Berlin in February 1946 was the campaign for and against the proposed merger, or 'Fusion', of the SPD in Berlin with the communist KPD. The campaign was the first time after the war that British authorities in Germany collaborated politically with Germans, their former enemies, and openly opposed the Soviet Military Administration.[38] As such it can be considered a precursor, or the first manifestation, of the Cold War within Germany. It also illustrates the processes by which many democratic socialists in both Britain and Germany, including Albu, Flanders and their *Neu Beginnen* and ISK comrades, moved from advocating a wartime alliance with communists against fascism, to opposing what they perceived as Communist Party 'totalitarianism'.

Although directly affecting only a few thousand SPD members in the city, the campaign to preserve the SPD as an independent party in Berlin highlighted some of the fundamental issues which Albu, Flanders and their socialist colleagues were grappling with at the time. Was a united working class 'popular front' essential to prevent a Nazi revival, as many socialists believed before and during the war, or was the best defence against fascism a strong two or three party democracy, similar to the British and US models? Was unity between the four wartime Allies essential to prevent a resurgence of German military power, or did the Soviet Union now represent a bigger threat to British and US interests and to peace and prosperity in Western Europe? Could different political and economic systems be established and maintained in the different zones of occupation, or would one system eventually prevail across the whole of Germany?

Fusion of the SPD and KPD was promoted by the Soviet Union, as a way of securing an electoral majority for a merged party that could not be achieved by the communists alone. Many members of both parties believed that if had they worked together more effectively in the 1930s, they could have prevented Hitler and the Nazis seizing power. In December 1945, the two parties agreed to collaborate on a common electoral programme.[39] In January 1946, the Central Committee of the SPD in Berlin, under pressure from the Soviet occupation authorities, decided in favour of the merger, but a significant number of SPD members remained opposed, unwilling to trust the KPD, fearing domination from Moscow, and recalling the disputes of the early 1930s, when the communists had labelled the SPD 'social fascists'.[40] On 1 March 1946, a meeting of SPD Berlin officials decided to hold a referendum on the issue, among members in the city.[41]

Some of the British staff in the political and intelligence divisions of the Control Commission in Berlin had been watching developments with concern as, if the merger between the two parties were to go ahead, it was highly likely that the merged party would gain a majority in any future elections, and it would be possible for the Russians to control the whole city through an elected German administration.[42] Furthermore, if the merger were subsequently approved across all four zones, Russian influence, acting through a strong combined German communist and socialist party, would extend to the western zones, arousing long-standing fears of a German-Russian alliance that could promote social revolution across the whole of Europe, as the Comintern had attempted to do in the 1920s.[43] Official British policy, however, was to remain neutral and not favour any one political party in Germany.[44]

A key role in the internal German opposition to Fusion was played by around 20–30 former *Neu Beginnen* members who had remained in Germany and re-formed as a group in Berlin after the end of the war.[45] Although *Neu Beginnen* had supported cooperation with the Soviet Union against Nazi Germany, the group's members remained deeply suspicious of Communist Party tactics. Similar views were shared by the great majority of socialists in exile in London, who had resisted attempts by German communists in exile in Moscow during the war to form a united front with social democratic and other anti-fascist parties.[46] Kurt Schumacher, the leader of the SPD in the British Zone, was also firmly opposed to any form of cooperation with the Communist Party. The Fusion campaign was therefore a battle for control of the SPD. The Berlin central committee, pressurized by the Soviet Union, declared in favour of Fusion. The opponents of Fusion, including the newly formed party in the British Zone, the London exiles and SPD members in Berlin who opposed a merger with the communists, were supported by the Western Allies. The stakes were high, as it was assumed that with the Nazis discredited and officially banned in all zones, the SPD would win any election for a future German administration and whoever controlled the SPD would control Germany.[47]

Though fully aware of the situation, Albu appeared uncertain what to do. Two days after his arrival, on 3 February 1946, he joined a meeting with Otto Grotewohl and Gustav Dahrendorf, the leaders of the Berlin SPD central committee, arranged by Christopher Steel, a former Foreign Office official and head of the Political Division in Berlin. Grotewohl and Dahrendorf appeared to be looking for British support to resist Soviet pressure for Fusion, even though they had already declared in favour of the merger. The meeting was not productive. The British representatives were unable to offer substantial support to counter Soviet influence in the city. Albu asked if an official statement from the Labour Party, opposing Fusion, would be helpful, but they doubted if this would make any difference.[48] Grotewohl continued to support Fusion, despite personal reservations, and later became the first Prime Minister (*Ministerpräsident*) of the German Democratic Republic (East Germany) in 1949. Dahrendorf changed sides shortly after the meeting, but played no further part in the campaign. He left Berlin with British assistance and moved with his son, Ralf Dahrendorf, to the British Zone.[49] Unable to influence the decisions of the Berlin central committee, British Control Commission political and intelligence staff gave informal encouragement to SPD members opposed to Fusion. Two weeks after the meeting with Grotewohl and Dahrendorf, Albu met Kurt Schmidt, the leader of the *Neu Beginnen* group in Berlin and put him in touch with Schumacher, whom his British colleagues had invited to Berlin to support those opposed to Fusion.[50]

In early March, after the decision was taken at a meeting of Berlin SPD officials to hold a referendum in the city on the issue, Albu decided that he needed to play a more active part in the campaign. Using language that demonstrated the strength of his feelings, he noted in his diary that he had decided to stay in Berlin until the referendum on 31 March, 'to try to organise the majority which was being raped by the Russ[ians] & the KPD.'[51] He wrote later that he was 'risking his reputation' as official British policy at this time was not to engage in internal German political disputes.[52] The precariousness of his position was illustrated when a small group of left-wing Labour MPs in London took the opposite line to his, and sent a message to the Berlin SPD central committee in support of Fusion. Albu and his colleagues felt they had to counter this by holding a press conference to state that the message reflected the views of only a small part of a very much larger British Parliamentary Labour Party.[53]

The campaign for and against Fusion became intense on both sides. The Russians, fearful of the result, banned the referendum in their sector of Berlin, but it took place with US, French and British support in the western sectors of the city. Albu still felt unable to declare British opposition to Fusion openly, but on the day of the referendum he issued a statement published in *Der Berliner*, the British newspaper in Berlin, urging SPD members to vote.[54] Newspapers in the Soviet sector had already announced there was no need for a referendum, as seven out of the eight SPD districts in their sector had decided in favour of a united party.[55] The result of the referendum was a decisive majority against Fusion, though voters also endorsed a second question, by a smaller majority, which supported collaboration with the communists but not a merger of the parties.[56] As a result, the SPD survived as an independent party in the western sectors of Berlin, whereas those SPD members who supported Fusion merged with the KPD to form the Socialist Unity Party (SED), the governing party in the Soviet Zone and subsequently in East Germany, until reunification in 1990.[57]

The result could be seen as a success for Albu, in helping to secure victory for his *Neu Beginnen* friends and the independence of the SPD in Berlin and the British Zone, but it was also a failure, as the SPD remained divided and he was unable to prevent its merger with the communists in the Soviet Zone. The issue demonstrated how little scope he had for positive action. British support for the opponents of Fusion was organized mainly through Intelligence staff working for the Control Commission's political division in Berlin and subject to approval by Foreign Office officials in London.[58] On this issue, as in many other cases, British influence was limited to creating space for the Germans to make their own decisions. It did not extend to determining the result.

As the campaign progressed, Albu's outlook on the economic and political situation became increasingly pessimistic. The tactics used by the Soviet Union appeared depressingly similar to those of the Nazis, and he was afraid that economic conditions would favour the communists rather than democratic socialists. A few days before the referendum on 31 March, when posters supporting *Einheit* (a united party) appeared in Berlin, he wrote in his diary:

> Fresh Einheit [Unity] posters every day, all over the town. Demagogic & nationalistic 'Einheit, Ein Reich ...'[59]

The posters actually said 'Ein Ziel, Ein Weg, Einheit' (one aim, one path, unity) which was uncomfortably close to the Nazi slogan 'Ein Volk, Ein Reich, Ein Führer'.[60] Albu set out his conclusions in a memorandum written during the campaign. There was a 'growing realization', he wrote, that Fusion would be 'but another step in the squeezing out of the other Allies from Berlin'. He believed that the SPD was the only party which could gain the support of the working class, resist communist pressure and remain democratic. It would, however, 'lose all influence in the eyes of the Germans if it appears as a puppet of the Western powers'. Hence any scope for direct action by the Allies to promote political reform was limited. Rather than looking to the British to implement a policy of social change, he recommended that the best way to counter communist influence was for German advisory boards (with a strong contingent of SPD members) to be invited to submit plans for socialization, land reform, social legislation and 're-activating German industry'.[61]

Three months later, after a visit to the Ruhr that left him deeply depressed by the economic conditions he encountered there, he wrote to his wife:

> I don't know if I can stick it. This is the worst area, of course. The people are on the verge of starvation, their industries are running out of raw material, pits & factories are closing down, there's no material for re-building ... It seems a nonsense to be talking politics under the circs ... Already people are getting hysterical ... Why the hell did I come here?[62]

Back in Berlin, he wrote to Robertson that their political activities were meaningless in the current economic situation as 'the only voice that will be listened to is that of a hysterical nationalist demagogy', now provided by the Communist Party, which was attracting former officers and Nazis into its ranks, just as the Nazi party in the 1920s had recruited former soldiers from the *Freikorps*. Echoing Montgomery's memo of 1 May, he added that their work in Germany would become futile, as the new nationalists would 'see the opportunity to rebuild Germany from the East' and the only purpose of military occupation would be to 'prevent the chaos spreading beyond the boundaries of Germany and ... prevent the Russians taking over our Zone, either directly, or through the Communist Party'.[63] Although he had started from a different set of assumptions, the conclusions he reached on the need for economic reconstruction and political renewal in Germany were similar to those of Montgomery and the army generals. The principal danger appeared to come from the communist East. A 'positive socialist policy' was now required, in his view, to promote better economic conditions and restrict the spread of communism, rather than, as the Socialist Clarity Group had argued during the war, to change the established social order, and prevent a Nazi revival supported by the 'ruling classes' of militarists, landowners and industrialists.

Promoting a positive socialist policy

Hynd's appointment of Albu and Flanders to influential positions in Germany runs counter to the widely held view that German socialists in exile in London had little influence on British policy.[64] This was undoubtedly true for the duration of the war and the three-month period leading to the Potsdam Agreement in August 1945, but not subsequently. The Labour Party, which had invited the SPD leadership in exile to move to London from Paris in 1940, after the defeat of France, ceased all official contacts and withdrew their political and financial support in 1942, in an acrimonious internal dispute within the Party which has been termed 'The victory of socialist Vansittartism', referring to Labour Party members who supported views expressed by the former Foreign Office Permanent Under-Secretary Robert Vansittart.[65] In a series of radio talks in December 1940, Vansittart claimed that all Germans including, by implication, opponents of the Nazis, were aggressive, militaristic, and could not be trusted. Edited extracts were published in the *Sunday Times* and the full text printed as a pamphlet, *Black Record,* which sold half a million copies in the first year.[66]

In late 1945 and 1946, however, the position was reversed and the new Labour government showed a cautious but clear preference for the socialist SPD over other political parties in Germany. Albu and Flanders had close links with German socialist groups, some of whose members returned to Germany from early 1946 onwards. In addition to Hynd's appointment as Minister for Germany, Philip Noel-Baker and Patrick Gordon-Walker, Albu's friend and colleague in the Socialist Clarity Group, were appointed as junior ministers in the government.[67] Both had supported the German SPD leadership in exile during the war and argued against the 'Vansittartists'. The 'Fight for Freedom Publishing Company', the organization which had championed the 'Vansittartist' position in the Labour

Party, became defunct[68] and one of its leading supporters, William Gillies, was replaced as secretary of the Labour Party International Subcommittee by Denis Healey, who was more sympathetic to the German socialists.[69]

Despite later claims that the British ignored their advice and failed to support Anti-Nazi German democrats, there are numerous examples of refugees from Nazi Germany working in influential positions for the British Military Government or Control Commission. Few German exiles were appointed to senior positions, but many more held positions at junior levels, where they could still be influential within their own areas of responsibility. In his study of the organizational structure of the British occupation, published in 1980 but still valid today, Ulrich Reusch commented that the 'widespread view' that the British made little use of the knowledge of German émigrés needed to be 'heavily qualified'. He found many examples of German exiles working during and after the war in Foreign Office research and intelligence departments, as legal advisers, in SHAEF, in the Control Commission press and other departments and in the joint US and British Bizonal control office in Frankfurt, established in 1947.[70]

Albu and Flanders therefore had some grounds for optimism in early 1946 when they took up their positions as members of the British Military Government. They could hope for support for an active socialist policy in Germany from at least some members of the government in London. Their friends among the German socialists in exile in London had overcome earlier divisions and re-established contact with the re-formed SPD in Germany. After some delays, leading socialist refugees were allowed to return to Germany in late 1945 and early 1946 to re-establish contact with former colleagues and take up political positions in the newly re-formed SPD and the trade unions. SPD, *Neu Beginnen* and ISK members who spent the war in exile in London later played a significant role in the political life of post-war Germany. Erich Ollenhauer, for example, was leader of the SPD from 1952 to 1963, and Willi Eichler, the leader of the ISK, played a key role in formulating the Godesberg reforms in 1959, in which the SPD formally abandoned Marxist principles and adopted a social democratic programme.[71]

There were, however, limits on the ability of British socialists to support their German comrades. Robertson and the generals who continued to hold the most senior positions in Military Government were not generally sympathetic towards a policy of supporting one political party over another, especially if they were expected to favour the SPD, when their natural sympathies were closer to those on the other side of the political spectrum. General Richards, the Commander of 8 Corps, responsible for the administration of Schleswig Holstein, wrote to Robertson in April 1946 complaining about political bias of the Control Commission's Political Division and interference in the work of his officers:

> I think the trouble is this. The Political Division – and it is not for me to say whether they are right or wrong – appear determined to put SPD members wherever they can into positions of authority and to eject everything to the Right of this... The means adopted to achieve this tend to be underhand and consist in proving that every Right-wing person is undesirable and unpleasant while everyone to the Left is excellent – a demonstrably idiotic assumption.[72]

Robertson's reply was sympathetic. He confirmed that the Labour government in London supported the SPD and wished to see them appointed to positions of authority in Germany, but suggested they should be wary of doing so in areas where the SPD was weak, as there was a 'conflict between this policy and that of placing in authority persons having the backing of the majority of the population'.[73] Albu, in turn, considered Richards' predecessor, General Evelyn Barker, a 'bloody reactionary' who 'practically lived with the Bismarck family' and 'got on very well with the captured German generals'. He was appalled when Barker was sent to command British troops in Palestine.[74]

Albu wrote to his wife that he felt lonely sometimes and had no friends. He told her that he got on well with his immediate superior, General Erskine, the Chairman of the Sub-Commission, who accepted his ideas and put his authority behind them, but his effectiveness was limited by the lack of firm policy direction from London.[75] He wrote around the same time that he felt increasingly isolated:

> With reactionary officers and utterly reactionary F.O. [Foreign Office] boys. T G Erskine seems both intelligent and politically reasonable. And there are many good soldiers. But good tho' they are at their jobs – so many have this militarism (almost Prussian) repressed emotionalism [*sic*] which makes them give vent to the most obscurantist ideas on subjects outside their own jobs. This includes an intense fear of 'politics'.[76]

His sense of isolation may have been reinforced by mixed feelings about going as a Jew to Germany immediately after the war. Although he referred to this only occasionally in his diaries and letters home from Germany, he wrote later in his memoirs that:

> Events of the previous five years had inevitably stirred up profound emotional feelings among British Jews such as myself, aware that only the Channel and the Royal Air Force had enabled us to escape the Holocaust in which the vast majority of our fellow Jews on the Continent of Europe had been coldly and scientifically destroyed.[77]

In June 1946 he visited a distant relation of his in Berlin, Käthe Schmidt, born Albu.[78] After describing meeting another relative, he added: 'Only those who lived during those appalling years while the Nazis ruled Germany can appreciate my astonishment and emotion at first discovering these two relatives alive.'[79]

It would, however, be wrong to overemphasize the differences between British socialists, like Albu and Flanders, and the more conservative Foreign Office diplomats and army generals. Flanders objected to 'the political outlook of many officers in Military Government (military and civilian)'[80] but claimed to have successfully influenced the views of his immediate superiors in Political Division, both of whom were former Foreign Office diplomats.[81] Albu's personal diaries for his first four months in Germany, together with his letters to his wife over the same period, show that his attitude to his British colleagues was ambivalent. He had little time for Ingrams, whom he considered well intentioned, but over-mechanical in his approach, inflexible in his ideas and 'such a waffler'.[82] He had more respect for the senior generals, some of whom appeared surprisingly receptive to his ideas. He wrote to his wife that:

> Whatever we are doing to the Germans the job of political education we are doing on the British army & its brighter officers is terrific. They seem to like it. The sincerity & as Robertson says 'sense of mission' is first class.[83]

He told her that he had discussed the need for a 'positive socialist policy' with Generals Robertson, Templer and Balfour.[84] He attempted to explain to them that socialists were suspicious of big businessmen and supposedly politically neutral administrators, who needed to be removed from power as much as the Nazis. In a social revolution, he continued, the ruling classes would have been purged, but this had not happened in Germany and it was now difficult for Military Government to 'make a revolution at the point of a bayonet'.[85]

Albu found Robertson impressive at their first meeting and they appeared to develop an excellent working relationship, despite differences in their background and political outlook. This may have been helped by a sense of mutual respect, both having trained as engineers and having managed sizable factories, Robertson for Dunlop in South Africa and Albu for Aladdin in West London. Initially, Robertson appeared to have been suspicious of Albu, concerned at his direct line to Hynd.[86] However, shortly after he arrived on a temporary contract, Robertson offered him a senior post in the administration. According to Albu, Robertson told him that they 'needed someone like me' and 'although I wasn't indispensable, he'd rather have me than a new man … I rather think that from R[obertson] it was a pretty high compliment.'[87] The post on offer was that of 'Deputy Chairman of the Governmental Sub-Commission', one of two sub-commissions that, according to Robertson, would determine policy and 'really rule the country'.[88] The salary, at £2,000 plus allowances, was generous, equivalent to that of a Major General.[89] Albu decided to accept and in April moved into a 'palatial office' in the generals' suite in the rather grandly named Lancaster House, the British headquarters building in Berlin.[90] His position in the administration seemed to be strengthened further in July 1946 when he replaced Ingrams as Chairman of the Control Commission's 'Standing Committee on Governmental and Administrative Structure' (SCOGAS) which, he told his wife, was the committee that would 'do the real policy stuff on the future constitution of this country'.[91] Yet despite his senior position within the administration, Albu considered that his influence declined while he was in Germany. His ability to implement policy was still limited by Hynd's lack of influence in the government at home and his own lack of executive authority.

Ordinance no. 57: The devolution of power to the German *Länder*

Before leaving Germany, Albu oversaw the implementation of a number of governmental reforms, which came under his area of responsibility.[92] These included the reorganization of regional government in the British Zone and the promulgation in December 1946 of Military Government Ordinance no. 57, which provided for the devolution of powers to local German administrations on a wide range of subjects, including education, local government and health. Reusch has argued that Ordinance 57 represented a turning point in British policy,[93] and could be considered the 'Occupation Statute for the British Zone' as it defined the powers of the German regional *Land* governments and legally regulated their relationship with the British occupation authorities.[94] According to Reusch, the policy of devolution of power was initiated by the Foreign Office,[95] but documents from the Control Commission archives tend to support Albu's claim in his memoirs[96] that British policy on the issue of the devolution of power and the future federal structure of Germany was largely based on his and his colleagues' work in Germany. The Foreign Office accelerated the process, but the Control Commission had been working for at least the previous six months on similar lines.

The origins of Ordinance 57 and a policy of devolution can be traced to a memorandum Robertson wrote in September 1945, on 'The Evolution of

Control of Government in the British Zone'.[97] Following comments from Control Commission staff, Montgomery issued two instructions, in December 1945 and March 1946. At the end of the first, he stated clearly that devolution of power to Germans was an essential part of the transfer from military to civilian rule:

> The real essence of the change ... is that under Military Government we govern our zone through the Germans ... Civil control, on the other hand, means that the Germans govern themselves subject to control and supervision by us.[98]

Montgomery's second instruction, in March 1946, made a similar point more forcibly: 'the best people to deal with the many difficulties which beset GERMANY today are the Germans', and there was a need to 'build up German administrations in our zone'.[99]

The Foreign Office was reluctant to intervene directly at this stage, preferring to observe and comment from the sidelines. An official minuted that Montgomery's March memo was a 'valuable piece of stocktaking' and the views expressed looked 'as if they owe a lot to General Robertson'.[100] Another official commented that it was an 'impressive document', though Troutbeck, head of the German Political Department, added a cautionary note against proceeding too quickly, which suggests that in late 1945 and the first half of 1946, the Foreign Office were opposed to devolution, rather than promoting it:

> Yes, but one wishes that we might be handing over a going concern to these new German administrators. They will be weak and untried organisations, hardly capable of coping with starvation and widespread unemployment. And if they fail, the loss will not be theirs alone.[101]

It was not until June 1946, following the failure of the Allies to agree a joint policy towards Germany at the Paris Council of Foreign Ministers, that Foreign Office officials showed a renewed interest in the administrative structure and organization of the British Zone and decided to take a more active role.

In an internal Foreign Office paper on the 'Future political structure of Germany', Patrick Dean, who had replaced Troutbeck as head of the Foreign Office German Political Department, outlined three reasons for a policy of decentralization: to collaborate with their Western Allies to counter Soviet advocacy of a highly centralized Germany, build up western Germany economically and politically, and reduce the cost of the occupation by devolving responsibility to Germans.[102] In order to minimize the risk of over-strengthening the powers of any future central German government, Dean also laid down three principles from which all policy should derive: maximum decentralization of power from the centre to the regions and localities; maximum devolution of power and responsibility to the Germans; and, subject to the above, maximum acceptability to the Germans of future constitutional arrangements, to ensure that these would last and not be changed by a future independent German government.[103]

In parallel with these developments, Albu, in his capacity as Deputy-President of the Governmental Sub-Commission, was working on the same issue. In June, he circulated a paper, 'Germany: The nature of Federal Government', in which he argued that the failure by the Allies to agree on central administrations for Germany as a whole (at the Paris Council of Foreign Ministers which was then in session) made it necessary to reorganize the structure of government in the British Zone. After referring to federal arrangements in the United States, Australia, Canada and Switzerland as possible models, he concluded that: 'if it is desired to weaken the future power of Germany to make war, as great a degree of decentralization should be imposed as possible'. He envisaged a gradual development, delegating powers to the *Länder* immediately, but requiring all German decisions at central or at regional level to be subject to Allied veto:

> In this way a radical change in the structure of the German state could be brought about immediately and for an adequate time would remain under supervision until there was a reasonable assurance that it was workable and had popular support.[104]

However, he qualified the need for decentralization by adding that if the central government did not have sufficient power to ensure stable social and economic conditions, there would be 'violent pressure' to achieve greater centralization, which could not be resisted.[105] Whereas the Foreign Office were advocating the maximum degree of decentralization, the Control Commission, advised by Albu, fought a determined and largely successful rearguard action, not so much, as claimed by Reusch, to preserve their ability to impose a British model of government,[106] but to maintain sufficient powers within central government so that a future SPD government in Germany could operate a planned economy on socialist principles.[107]

Dean travelled to Berlin in August 1946 for a series of high-level meetings with Robertson, Albu, Flanders and William Strang, the political adviser to the Military Governor and the principal Foreign Office contact within the Control Commission. During the visit, Strang added marginal notes to a briefing paper Dean had prepared before the visit,[108] commenting that the Germans would not be attracted by a '*Staatenbund*', a loose federation of independent states, but would accept a '*Bundestaat*', a federal state. In a letter to his wife on 14 August, two days before Dean's visit, Albu used similar language to describe the highly decentralized regional structure in the US Zone, as either a body of three dictators, one in each of the *Länder* in the zone, or 'a *Staatenbund* – that most inefficient of governments' and widely disliked within the Control Commission.[109] On his return to London Dean reported that their views were closer than he had expected.[110] The terms *Bundestaat* and *Staatenbund* were adopted, after Dean's return to London (in the original German) in a Cabinet Paper on 9 September. In a speech to Parliament on 22 October, Bevin used similar language saying that Germany should 'avoid the two extremes of a loose confederation of autonomous states and a unitary centralized state'.[111] The Foreign Office and Control Commission now agreed on a policy of decentralization and the further devolution of power to German authorities, but not to the extent of creating virtually independent regional states, as Albu and his colleagues in the Control Commission feared was happening in the US Zone. With the approval of the Prime Minister, the Foreign Office invited Robertson and Strang to a meeting with Bevin in Paris to discuss a new draft directive, subsequently approved by the Prime Minister and Cabinet, instructing the Military Governor to accelerate 'the process of decentralization territorially and devolution of powers to the Germans in the British Zone'.[112]

Ordinance 57, which gave practical effect to the policy of devolution, came into effect from 1 December 1946.[113] In a talk to the German press, Albu responded to criticisms from German politicians by referring again to the need to preserve adequate central government powers:

> The powers which have been reserved to the centre are those powers which are necessary to ensure the economic revival of Germany and to enable a reasonable degree of economic planning and of the distribution of very scarce raw materials ... I must again emphasise that until there is a Central Government for Germany there is no other way than the exercising of these powers by Military Government.[114]

Albu succeeded in his aim of creating a federal structure in the British Zone that preserved a significant role for a central zonal authority, rather than a highly decentralized, loose confederation of regional governments, as had been established in the US Zone. But over the following year, as US influence over economic issues in the joint British and US 'Bizone' increased, it became clear that the powers reserved to central government would not be used in the way he had hoped, to facilitate a planned economy on socialist principles. Albu grew increasingly pessimistic as to the prospects for a socialist Germany and his ability to make a positive contribution to the British occupation.

By the time he left Germany in November 1947, Albu believed there was little more he and his colleagues could achieve. He was no longer especially concerned about security, writing that 'this time we really have destroyed the German army, both its personnel and its physical assets'.[115] Nor was he unduly concerned, as he had been at the time of the Fusion campaign, that a united Germany might be dominated by the communists, now ascribing this view to the Foreign Office.[116] In a British Forces Network broadcast in March 1947, he said that, now that the regional *Land* governments had taken office, 'the giving of orders no longer rests with Military Government officers'. German administrations needed to be monitored and controlled, and the British had to act as 'guides, philosophers and friends' of the German politicians.[117] Flanders used the same words to describe the 'most important sphere of his work' in his notes to his comrades on leaving Germany.[118]

In September 1947 Albu recommended that the size of the British Control Commission be reduced to 2,178, roughly a tenth of its current size.[119] Reductions of this magnitude were not achieved until after 1950,[120] but the overall direction was clear. Apart from exercising the power of veto, there was little the British could do, as an occupying power, to promote either democratic renewal or a positive socialist policy. Those who remained would have to depend on their personal relationships with their German colleagues and friends to promote what they considered positive reforms. Albu and Flanders decided they had done what they could in Germany and it was time to return to Britain.

Disengagement from Germany and return to Britain

Albu's achievements in the area of governmental reorganization did not change his pessimistic outlook on the economic and political situation, which dated back to his perception acquired during the Fusion campaign soon after his arrival in Germany, that Russian tactics were similar to those of the Nazis and economic conditions would favour the communists rather than democratic socialists. In March 1947, after a year in post, he wrote to Hynd that 'on some quite crucial matters the Foreign Office have departed from the principles which I think both you and I felt were essential here'. He was concerned that without at least some degree of centralized planning, economic conditions, aggravated by the influx of millions of refugees, would 'create a demographic and economic position in Germany which was just impossible'. He was also 'intensely pessimistic' about the Bizonal agreement recently concluded with the Americans and feared that the continued policy of reparations would make it increasingly difficult to secure cooperation with local German administrations. Finally, if the Russians continued their current policy of taking reparations from current production, there would be no alternative to 'bringing the iron curtain down'.[121]

In April 1947 Hynd was replaced as Minister for Germany by Frank Pakenham, Lord Longford, and responsibility for the British administration of Germany was transferred to the Foreign Office from the Control Office for Germany and Austria (COGA), which until then had functioned as separate government department. Albu stayed until October to complete his work of governmental reorganization, before returning home to find another job and pursue his ambition of entering Parliament. Soon after his return from Germany, he was elected as Member of Parliament for Edmonton, in a by-election following the death of Evan Durbin.[122] Apart from a brief period as a junior minister from 1965–6, he remained on the back benches. He had little involvement in foreign affairs or matters concerning Germany, but was an early supporter of Britain's entry to the Common Market. Perhaps his earlier belief in a 'federation of free, democratic Socialist states of Europe' played a part in this, though it was to be a capitalist, not a socialist, community of nations that helped to make another war in (Western) Europe impossible.

Allan Flanders left Germany shortly after Albu, equally disillusioned. An article in *Socialist Commentary*, published in November 1946 while he was still in Germany,[123] endorsed British government policy of promoting economic recovery and making Germany, or at least the British Zone, self-supporting, but criticized the failure to implement a positive socialist policy. A decision to take the coal and heavy industries into public ownership had not been implemented. No progress had been made on land reform. Currency reform was 'long overdue' and, in the meantime, the black market flourished, preventing sound economic development. The government in London had failed to provide clear guidance or a coherent plan for the economy. Many Military Government officers regarded any plan as 'too socialistic' and spoke contemptuously of the Labour government in their officers' messes. Within Germany there was a shortage of suitably qualified socialists able to take over administration from supposedly politically neutral, but deeply traditional and conservative, German civil servants.[124]

In a report to his friends in the Socialist Vanguard Group a year later,[125] Flanders emphasized the personal benefits of his going to Germany, but could point to few concrete achievements. His department had been responsible for a few 'restrictive measures', banning those who made overtly nationalist speeches from political activities. He was able to help his 'own comrades' in the ISK in a few minor ways, such as approving the licensing of a new journal *Geist und Tat* (Spirit and Deed), edited by Willi Eichler.[126] In general, however, he wrote that the main purpose of his work appeared to be negative, that of 'stopping worse things happening'.[127] The one 'hopeful factor' he could point to was the strength of the German Social Democratic Party (SPD), his ability to assist in its development, and the personal contacts he had been able to establish with Kurt Schumacher, the party leader, and his colleagues. He left Germany at the end of 1947, spent a year in the United States, and then built a successful career in academia as one of the UK's most highly respected experts on industrial relations.[128] He continued to act as chair of the editorial board of *Socialist Commentary* until he died in 1973.[129]

Albu and Flanders were in a difficult position and had limited scope for positive action. They left Germany before currency reform in 1948 and the 'economic miracle', which Albu wrote later they could not have foreseen.[130] As outsiders in what was effectively a Military Government, they had neither the authority that Montgomery and his generals possessed as military commanders nor the control of the bureaucratic apparatus exercised by Robertson as deputy Military Governor and head of the Control Commission. Despite holding senior positions in policy-making divisions at headquarters, they had no opportunity to exercise direct authority on the ground. Their opportunities for indirect influence, through informal links and discussions with like-minded colleagues, were limited.

On Albu's resignation from the Control Commission, Robertson sent him a letter of appreciation of the work he had done, which reflected the nature of their relationship and the difference in approach between them. Albu was disappointed because his achievements did not match up to his original hopes and expectations. Robertson replied with his understanding of their task in Germany:

> You say that you wonder what you have achieved. Each of us makes a contribution, no man more than that, to the British effort in Germany. I believe very firmly that history will justify the British effort. Your contribution has been to bring to bear on our problems the influence of your liberal and well-trained mind. That is a very worth-while contribution, and there is no need to go further to seek concrete achievement.[131]

The contribution Albu and Flanders made to political renewal in Germany was not to impose their own vision, but to help 'smooth the path'[132] by assisting their German comrades where they could, in the Fusion campaign in Berlin, through facilitating the devolution of power, and in the creation of a federal structure for the future Federal Republic. Although disappointed by what they had been able to achieve, they formed a bridge between the occupation authorities and the German socialists they had known in exile in London. They recognized the limits of what could be achieved by the British Military Government, and by stepping back, allowed democratic German politicians to take responsibility for their own actions. Many of their colleagues in *Neu Beginnen* and the ISK, in both Britain and Germany, followed similar trajectories, from pre-war idealistic international socialism, through the desperate struggle against fascism and the experience of the Holocaust, to the acceptance of a mixed economy, opposition to communist totalitarianism and pragmatic national, rather than international, social democracy.

7

Conflict and Cooperation in Hamburg

When Henry Vaughan Berry died in 1979, Helmut Schmidt, the Chancellor of the Federal Republic of Germany, sent his widow the following tribute:

> It is with deep personal regret that I have learned about the death of Sir Henry. I will always remember the interesting and inspiring hours I spent in Sir Henry's house in Hamburg Germany and I personally lost a friend.[1]

Berry was the British Regional Commissioner for Hamburg from 1946 to 1949. He could not have foreseen then that one of the young students from Hamburg University, taking part in a series of informal discussions at his house, would one day become the German Federal Chancellor, but one of his aims as Regional Commissioner was to establish dialogue and build trust with those people most likely to form part of a governing elite in post-war Germany.[2] Berry wrote in a Christmas letter to his great-niece in 1975: 'It is a matter of some pride to me that the present Chancellor, Helmuth [*sic*] Schmidt, was in my time one of about 15 students who used to come to our house regularly for informal discussion.'[3]

Hamburg could be considered the most favourable of all the *Länder* in the British Zone for effective cooperation between British and Germans. The city had a long tradition of self-government and well-established trading connections with Britain and the United States. Economic revival after the war was adversely affected by Allied restrictions on foreign trade, the destruction of the German merchant marine and dismantling of the shipbuilding industry, but Hamburg still had great strategic importance as the largest city in western Germany and the main port of entry for goods and supplies.[4] Though badly destroyed by Allied bombs in the firestorms of 1943, conditions at the end of the war were not as bad as had been feared. Half the living accommodation had been destroyed and 100,000 inhabitants had lost their lives, but the city was not damaged in the land-based campaigns in April and May 1945, surrendering without a shot being fired. Telephone connections, electricity and water supplies continued uninterrupted.[5] But if Anglo-German relations were generally better in Hamburg than elsewhere, the city was not exceptional in providing examples of cooperation between occupiers and occupied. The group of students meeting at Berry's house was just one of several thousand Anglo-German discussion groups established in the British Zone by 1948.[6]

Berry's tenure as Regional Commissioner was considered at the time to have been highly successful by both British and Germans. He received glowing tributes from the German press when he left Hamburg,[7] and was awarded a knighthood on his return to Britain. Recent historians have been more critical, highlighting opposition to British military rule and conflict as well as cooperation. This chapter discusses Berry's aims and intentions and some of the successes and failures of British occupation rule in Hamburg.

Personal background and appointment as Regional Commissioner

In May 1946, in an attempt to 'civilianise' the British administration of Germany, four Regional Commissioners were appointed to replace the military Corps Commanders. The appointments were a key element of the policy to decentralize government of the British Zone, devolve power to the *Länder* and govern by indirect rather than direct control. The commissioners were nominated by John Hynd, the Minister for Germany, and approved by the Prime Minister, Clement Attlee, and the Foreign Secretary, Ernest Bevin.[8] Three of the commissioners were civilians and active Labour Party supporters, the fourth an army general.[9]

Unlike Hynd, Albu or Flanders, Berry had no links with German exiles in London. Unusually for a Labour Party activist, he worked between the wars in a senior position in the City of London, as assistant manager of the Union Discount Company.[10] Concerned at what he perceived to be a lack of understanding of financial matters among the Labour leadership in the 1930s, he founded an influential pressure group of Labour sympathizers in the City, the XYZ Club.[11] Yet despite his financial background, he was not involved in discussions regarding economic policy for the British Zone, or the proposed currency reform implemented in June 1948. His main qualifications for his appointment appear to have been his ability to speak German fluently, his experience as a young man on the staff of the Inter-Allied High Commission for the occupation of the Rhineland after the First World War and his personal connections with leading members of the Labour Party, including Herbert Morrison and Hugh Dalton.[12]

Figure 7.1 Sir Henry Vaughan Berry in 1947–8. Photo courtesy Kate Owen.

Berry was born in 1891 and was therefore closer in age to Harold Ingrams and the generals considered in Part One, than to his fellow socialists Austen Albu and Allan Flanders.[13] Berry said later that he became a socialist after the First World War, influenced by events in Germany,[14] though it seems likely that his political beliefs were strongly influenced by his childhood and education. His father moved from the small Wiltshire town of Melksham to London and then to Madras in India, where he worked as a stockbroker, lived in a grand house and appeared very wealthy. When Berry was four years old his father died of pneumonia. His fortune disappeared and the family was left with a 'few hundred pounds', generating an annual income of £40, not enough to live on. His mother had to leave home to work as a governess and Berry and his two sisters moved to Bath, where they lived with two maiden aunts, who had depended on his father for their livelihood.[15]

Berry's early life was a struggle to obtain an education that matched his ability. With help from his godfather, he left home age seven, to attend a boarding school, the Royal Asylum of St Anne's, at Redhill in Surrey. He described it later as a 'charity school' for 'those who had come down in the world',[16] quite different from the public and preparatory schools attended by the middle and upper classes, adding that it was an 'amoral and stupid system ... to educate the rich separately'.[17] At age sixteen, he obtained a scholarship to the City of London School to continue his education. He won another scholarship to Cambridge University, but was only able to accept the place after receiving financial assistance from an education trust established by a Scottish peer.[18] His later socialism was meritocratic, placing greater emphasis on equality of opportunity, 'from each according to his abilities', than the redistribution of wealth and alleviation of poverty, 'to each according to his needs'. He was opposed to unearned wealth and privilege, but remained elitist rather than egalitarian, believing that those with ability should have the opportunity to progress to positions of responsibility in society.[19]

He studied French and German at university and spoke both languages fluently, having spent six months in each country through a school scholarship in 1909. He served in the First World War as an officer in Salonika, Ireland and France, where he was wounded.[20] Towards the end of the war, a chance encounter in London with his former university tutor led to a transfer to the Intelligence Corps and a posting with the army of occupation in the Rhineland.[21] The inflation of the early 1920s made a deep impression on him and, in later life, he would speak of how 'the hardships experienced by the middle classes were one of the chief recruiting grounds for Hitler'.[22] In notes for a speech he gave in 1962, he outlined his understanding of the period: the young Weimar Republic never had a chance; the steps taken by the Allies were all too little too late; in the late 1920s, Germany was hit by the world economic crisis; it was the 6 million unemployed that gave Hitler his real opportunity and within three years he was in power. There were clear parallels, his notes continued, between his experiences after the First World War and when he returned to Germany in 1946. On both occasions he had seen hunger and inflation in which people lost nine-tenths of their savings. The scale of destruction and disruption to society was even worse after the Second World War than the first. Above all there was no government or authority with which to deal. The conclusion he drew was that to avoid continuing chaos, 'the Allies had to take steps to rehabilitate Germany'.[23] His conclusions were similar to those of General Robertson and other senior army officers described earlier (see Chapter 2), that while disarmament was necessary, a harsh occupation based on a desire for revenge was not only wrong but counter-productive. However much the British may, as Berry wrote later, have 'hated and detested Germany and the Germans as a result of the war',[24] the only alternative, in their own interest, was a constructive policy of economic reconstruction, active support for democratic German politicians and personal reconciliation.

Berry claimed later that he was offered and accepted the position as Regional Commissioner in Germany due to chance. Following the election of the Labour government in 1945, he had hoped to be appointed a director of the Bank of England. These hopes were not realized, so he negotiated early retirement from the Union Discount Company and made arrangements to retire to the country. According to Berry, Morgan Philips, the general secretary of the Labour Party, told him, when they met by chance at the House of Commons after an XYZ Club meeting, that 'the government needed people who shared its political convictions'.[25] In due course Berry was offered the post of Regional Commissioner in Germany. Although he was interested, his wife was reluctant to move. The older of their two sons, Michael, had died in July 1944 from an unknown illness in Egypt. Berry was about to decline the offer when another personal tragedy changed their future outlook and expectations. Their second son, Peter, who was training to be a doctor, was killed in a motorcycle accident. Their 'dream of having two fine sons each in a fine profession', which he 'had sometimes said was too good to be true', was shattered.[26] Peter's death

> after that of Michael two years before ... was a shock in the real sense of the word. But when it came to deciding our own next moves, it seemed clear, or at any rate very likely, that a totally different sphere and a totally different world would be best for both of us.[27]

Rather than retreating into private life, he accepted the position in Germany.

Shared ideals and aims

Berry claimed later that he received no serious briefing on his role as Regional Commissioner and 'no hint ... of the kind of policy we were to adopt in our different regions'.[28] He appeared unaware of the planning that had been done for the occupation and the numerous directives issued to Control Commission staff. After a brief spell as Regional Commissioner for Westphalia, before the merger with North Rhine Province to form the new *Land* of North Rhine-Westphalia, he moved to Hamburg in September 1946.[29] Elections were held soon after he arrived, resulting in victory for the SPD. The previous *Bürgermeister*, a conservative who had been appointed by Berry's predecessor, Brigadier Armytage, was replaced by a socialist, Max Brauer, who had returned from exile in the United States and was untainted by any connection with the Nazis.[30] Without being specific as to how this affected their relationship, Berry claimed that their sharing a socialist 'fundamental philosophy ... proved to be of enormous help to me during the ensuing three years'.[31]

Berry was concerned that both he and his staff should establish a good working relationship with the German administration in Hamburg. He took great care over a speech he gave on 22 November 1946 at the ceremonial opening of the *Bürgerschaft*, or city parliament.[32] The content of the speech was unremarkable, emphasizing that free elections had been held in the city for the first time in fifteen years, that he was a civilian and not a Military Governor and that during the election campaign he had permitted the greatest possible freedom of speech, including criticism of the British Military Government. More important was the tone, which he intended to be as conciliatory as possible, and the fact that he delivered the speech in German. He said later that had he spoken in English, 'they probably would have paid little attention, taking it as a mere formality', but

> Germans are very conceited about their knowledge of foreign languages and would sit up and take notice if they found their new civil governor speaking to them in what I flatter myself was fluent German.[33]

At the end of the speech he referred to his officials being 'ready at all times to discuss your problems in a spirit of co-operation'. The ceremony was followed by a dinner, at his own expense, to which he invited the new 'senators', as the ministers in the city government were called, and some of his own staff. This, he believed, was 'well worth any expense, because it meant that the new administration started off at least on a friendly basis with my senior officials'.[34]

Berry arrived in Hamburg at a difficult time. The winter of 1946–7 was the worst in living memory. The river Elbe froze and ships carrying essential supplies could only reach the port through a channel cut by icebreakers. Unable to dock at the wharves, they had to unload into lighters in mid-stream.[35] In January and February, 85 people froze to death, and a further 200 died each month from inflammation of the lungs.[36] Due to a shortage of coal, the supply of electricity was reduced to maintain essential services.[37] The suburban railways ceased to run, trams stopped at 8.00 pm and theatres and cinemas remained closed.[38] Building was at a standstill.[39] Because no coal was available for domestic heating, there was massive thieving of coal from freight trains arriving in the marshalling yards, with crowds of up to 30,000 taking part.[40] Berry reported that 6,000 people were arrested for stealing coal in January, 17,000 in February and 11,000 in March.[41] Unsurprisingly, he expressed concern over the authorities' ability to keep order. Unable to resolve shortages of food and fuel, he decided on a token gesture of increasing unemployment relief to a level sufficient to purchase 'rationed necessities'. 'Without the prospect of this particular concession,' he wrote, 'which at least gave evidence of a sympathetic attitude with the plight of the people, public order would not have been maintained'. 'The price was cheap' he added in his report.[42] He retained the support of the *Bürgermeister*, Max Brauer, and 'responsible trade union leaders', and there were relatively few disturbances in the city over the winter.[43] In April, he was able to report that Brauer had authorized the German police to use firearms, and arrests for stealing coal ceased with the warmer weather.[44]

Berry appears to have made many of Brauer's aims his own, and in so doing established excellent relations with him and the German administration.[45] In his first monthly report as Regional Commissioner for the city in January 1947, Berry outlined his four principal aims for the year: to deliver the full ration of 1,550 calories, create a reserve of fuel, remove uncertainty over reparations and complete the process of de-nazification.[46] These were all issues of immediate concern to the local population. At the end of the year, in a speech to the *Bürgerschaft*, again in German, Berry reviewed progress against his four aims, again striking a conciliatory tone.[47] All of his aims except the first, he said, had been achieved, though significant problems remained. They had all expected too much, too soon from the peace, in Britain as well as in Germany. For two and a half years, English and German officials had worked side-by-side, learning to understand, trust and respect each other. He concluded by referring to the great fire of Hamburg in 1842 when much of the city had been destroyed, saying he trusted that the same spirit which guided its reconstruction then was still alive in the city.[48]

Throughout his tenure as commissioner, Berry represented the interests of the city to the British authorities and advocated special measures, such as subsidized inland transport rates, which would benefit the port.[49] In his first monthly report, in January 1947, he wrote that 'I feel it is still necessary to stress the fact that a big metropolis always presents special difficulties.'[50] Later in the year, the city was declared an emergency area (*Notstandsgebiet*) after the food ration was cut by a third to an average of 1,000 calories a day and 200,000 people attended a hunger demonstration.[51] Berry wrote in his monthly report:

> It is high time that the Bi-Zonal food authorities paid some attention to Hamburg's plea for special consideration.[52]

The food situation improved, but he continued to advocate special treatment for the city in other ways. When a list of factories to be dismantled was published in late 1947, he reported that the reaction from the city's population was generally reasonable, but there was 'of course one reservation for Hamburg'. The future permitted level of the shipbuilding industry had not yet been decided and it would be 'a great mistake to settle what for this great Port is a vital matter without consultation with the people of Hamburg'.[53]

Berry's pre-eminent concerns, however, as expressed in his monthly reports to the Military Governor and senior British headquarters staff, were to keep order, avoid discontent and represent British interests. The welfare of the inhabitants and good relations with the city's German administration were the means by which he achieved these ends. If Berry assisted Brauer by advocating special treatment for the city, Brauer helped Berry maintain order, defuse conflicts and restrain public opposition to the occupation.[54]

The 'Hamburg Project': Defusing conflict

Shortly before Berry's appointment as Regional Commissioner, relations between the British occupiers and the local German population in Hamburg had started to deteriorate, following widespread protests against the continued requisitioning of houses for occupation personnel.[55] The city was badly overcrowded, with little prospect of any improvement in the immediate future, due to British plans to build a new administrative headquarters for the Zone in Hamburg, replacing the Control Commission's divisional headquarters, scattered among the small towns in Westphalia where the army had been stationed at the end of the war. The scheme, known as the Hamburg Project, became the focus of opposition to the occupation in the city. The British authorities decided that a new headquarters was no longer required and work ceased. Once the decision had been taken to abandon the project, Berry worked closely with the German administration to defuse the situation, save face and salvage something from the debacle.

The Hamburg Project had been agreed in 1945. The original scheme envisaged an imperial-style 'enclave', requiring the evacuation of up to 50,000 German civilians to make room for around 30,000 British personnel.[56] In June 1946, before Berry's appointment as Regional Commissioner, a revised, slightly smaller, plan was announced and work started, resulting in the eviction of 650 German civilians.[57] A peaceful protest by 500 German women, handing in a petition at the Town Hall, grew rapidly over the course of the day to around 10,000 people. The mood of the demonstrators deteriorated and they became increasingly antagonistic to the British, shouting 'we are not Indians or coolies' and singing the German national anthem.[58] Brauer's predecessor as *Bürgermeister*, Rudolf Petersen, tried to speak to the crowd from a balcony but was shouted down.[59] Ten demonstrators were arrested and a few days later sentenced, in a special session of the British military court, to a total of twenty-seven years' imprisonment.[60] Berry claimed later that he threatened to resign if the plan was not abandoned. He recalled in his memoir that he considered it 'politically disastrous' as:

> It seemed to be treating a very ancient city in Europe in much the same way as a town in India or China with its cantonments and its international settlements and to preclude any possibility of furthering reasonably good relations between the occupation and the Germans.[61]

He added that he made his views known to the Military Governor, Sholto Douglas, and his deputy, Brian Robertson; the matter was discussed at the Regional Commissioners' conference in Hamburg and it was decided to abandon the project.[62]

Although Berry's memoir is generally reliable and consistent with documents in the archives, I have been unable to confirm his claim that he offered to resign. The minutes of a Regional Commissioners' conference held in Hamburg in December 1946, shortly after Berry arrived in the city, made no reference to the project,[63] although it appears, from references in other documents,[64] that a decision to suspend it was taken at an earlier, unrecorded, high-level meeting. Berry may have attended this meeting, as he flew to London at the end of December to advise the government of the decision to abandon the project. He wrote to Robertson from London to say he had notified Hynd who, he continued, was annoyed as he had prepared, but not submitted, a Cabinet paper recommending the project's continuation.[65] Robertson replied to Berry that 'Hynd's reaction to our decision' surprised him, but he hoped to 'smooth him down' on his next visit to Germany.[66] The exchange of letters indicates that although Robertson had originally strongly supported the project, the decision to suspend it was probably more consensual than Berry suggested in his memoir.

Berry was not alone in his opposition to the project. It had been extensively criticized in Parliament, notably by Richard Stokes MP, who referred to it in a House of Commons debate in October 1946 as the 'Hamburg Poona', alluding to similarities with imperial enclaves in India, from which the native inhabitants were excluded.[67] Berry's predecessor as Military Governor in Hamburg, Brigadier Armytage, had also opposed the project, writing a strongly worded memo to Robertson in July 1946, drawing his attention to the 'extremely serious situation' which had arisen due to evictions required for the Hamburg Project, evictions elsewhere in the city to provide accommodation for British families and the general shortage of building materials.[68] Armytage estimated that by September, 6,000 German families would need to be evicted. Due to the shortage of alternative accommodation, they could only be housed by 'doubling up' with other families in already overcrowded homes. He told Robertson he had agreed with the *Bürgermeister* (Rudolf Petersen) that alternative accommodation would be found for 6,000 families, but no more. He would not 'agree to any further evictions than those already referred to unless I receive direct orders from you to do so'.[69]

An equally strongly worded memo was written in September 1946 by the officer commanding army intelligence for the city, Lt. Col. Philip Ramsbotham.[70] He stated that Hamburg was 'undoubtedly an unfortunate choice' as the designated headquarters of the Zone, due to 'chronic overcrowding' in which 'some 30,000 persons are living in appalling conditions in cellars, bunkers and attics'.[71] There had been, he continued, a 'marked change from undoubted goodwill to open hostility', the 'feeling amongst the Hamburg population' was already intense and increasing and 'the hostility of the Hamburg populace, half-starved and entering a second winter of "peace", may reach a dangerous level'. A further reason for cancelling the project, Ramsbotham argued, was that Hamburg was no longer the most suitable location for British headquarters. The recent decision to merge the British and US Zones economically to form the 'Bizone', and the city's closeness to the Russian Zone, made it preferable to locate headquarters in a small town 'not yet openly hostile to Military Government', in the southern part of the British Zone.[72]

Opposition to the scheme therefore reflected differences among the British in addition to tensions between British and Germans. Robertson, the original proponent of the plan, was concerned about the effectiveness of the central administration, whereas regional officials, such as Berry, Armytage and Ramsbotham, wished to maintain a harmonious relationship with the local German population. The main reason the project was abandoned, however, was that by the end of 1946 it had become redundant. A large central British headquarters was no longer required once the decisions had been taken, following the Paris Council of Foreign Ministers' meeting in the spring and summer of 1946, to merge the British with the US Zone and reduce the total number of Control Commission staff. However, the project had acquired a momentum of its own, and criticism in Parliament and from the press in both Britain and Germany made it difficult to cancel, without damaging the prestige of Military Government.

Once the decision had been taken to abandon the project, Berry and his colleagues were able to use their good relations with Brauer and the German administration to pre-empt criticism. British staff were told that the project had not been abandoned, but temporarily suspended due to a shortage of building materials.[73] At a Regional Commissioners' conference in January 1947, attended by Robertson and Hynd, it was agreed that work should not cease immediately, but should continue to complete the foundations of blocks of flats under construction.[74] Rather than taking the opportunity to criticize the British, the SPD administration in Hamburg decided it was in their interest to help manage the presentation of the issue to the public. Brauer agreed with Berry that the project should not be stopped completely but 'slowed down':

> A complete abandonment of the project after such great investments would justify any reproach by the public that the planning had lacked the necessary foresight. The point that much greater use could have been made of the material spend and the labour employed for the building and the repair of other flats in Hamburg could then not be countered effectively.
>
> On the other hand ... after the present work has been completed to a certain extent, it should be slowed down. Thus the reproach would be avoided that for the continuation of the Project an incomparably great amount of material would be used in contrast to the civil housing programme.[75]

A few days later the issue was discussed again at a joint meeting of British and German officials, chaired by Berry. Brauer reiterated his view that the British and German authorities were 'in the same boat' and if the project was abandoned, both would be blamed for spending money unnecessarily. However, he added that the flats should not be completed before 1950 or possibly later.[76]

The project continued slowly. Both sides understood that the buildings would never be used to accommodate British personnel, although this was tacitly assumed, not stated explicitly. It had always been intended that the British 'enclave' would be handed back to the Germans after the occupation. On 10 March 1948 a meeting was held to discuss the 'final hand-over of the residue of the Hamburg project to the Germans'.[77] A year later, in February 1949, Robertson wrote to Berry, after learning that the German administration in Hamburg was going to resume work on the flats:

> I am of course delighted to hear that the Hamburg project is to be restarted. I always held that the work which we did would be of benefit to the City and I am glad to see myself being justified.[78]

His comment reflected a sincere, if optimistic, belief that the occupation would ultimately benefit the Germans, despite the original plans for the Hamburg Project requiring the eviction of 50,000 local residents from their homes, with no alternative accommodation, in an already overcrowded city. The *Grindelhochhäuser*,[79] as the blocks of flats originally designed to house British occupying forces were called, were completed in 1956. They were renovated between 1995 and 2006 and now stand under historic buildings protection.[80]

Personal reconciliation through Anglo-German discussion groups

Once power was devolved to local German administrations, the British authorities could no longer issue detailed instructions or tell the Germans what to do, but they still wished to influence the future development of the country through acting as advisers. Following various initiatives undertaken by individuals in the Control Commission's Political Division and Education Branch, Frank Pakenham, who succeeded Hynd as Minister for Germany in April 1947, wrote to Robertson asking him to ensure that in the light of 'the gradual transfer of power to the Germans ... our whole personnel establishes such personal relations with the Germans as to exercise the greatest possible influence'.[81] Staff were encouraged to develop personal relationships and hold informal discussions with Germans in responsible positions in government, business, the media and education. Frances Rosenfeld has documented the many ways in which British occupation officials in Hamburg created a 'successful arena' for 'post-war reconciliation and cultural exchange' through promoting a network of interlocking Anglo-German clubs and associations, supported by officially sponsored reading rooms and information centres, known as *Die Brücke* (The Bridge).[82] Over time, informal discussion groups developed into social and cultural clubs and societies and were complemented by other activities designed to promote mutual understanding, such as exchange visits between Britain and Germany. Hamburg was not unique in this. Similar initiatives took place throughout the British Zone.

The first Anglo-German discussion groups were formed on an entirely voluntary basis, outside their normal working hours, by individual Control Commission staff.[83] The idea was taken up, in slightly different ways, by Political Division and Education Branch. A proposal for an 'informal re-education scheme', modelled on the 'Education for Citizenship' activities developed by the British Army Bureau of Current Affairs, was approved in July 1946.[84] Meanwhile Education Branch promoted the idea of informal discussion groups, run voluntarily by enthusiastic individuals.[85] A branch memo in November 1946 suggested that Germans tended to view all official news sources with suspicion and would gain a better understanding of the 'British way and purpose' through personal contacts.[86] The idea was endorsed at a Regional Commissioners' conference in September 1946.[87] An article in the *British Zone Review* in January 1947 announced that the Commander-in-Chief (Sholto Douglas) had given formal approval for groups to be promoted and encouraged throughout the Zone, so that:

> Through personal contact and free discussion, the Germans will gain a fuller appreciation of the British way of thought, and conversely the British will reach a better understanding of the German mental outlook.[88]

Practical guidelines were offered on how to run the groups. A 'sufficiently keen and capable' British person should act as sponsor. Thirty should be the maximum number of participants; if there were more, it was difficult to hold a genuine discussion. Until the group had existed for some time, controversial subjects were best avoided, but topics should be of current interest, such as housing, food, education reform, films and music.[89] By 1948 several thousand groups had been formed in the Zone, including at least twenty-five established Anglo-German groups and sixteen other regular discussion groups in Hamburg.[90]

Other initiatives to promote mutual understanding and personal reconciliation were initiated at the highest levels of the Control Commission. In July 1946, soon after their appointment, Regional Commissioners were told that Robertson, the Deputy Military Governor, believed it desirable that they should develop social contacts with 'German officials, political leaders, Trade Union leaders and so on', as 'many things can more suitably be discussed unofficially at a cocktail party or a dinner party than officially in an office'.[91] In May 1947 most of the restrictions on personal and social contacts between British and Germans were lifted in a new 'Special Order', the preamble to which stated that 'British policy aims at encouraging the democratic way of life among the Germans'.[92] Control Commission staff were encouraged to visit German families (but not to 'spend the night with them') and to entertain Germans 'both officially and as private individuals'.[93] A year later the regulations were revised again to state that British personnel should 'behave towards the Germans as the people of one Christian and civilized race towards another, whose interests in many ways converge with our own and for whom we have no longer any ill-will'.[94]

As Regional Commissioner, Berry provided official endorsement and gave his personal support to some of the most high-profile activities, such as the Hamburg International Club, for young men and women aged between 18 and 30, and the elite Hamburg Anglo-German Club. At the inaugural meeting of the International Club, Berry spoke of a need for mutual tolerance and understanding. The club's German members, he said, had 'a difficult past to face'. Although many were only children at the time, they had to face the fact that:

> The Nazi Government, which was enthusiastically supported by large masses of the German people, committed unspeakable crimes against humanity, and you must not expect that these things can be quickly or easily forgotten, especially by your Eastern neighbours.[95]

British members, on the other hand, Berry added, should 'not be too critical of those Germans who spent their childhood under the Nazi regime'.[96]

Whereas the International Club was for young people, the Hamburg Anglo-German Club was deliberately modelled on a traditional English gentlemen's club and was intended to cater for the city's elite. Founder members included Berry, his deputy and later successor as Regional Commissioner, John Dunlop, Brauer, and some of the city's leading German politicians and businessmen.[97] After the currency reform in June 1948, Berry complained that British officials could no longer afford the costs of returning hospitality offered to them by 'affluent Germans' in the club. This, he believed, was unfortunate as it was in clubs such as these 'that we can reach the ruling 5 per cent of the population'.[98] The Hamburg Anglo-German Club survived proposals to close in 1951 and still exists in 2016.[99]

From 1947 the British made a deliberate effort, in Berry's words, 'to impress our ideas on the small elite of the population who lead in administration, industry, education and arts, journalism and so forth',[100] but this did not extend to courting popularity among the German population as a whole. As an unelected Military Government, imposed on a defeated nation by force, there was no obvious need to do so. Berry wrote in February 1948 that the 'occupation is not exactly popular and we make little effort to win the support of the German people'.[101] A few months later, he warned that although the air-lift had resulted in a more favourable attitude towards the Western Allies in Berlin, in the British Zone the occupation was:

> Intensely disliked and we must not be misled by the excellent relations which exist between the Administrations on both sides. It is not so much that we ourselves are becoming more unpopular as that the Germans are finding their feet.[102]

Berry asked his staff to investigate further. They reported that the British were disliked for their alleged aim of exploiting Germany, 'muddlesome inefficiency', and because the Germans held them responsible if anything went wrong.

There was 'admiration for individual British integrity' but 'very little for our administrative ability'. 'British psychology in official relations with the Germans' was considered poor and 'the only virtue seen in the British occupation is that it keeps the Russians out'.[103]

Despite concerns over the unpopularity of the occupation, Berry's later reports showed satisfaction with progress. In March 1948 he attached a declaration from the city government welcoming the Marshall Plan. This showed, he commented, that 'the right spirit rules in the Senate of Hamburg'.[104] In June 1948, as the availability of food improved for the first time since the end of the war, he reported that: 'For the first time in Occupation history food has not been the most absorbing topic.'[105] The following month, as tensions over Berlin eased, and fears lessened that the Western Allies would give way to Soviet pressure and evacuate the city, he reported that, for the first time in the occupation: 'The majority of Hamburgers are openly and vigourously [*sic*] championing Western democracy against Russian totalitarianism.'[106] The economic transformation following currency reform had been 'quite remarkable' and the city's finances were much improved.[107] In his last report as Commissioner, for April 1949, he could state that: 'A spirit of optimism prevails at the moment among all responsible elements and general morale has probably never been higher since the Occupation began.'[108]

'Yesterday's enemies, tomorrow's friends'

By the time Berry left Hamburg in May 1949, to take up a position as the British representative on the International Authority of the Ruhr, his aim of establishing a good working relationship with the city's German administration had been achieved. In a study completed in 1974, Hilary Balshaw conducted interviews with a number of Hamburg senators, all of whom spoke of the 'respect and admiration' he inspired in them and praised him in exceptional terms as, for example, 'a most marvellous man'.[109] In January 1949, Robertson provided further endorsement of the strength of his relationship with his German colleagues by telling Berry that he had recently asked the heads of government of the four *Länder* in the British Zone for their views on the current state of Anglo-German relations. Brauer had replied that:

> Relations between the Germans and the British and between the City Administration and the British occupation authorities can properly be described as ideal. That is largely due to your Regional Commissioner [i.e. Berry]. There

> are of course difficulties from time to time but we always manage to straighten them out. In my view the difficulties are not greater and probably less, than they would be if we had a German garrison in the town.[110]

Berry was able to look back on his achievements in Hamburg with satisfaction. In a speech during a celebratory return visit in 1959, he attributed much of his reputed success, and that of the City of Hamburg, which now 'formed part of the German miracle', to the 'far-sighted and humane policy of the Western Allies', adding that he retained his admiration for men such as General Robertson and Robert Birley, the education adviser, who had directed British policy in the Zone.[111]

Recent historians of the occupation in Hamburg have not agreed with the self-congratulatory view, expressed by Berry and many of his former colleagues in the 1950s and 1960s, that far-sighted and humane British policies contributed to the political and economic success of a democratic West Germany. Axel Schildt has argued that it is an oversimplification to see the occupation from 1945–9 as harmonious throughout. Growing trust was paralleled with tense conflicts, of which the Hamburg Project was one.[112] Similarly, Arnold Sywottek has highlighted German opposition to British Military Government, as well as initiatives by both sides to promote mutual understanding.[113] These comments are valid in correcting an overly rose-tinted view of growing trust and uninterrupted harmony but, in Hamburg, unrest was successfully defused and had little impact on the ability of the British to achieve their primary aims.

In the conclusions to his thorough and wide-ranging study, *Die Briten in Hamburg*, Michael Ahrens argued that the occupation was over-complicated and badly planned. The cost was too high, the British and Germans lived in 'parallel worlds', there was a 'deep division' between the civilian and military arms of the occupation, and no single point of contact for German authorities to deal with.[114] These criticisms are valid from a German perspective. They describe various ways in which the occupation made life more difficult for Germans in Hamburg, and they question the extent to which the British goal of mutual reconciliation was achieved. The Germans paid the occupation costs, resented the privileges assumed by the occupiers, such as travel in reserved compartments on overcrowded trains, and were annoyed by sometimes having to deal separately with British civilian and military authorities. None of these issues, however, significantly hindered British achievement of their primary aim of creating a peaceful and democratic Germany.

Frances Rosenfeld considered that the encounter between British and Germans in Hamburg was a 'unique experiment in post-war reconciliation and intercultural understanding' of which both sides were proud at the time, but which was achieved at the cost of ignoring difficult situations and topics: the German Nazi past, the British colonial legacy of separation from the natives and the Allied fire-bombings of the city.[115] The Hamburg bourgeoisie claimed, incorrectly, that they had opposed the Nazis during the war. They looked back to the city's pre-1933 liberal and cosmopolitan traditions and in so doing reasserted their own social, economic and political pre-eminence in the city. British policy, on the other hand, Rosenfeld claimed, was unduly influenced by an outmoded colonial model and 'reflected the essentially conservative values and self-image of the Foreign Office establishment, by projecting a generally old-fashioned, rose-tinted, middle and upper class view of British life'.[116]

Rosenfeld was surely correct that part of the price paid for mutual reconciliation was that both sides avoided and rarely discussed difficult but important issues, such as the city's Nazi past and, on the British side, the wartime bombing. These issues remained unresolved and re-emerged in later years as a source of conflict between the British and Germans and in public debates within Germany. Her claim that British policy was unduly influenced by an outmoded colonial model, however, was a generalization that was true of many members of the occupation but not of Berry. As discussed previously, there were strong 'echoes of empire' in British occupation policy as formulated by men such as the former colonial official Harold Ingrams, Field Marshal Montgomery, and Generals Robertson and Bishop. Although Berry was of similar age and could be considered part of the same 'generation', his personal experience of Empire was negative. His father had become wealthy in India, but lost all his money when he died and left his family to live in genteel poverty. Berry's life history was an illustration of an alternative grand narrative, also highlighted by Rosenfeld, of Britain as a great power in Europe.[117] He studied French and German at university, spoke both languages fluently, fought in the First World War, served in the occupied Rhineland and worked in the City of London, then, as now, the leading financial centre in Europe. Berry's role as the representative of British interests in occupied Germany was a natural extension of his earlier career, and illustrates an often neglected aspect of the occupation: the British attempt to maintain a pre-eminent role in post-war Europe.

Berry did not act as the representative of a power in decline. He was supremely confident in his own values, ability and judgement, based on his personal experience and the conclusions he had reached from his work in politics and business between the wars. He understood and respected local traditions and never treated Germany as a colony. He did not share the wartime 'Vansittartist' prejudices of some of his Labour Party colleagues against the German Social

Democrats and accepted without question that they represented a progressive movement with similar ideals to his own. He represented the interests of his city to the central British authorities, but he was willing to reprimand and overrule the local German government if he considered this necessary. His experiences in the Rhineland from 1919 to 1925 were more important than the emerging Cold War in influencing his policy and attitudes. Over time, they reinforced each other and the conclusion he could draw from both was that he and his British colleagues had a vital role in actively supporting and encouraging democratic forces within Germany.

Berry's principal aim was simple and uncontroversial: to create a peaceful and democratic Germany that would never again threaten the national interests of Great Britain. He believed that this aim could best be achieved by establishing a good working relationship with the German SPD administration and promoting mutual reconciliation as a means of preserving British influence among the German governing elite. In his farewell speech at a reception on leaving the city he said that:

> Dem Gegner von gestern, dem Freunde von Morgen
> Das ist das Ziel, dem wir nachstreben sollten.
> [Yesterday's enemies, tomorrow's friends, that is the goal we should strive for.][118]

As recent historians have shown, there were periods of tense conflict in Hamburg, as well as cooperation between occupiers and occupied. Some actions of the British, such as the requisitioning of houses for the Hamburg Project, were unnecessarily high-handed and antagonized the local population, and some difficult issues were ignored. There is little evidence of any long-term British influence on the city arising from the occupation, apart from the continued existence of a few blocks of flats and the Anglo-German club. On the other hand, Berry established excellent relations with the German administration on a basis of mutual trust. He kept the peace but tolerated dissent, provided a channel for the discussion of grievances and defused difficult situations. He oversaw the transfer of power from direct British rule to an independent German administration. Overall, despite criticisms from some historians, his tenure in Hamburg still offers a reasonable model for the benevolent occupation of a defeated enemy.

Part Three

Personal Reconciliation: Young Men with No Adult Experience but War

8

A Younger Generation?

Jan Thexton worked briefly in an accountant's office before the war, but six years on in 1945, he felt it was too late to return:

> I just didn't really know what to do. I was far too old to start again for accountancy or anything like that. I had no other qualifications apart from my basic educational qualifications. I was no good to anybody really.[1]

Whereas the Military Governors, generals and senior civilian administrators discussed earlier were at the peak of their professional careers, younger and more junior officers and NCOs were at the start of their working lives, uncertain what to do next, with no relevant experience apart from war. Most had fought with the Allied armies in the Normandy landings and across North-West Europe; some were posted to Germany when the war was over, from the navy, the RAF or from the Far East. They had survived the war but had no career to return to. The skills they had learnt and the experiences they had gained as soldiers, sailors or airmen were unlikely to be of much benefit in civilian life. In the meantime they had to stay in Germany and wait a further one or two years, depending on their age and length of service, before they were demobilized and could return home.

Part Three of this book examines four young officers responsible for the implementation of British policy in occupied Germany. All four held responsible positions, despite their youth, and formed part of a 'governing elite' of military officers and civilian administrators in the British Zone of occupied Germany. John Chaloner, a former tank commander, was Press Officer in Hanover, where he created the news magazine *Der Spiegel*. Michael Howard was Intelligence Officer for T-Force, the unit within the British army responsible for 'evacuating' German equipment, research laboratories, scientists and technicians to assist British economic recovery after the war. Michael Palliser was also a tank commander during the war. He remained in Germany as part of the army of occupation until he was demobilized in January 1947. Jan Thexton served during the war as a non-commissioned signals officer and joined the Control

Commission for Germany after he was demobilized in 1946. He met and married his wife in Germany. The experiences of these four young officers are contrasted with those of their seniors and illustrate how personal relationships – working together with Germans or meeting them socially as individuals – contributed to reconciliation between former enemies.

There is less written material in the archives relating to younger and more junior officers, so to compensate for any bias in the source materials, which were inevitably more personal than those used in previous chapters, I have also drawn on interviews held at the Imperial War Museum Sound Archive (IWM SA) with twenty young British men and one woman, who worked for Military Government or the Control Commission in an official capacity, for at least one year between 1945 and 1948. Although experiences were diverse, those discussed were fairly representative of young British soldiers, sailors and airmen who were based in occupied Germany between 1945 and 1948. Thexton, Palliser, Chaloner and Howard were born between 1920 and 1926 and came from a similar, professional middle class family background to the senior officers discussed in Part One. Eleven of the IWM interviewees were the same age as the four young officers and ten a little older, born between 1913 and 1919. Some were from less established or affluent family backgrounds. They also covered a greater diversity of roles in occupied Germany, including intelligence, the care of Displaced Persons (DPs), the Judge Advocate General's department responsible for prosecuting war crimes, RAF ground crew, two naval officers on minesweeping and customs and excise patrols, one man and one woman working on de-nazification, two volunteers working for Friends' Ambulance and Salvation Army units, and a Russian interpreter.[2]

It has been common practice in German historiography and culture to classify people as belonging to a particular age group or 'generation',[3] following theoretical work by Karl Mannheim and Helmut Fogt, according to which, for a 'generation' to be of historical significance, a group of people need to share common experiences and have a similar understanding of the meaning of historical events, as well as having been born within the same period of time.[4] The concept of 'generation', however, has been little used in studies of British history, which have tended to focus on other categories of analysis, notably social class, gender and political allegiance. There are no British equivalents for the various overlapping 'generations' described by German historians, such as the *'Hitler Jugend'* (Hitler Youth), the *'Flakhelfer'* (Anti-aircraft auxiliaries) or the '1945ers', born between 1921 and 1933 and therefore too young to have been actively involved with the Nazi Party, except as children.[5] In Britain, differences between people of a similar age generally appear more important than any similarities.

The Military Governors and army generals discussed in Part One of this book were born within a few years of each other; Robertson in 1896, Bishop in 1897, Douglas in 1893 and Montgomery, the oldest, in 1887.[6] They shared similar experiences in their early lives and possessed a common understanding of historical events, so they do appear to meet the criteria required for consideration as a historical 'generation'. One might call them the 'Empire Builders'. They all received a traditional public school education, followed (with the exception of Douglas who went to Oxford University) by attendance at the Military Academies at Sandhurst or Woolwich, where they were commissioned as officers. They fought as young men in the First World War, when Montgomery, Bishop and Douglas were wounded, and stayed on as regular soldiers or re-joined the forces later. In the interwar years they served in the British Empire, in India, the Middle East or Africa, and attended or taught at the army or RAF staff colleges. Though not from especially wealthy or aristocratic families, they were very much part of the British professional establishment. They had grown up at a time when the British Empire was at its height, fought to defend the Empire in the First World War and worked to protect and preserve its power and influence in the interwar years.

The civilian diplomats and administrators considered in Part Two, on the other hand, do not fit easily within a generational framework. Berry was born in 1891, Ingrams in 1897, Albu in 1903 and Flanders in 1910. Ingrams, the colonial administrator, shared a similar outlook to his close contemporaries, Generals Robertson and Bishop, but had little in common with Berry, despite both having served as officers in the First World War. Although Berry was an active Labour Party supporter, his experiences before the war were also very different from those of his fellow socialists, Albu and Flanders. Individual factors such as personal background and beliefs, education, political allegiance and pre-war experiences at work appear to have been more important in determining their aims and activities in Germany than membership of any age cohort or 'generation'.

Although the four young officers and twenty-one IWM interviewees discussed in Part Three all served in the armed forces during the Second World War (except for two conscientious objectors who served in medical units), and all worked in an official capacity in occupied Germany afterwards, their earlier experiences before joining the forces were very different. There were significant differences in outlook even within the small group of university students at Oxford during the war. For example, one IWM interviewee said that there were no pacifists at Oxford in 1942, all were servicemen and 'deeply engaged on the whole thing',[7] while another, also a student at Oxford but himself a pacifist and conscientious objector (CO), recalled that there were 'quite a lot of students at Oxford who were also COs'.[8] Class and social background, religious convictions, their expectations of what to do when the war was over, and their personal skills, training and aptitudes appear to have had at least as great an influence on their understanding of their task in Germany as any shared experience as a generational cohort.

Yet despite diversity in personal background and outlook, all four young officers and many of the IWM interviewees later remembered the war and its aftermath as a significant formative influence on the rest of their lives. Michael Palliser, for example, said that his experience in Europe and Germany at the end of the war had made him a convinced European, as this was the best way of trying to ensure that the devastation and destruction he saw then would never be repeated and war between two European countries, such as France and Germany, would become unthinkable.[9] On a more personal level, John Chaloner referred, in a semi-autobiographical novel published in 1991, to the combination of starting his first successful publishing venture and experiencing his 'first love affair of timeless but futureless passion', as 'a pattern he would always seek for the rest of his life'.[10] To some extent, therefore, the 'younger generation' of young men and a few women in occupied Germany did share a common experience during the war and after, and a comparison with the older and stronger 'generation' of senior officers can reveal similarities and differences between the two groups.

Personal fulfilment rather than collective goals

The four young officers and twenty-one IWM interviewees discussed in this chapter were generally practical, realistic and conscientious. Personal goals, and concerns as to what they could do when they were demobilized and returned home, were generally more important for them than collective national aims. None recalled hearing or reading the exhortations from Montgomery, Robertson or other senior officers to 'save the soul of Germany' or 'rebuild civilisation' let alone being influenced or inspired by these.[11] Similarly, none mentioned reading articles in the *British Zone Review*, Montgomery's proclamations to the German people or listening to talks on British Forces Network radio broadcasts. Most knew little about the activities of other divisions or how their actions related to the overall aims of the occupation. They had no doubts that the war had been just and necessary but, with a few notable exceptions, they were not motivated by high ideals or the need to serve their country or the British Empire. Now that the war was over, there was a retreat from the public to the private sphere and they were, above all, concerned for their own welfare. Having accepted during the war that this had to be subordinated to the greater good, they could look to the future and start to think again about their personal needs and ambitions.[12]

British soldiers were not demobilized immediately after the end of the war. Most of those serving in Germany had to wait between twelve and eighteen months before they could return home. Demobilization rules were based on age and length of service. Older men who had served longest were released first, and priority was given to those who had worked before the war in occupations considered vital for reconstruction, such as coal mining, teachers and the police. The young men at the end of the queue, who had joined the services in 1940, after the start of the war, were not released until the end of 1946. Those who enlisted in 1943 or 1944, when they were seventeen or eighteen, had to wait even longer until the end of 1947. Although demobilization generally worked reasonably well (unlike after the First World War, when the original scheme degenerated into chaos and had to be abandoned), lack of information, delays and the general uncertainty over future prospects contributed towards a sense of disillusionment for many, after the intensity of their wartime experiences.[13]

Jan Thexton was born in April 1920 in Plymouth and spent his early childhood in Bermuda. His father, a non-commissioned officer in the army, was Garrison Chief Clerk to the Governor, before he returned to the UK with his family to take up a position as a civil servant in the Military Secretary's branch of the War Office. After leaving school, Thexton joined the Middlesex Yeomanry as a territorial and was called up shortly before the start of hostilities in 1939, to help prepare for mobilization. He was posted to a signals unit in an armoured tank division and fought in North Africa and Normandy, landing on D-Day plus one. At the end of the war he was in Hanover. His rank at the time was sergeant. He claimed later that he and several others in his unit were offered commissions but declined, because everyone who accepted was sent to the Far East, to fight against the Japanese.[14]

When he was demobilized, he decided to join the civilian Control Commission and stay in Germany, rather than return home.[15] Though officially designated as civil servants, Control Commission staff were offered temporary contracts, with no security of employment. As staff numbers were progressively reduced from 1948 until the end of the occupation in 1955, most had to leave government employment, but Thexton successfully applied for entry into the permanent UK civil service and stayed in Germany for over twenty years. His first position was in the reparations branch of the Control Commission, where he was responsible, with a team of forty-five German staff, for compiling lists of armaments factories

Figure 8.1 Jan Thexton in 1945. Photo courtesy Robert Partridge.

and equipment to be made available as reparations for the British and other Western Allies.[16] He then moved to the Mandatory Requirements Office, which procured materials that the Germans were obliged to provide to the British and the other Allies, in accordance with the terms of the Hague Conventions and later Occupation Agreements with the Federal German government.[17] Thexton was responsible for purchasing equipment and supplies for the British, Belgian, Norwegian and Canadian occupation forces from the German economy, and obtaining reimbursement of the costs from the German authorities. In the 1950s he joined the British Embassy as a liaison officer, selling British-made weapons to the newly formed German armed services.[18] He met his wife in Germany soon after the end of the war, when he was working, as an army signals engineer, on restoring the German telephone system and she was a supervisor in the Hanover telephone exchange, though they were not able to marry until June 1947.[19]

Michael Palliser was born in 1922 to a family with significant naval connections on both sides. His father, Admiral Sir Arthur Palliser, joined the Royal Navy as a young man in 1907, rose to command first a destroyer then a battleship and, from 1938 to 1940, was captain of the gunnery school HMS *Excellent* at Whale Island near Portsmouth. At the end of the Second World War,

Figure 8.2 Sir Arthur Michael Palliser, December 1942, by Elliott & Fry, December 1942. © National Portrait Gallery, London.

he was Fourth Sea Lord at the Admiralty. Palliser's mother was the daughter of a distinguished naval engineer, who had been in charge of naval dockyards at Simon's Town in South Africa and Cockatoo Island, Sydney, Australia.[20] Palliser went to school at Wellington College,[21] finishing in the summer of 1939. He remembered spending most of July that year digging air raid shelters at school. Although the war had started, he was able to attend university at Oxford, where he read classics for a little over a year, before joining the Coldstream Guards. After initial training and six months at Sandhurst, he was commissioned as an officer in an armoured tank battalion. He spent a further two years with the regiment in England preparing for the invasion of Normandy and landed in France two weeks after D-Day. He fought with the army through France, Belgium and Holland, across the Rhine to Germany, and on VE Day had reached Neumünster, a small town in Schleswig Holstein, north of Hamburg. He stayed in Germany as part of the army of occupation until his demobilization in January

1947, stationed mainly in Berlin and later in Bad Godesberg, near Bonn.[22] After leaving Germany in 1947 he had a distinguished career in the Foreign Office, appointed Permanent Under-Secretary in 1975, and played a significant role in British applications to join the European Community under both Labour and Conservative governments.

John Chaloner was born on 5 November 1924.[23] Both his parents were journalists and writers.[24] When he was ten years old they sent him to the Beltane School in Wimbledon, where many of the other pupils were the children of German Jewish immigrants.[25] The co-director of the school, Ernst Bulova, had formerly been the principal of the Montessori Dahlem School in Berlin.[26] Chaloner volunteered to join the army as a private, but was soon promoted to sergeant and identified as a potential officer. He was accepted at Sandhurst and commissioned as an officer in the Westminster Dragoons.[27] He took part in the invasion of Normandy and subsequent battles in France, the Netherlands and Germany as commander of a Sherman flail tank. On one occasion his tank was destroyed by enemy fire and, though one of his crew was killed, he survived unharmed.[28] At the end of the war, by now promoted to captain, he heard that there were opportunities for officers with experience of publishing to join Military Government Information Services Control units. As he could speak German, though not fluently, and saw this as an alternative to a possible posting to the Far East, he applied and was accepted.[29]

Michael Howard, the youngest of the four officers, was born in May 1926 in Fiji, where his father was a Colonial Administrator. He left Fiji when he was eight years old to attend boarding school in England. At the outbreak of war in 1939 he was at school at Rugby.[30] He volunteered to join the forces as soon as he could, on his seventeenth birthday in May 1943, but was not called up for another fifteen months, too late to see active service. He was commissioned as an officer in the Rifle Brigade in August 1945, three months after the end of the war in Europe.[31] He was sent to a holding unit, in Osnabrück in North West Germany where, in a conversation with another newly commissioned officer, John Kirby, whose father was Deputy Chief of Staff for the Control Commission, he learned about a new unit, supposedly engaged in secret and interesting work.[32] T-Force had been established a year earlier, to examine and secure factories and research laboratories, by-passed by the front-line troops as they advanced. After the end of the war the unit's role broadened to support teams of scientists and businessmen sent to Germany by BIOS, the British Intelligence Objectives Sub-Committee, to investigate German scientific and technical capabilities and 'evacuate' documents, blueprints, machinery and people – German scientists and technicians – to Britain as reparations.[33] Howard had been offered a place at Cambridge University and originally hoped for as short a stay in the army as possible. However, he became absorbed in his work, rapidly received promotion from Second Lieutenant to Captain and stayed until he was demobilized in December 1947, by which time the work of T-Force was largely complete and the unit was wound down.[34]

Most of the twenty-one IWM interviewees were in Germany when the fighting stopped and had to stay while awaiting demobilization. Others, such as two naval officers and a Russian interpreter, were posted there when the war was over. Only one, a conscientious objector, who had a strong commitment to voluntary work and community service, made a deliberate decision to go to Germany.[35] Most of the others were filling in time before they could progress to their chosen career, such as one IWM interviewee who wanted to train as a teacher, but was faced with a two-year waiting list before he could take up his college place.[36] The only woman out of the twenty-one worked during the war for the Foreign Office and was able to transfer to a job in Germany to be with her husband, who was an intelligence officer in the Control Commission.[37] The two naval officers were reluctant to return to civilian life after six or seven years at sea, and took advantage of an opportunity to join the regular service, rather than being demobilized.[38]

Despite not having made a deliberate choice to work in Germany, all four of the young officers and many of the IWM interviewees took their work extremely seriously. Jan Thexton, for example, spoke of working long hours when he was compiling lists of war plants and machinery available for reparations. He was in the office from 8.00 am until 8 or 9.00 pm. Sometimes when he was travelling he did not return home for days at a time.[39] Others, however, treated their work more casually. For some in the army of occupation or the air force in Berlin, the end of the war meant a return to peacetime soldiering, but in a foreign country. One IWM interviewee spoke of 'going back to polishing things again'.[40] Another could not remember what he did in Germany, referring to 'staff duties' or 'something like that'.[41] One had 'a jolly twelve months' in a jazz band at HQ British Air Forces of Occupation at Bückeburg, playing there or at nearby locations most nights in the week. He had a 'sainted life', he said, and could do more or less as he liked. They were just waiting for demobilization but 'it was a lovely way to do this … It was just one big ball actually while we were there'.[42]

Despite their differences, both senior and younger officers were more concerned with the future than the past, which led them to focus on reconstruction rather than restitution and reparations. The senior officers understood their role to be the restoration of order and the prevention of disease and social unrest, which presupposed a reasonably effective civil administration and a functioning economy. Facing an uncertain future, in the interlude between the end of the war and returning home, the younger generation adjusted to a peacetime mentality and started to rebuild their lives.

Reactions to death and destruction

The statistics of the scale of damage to the major towns and cities in Germany are well known, with official British figures stating that in Cologne, for example, 66 per cent of the houses were totally destroyed and in Düsseldorf 93 per cent were uninhabitable.[43] According to government statistics, around 600,000 civilians in Germany were killed by bombing raids, compared with 62,000 in Britain. A further 900,000 civilians were wounded and 7.5 million made homeless.[44] Many more civilians, of course, were killed in Eastern Europe and the Soviet Union during the German invasion and retreat,[45] but British soldiers did not see this for themselves.

Whereas the senior officers quoted previously, and other observers including journalists and war correspondents, reacted with apparent shock and wrote that 'you have to see it to believe it', only a few of the young officers and IWM interviewees discussed in this chapter responded similarly to ruined buildings and the scale of destruction in the German cities. The senior officers could tell a relatively simple story, which emphasized their own achievements, of chaos and destruction followed by the restoration of law and order. The younger generation may have related the ruined cities they saw in Germany to their personal experiences, which were largely those of wartime, and assumed that death and destruction were an obvious consequence of war, too well known to be worth mentioning.

The few who did refer to the scale of destruction in Germany showed a mixed response. Two IWM interviewees described it as shocking and unjustified.[46] The scale of destruction in Berlin and the industrial towns of the Ruhr made a lasting impression on those stationed there, such as one young man, who was part of the British advance guard sent to Berlin in 1945:

> It was like the rest of Germany really… No-one who didn't see Germany in 1945 and 1946 knows what bombing's all about… It really appalled everyone… You don't let much worry you at that age [but] it appalled me.[47]

He remembered that there were still many bodies buried under the rubble. The summer of 1945 was very hot and after it rained the smell was terrible. He added that he could understand why Bomber Harris was ostracized after the war and that the destruction of Dresden could be compared to a war atrocity.[48] Others, however, assumed that destruction on this scale was an inevitable consequence of war, perhaps regrettable, perhaps a notable achievement which had contributed to winning the war, but no more than the Germans deserved and had inflicted on others.

Michael Howard had not seen active service in the war. When asked in his oral history interview for the IWM in 2008 about the condition of Osnabrück, he replied that it was severely damaged, but what struck him most was that it must have been the target for medium artillery, as many houses had lost their roofs and top floors: 'Yes, it was a pretty desolate place', he added. The barracks where he stayed were relatively undamaged but the town was a heap of rubble. This was much as expected and made no particular impression on him: 'It was much as it ought to be.'[49] Contemporary letters to his parents published in his book *Otherwise Occupied* give a slightly different, but not inconsistent, picture. The scale of destruction, he wrote, was an 'amazing sight', but he did not draw any conclusions from this, apart from describing his concern for the animals and children (who presumably, in his view at the time, did not share responsibility for the war with the adults) and expressing the conventional view that the bombing had been effective in destroying Germany's ability to wage another war for 'some forty years'.[50]

When I asked Michael Palliser in 2010 if he was surprised by the destruction he saw in German towns and cities, he related this to his own experiences of bombing in Britain, fighting in Normandy, and having to 'knock out' church spires in Holland, which might 'appear savage', but was necessary as they made an ideal observation and sniper post for the enemy.[51] Without being explicit, he appeared to be making two points: that the destruction was not unique to Germany, and that destruction was sometimes an undesirable but necessary means to an end. Later in the interview, he told the story of a conversation with a Swedish businessman, in the restaurant car of a train travelling through the industrial cities of the Ruhr. The Swede looked out of the window at this 'absolute lunar landscape' and 'banged on about how dreadful we'd been to bomb the Ruhr'. Palliser was furious with his companion who 'had enjoyed his neutrality during the war' and replied that if he looked at cities like London and Coventry, he would soon realize that the Ruhr was not unique.[52]

Palliser was incorrect in telling his Swedish travelling companion that the extent of damage caused by Allied bombing in the Ruhr was similar to that in

London or Coventry, though he may have believed this at the time. As the official statistics showed, the destruction of buildings and number of civilian casualties were far greater in Germany than in Britain and far greater in the Soviet Union and Eastern Europe than in Germany. But Palliser was surely correct that the destruction of the Ruhr and other German cities was not unique, and needed to be placed in the wider context of whether the end justified the means.

War crimes and Holocaust survivors

Only a few of the young British officers and NCOs discussed in this chapter made any mention of the Holocaust, war crimes or atrocities, in contemporary accounts or later oral history interviews. This was not exceptional. Historians have criticized the British occupiers for not giving sufficient priority to the care of concentration camp and Holocaust survivors.[53] Their apparent lack of concern may, however, have been due to the relatively low number of Jewish Displaced Persons in the British Zone compared to the US Zone. Estimates vary, but in June 1946 the number of Jewish DPs in the British Zone was calculated by UNRRA as 19,373 and remained fairly constant throughout the occupation. Around half were accommodated in Hohne camp, near Bergen Belsen, and most of the remainder in cities such as Hamburg, Cologne, Düsseldorf, Hanover and Kiel.[54] In the US Zone the number was higher, around 36,000 in January 1946,[55] and increased rapidly in the following two years due to immigration of around 250,000 Jews from Eastern Europe, the vast majority of whom were accommodated in camps in the US Zone.[56] British soldiers and administrators recognized that the murder of millions of Jews and other war crimes committed by Germans were 'absolutely horrific', but except for British Jews such as Albu, German Jewish exiles returning to Germany, or those responsible for investigating and prosecuting war crimes and atrocities, the Holocaust could appear as something that had occurred in the past, rather than a major concern for the present and future.

The attitudes of the 'younger generation' in this respect were no different from British people in Germany generally. Most of the British occupiers did not experience the liberation of the camps or meet the few Jewish survivors who were still alive in Germany in May 1945. Many more would have encountered Russian, Polish and Eastern European forced labourers, of whom there were over two million in the western zones at the end of the war. Over 200,000 remained in the British Zone as DPs in August 1947, unable or unwilling to return home.[57]

British soldiers and administrators also had to cope with five million ethnic German refugees who arrived in the Zone, sometimes in extreme distress, between 1945 and 1951, after having been expelled from Czechoslovakia and the former eastern German territories ceded to Poland.[58] This does not imply that British people in Germany were not aware of the Holocaust, or that it was not a major concern morally. It clearly was. However, there were relatively few Jewish DPs in the British Zone and there was nothing they could do to bring the millions of those murdered back to life. It took many years for people in all countries to come to terms with the implications of the Holocaust.

The attitudes of the more senior British army officers and civilian administrators to Jewish refugees and Holocaust survivors can be illustrated by the following two examples: firstly, Robertson's reply to one of his generals, who complained about criticism of the British from a Jewish survivor at Belsen and, secondly, Berry's report on the final stage of the *Exodus* affair, the enforced disembarkation from three ships in Hamburg of several thousand Jewish refugees, who had previously been prevented by the Royal Navy from landing in Palestine.

At the unveiling of a memorial to the victims at Belsen on 15 April 1946, the first anniversary of the camp's liberation, the secretary of the Central Committee of Jewish survivors, Norbert Wollheim, was reported by a British officer present at the ceremony, to have denounced the British for not providing the survivors with better living conditions, and also for not offering sufficient assistance during the war 'to the Jews in their desperate struggle against extermination'.[59] According to the report, Wollheim claimed that the murder of six million Jews was 'a crime for which the <u>BRITISH</u> should hang their heads in shame'. The British authorities were sensitive to criticism of this nature. General Galloway, the military commander responsible for the region, told Robertson that he found it 'intensely objectionable' that Wollheim was able to say 'offensive things about the British without any action being taken to stop it'. Robertson replied that he had discussed the matter with Colonel Robert Solomon, the recently appointed British special adviser to the Control Commission on Jewish affairs, who had told him that Wollheim was a 'young man with rather fanatical ideas and undue importance should not be attached to his outburst'. Robertson added that if Wollheim committed 'a further indiscretion' in future, 'steps will be taken against him just as they would be against any other German for a similar offence'.[60] At the time British policy was to treat Jews in the British Zone as German nationals, rather than recognizing the survivors' claim to be part of a separate Jewish nation.[61]

Jewish opposition to the British in Germany was directly linked with restrictions on emigration to Palestine and reached a peak in August and September 1947, when 4,500 Jewish refugees carried by the *Exodus 1947*, a converted US packet steamer, were prevented from landing in Palestine by the Royal Navy and forcibly transferred, after a bitter three-hour fight, to three other ships, the *Ocean Vigour, Empire Rival* and *Runnymede Park*. Unable to return the refugees to France, where they had originally boarded the *Exodus*, the British government decided they should be sent to Germany, a decision met with incredulity by Zionist sympathizers in Britain, France, the United States and around the world.[62] Jon and David KImche, the authors of *The Secret Roads: The 'Illegal' Migration of a People*, wrote that:

> The episode of the *Exodus*... shocked the world by its sheer uncomprehending stupidity and again poisoned Anglo-French relations.[63]

As Regional Commissioner, Vaughan Berry was responsible for the refugees' disembarkation from the ships after they docked in Hamburg, and their transfer onto trains to be taken to DP camps in Lower Saxony. This final stage of the affair, inappropriately named 'Operation Oasis' (as no Jew was likely to perceive a refugee camp in Germany as an oasis in the desert), was completed relatively peacefully. Most left quietly but some had to be carried off the ships by British troops and some were injured.[64] Two years later, after British withdrawal from Palestine and the creation of the state of Israel in May 1948, the *Exodus* refugees forced to return to Germany had emigrated a second time, and Jewish DPs were no longer accommodated in camps in the British Zone.[65]

In his report on Operation Oasis, the disembarkation of the refugees from the ships in Hamburg, Berry distanced himself from the origins and wider implications of the issue, claiming that he had received instructions to transfer the refugees only a few days previously, and no one in Hamburg had been consulted. He reported that there had been no injuries when the refugees left two of the ships, although soldiers searching the *Empire Rival* afterwards discovered a bomb and removed it to a safe place where it exploded. Had this not been done the ship would have sunk. On the third ship, the *Runnymede Park*, there had been thirty-three minor casualties when refugees had to be forcibly removed by British soldiers.[66] At the end of his report, Berry stated that on one of the trains carrying the refugees from Hamburg to Lower Saxony, the iron mesh on a window was pushed outwards and struck another train passing in the opposite direction, injuring four German passengers, one seriously. He added that it was an 'unfortunate commentary' on the affair that the most serious injury was to 'a German in no way connected with the operation'.[67]

Robertson's reference to a concentration camp survivor as 'any other German' and Berry's reference to a German injured in the train accident as 'in no way connected' to the Jewish refugees now appear inappropriate and grossly insensitive to Holocaust survivors and victims of Nazi persecution. Such attitudes, however, were typical of many of the British occupiers, who did not wish to emphasize German guilt for war crimes and atrocities more than had already been done by the Allies immediately after the end of the war and who now perceived the care of survivors as peripheral to their main tasks and priorities. Bishop's responsibilities as head of Public Relations and Information Services Control (PR/ISC), for example, included deciding whether newsreels and documentary films of the concentration camps should be shown in cinemas in the British Zone. He wrote later that, although it was 'clearly desirable' that German people should know about the conditions in the camps, he doubted whether showing the films would 'help us in what was then our primary task of restoring order in the country'.[68]

John Chaloner was the only young officer considered in this chapter who was present at or soon after the liberation of a concentration camp. His sister wrote that seeing Belsen soon after liberation was an experience that affected him deeply and the memory stayed with him for the rest of his life,[69] but there is no record of his referring to it in any public context. He did so only in private conversations and in fictional works based on his experiences in Germany. In his novel *Occupational Hazard*, he described the reaction of a tank crew after seeing Belsen for the first time:

> Two of my men who have after all, seen a few things, were very quiet, and then suddenly sick. They lay on the grass. We brewed up tea, and they had a cigarette and everyone said that nothing was too bad for the Germans.[70]

Although the experience was deeply moving, it did not prevent him from making lasting personal friendships with German journalists and editors he met later when re-establishing newspapers in Osnabrück, Lüneburg and Hanover.[71] His sister recalled a long conversation with him about Belsen. She believed that of all his wartime experiences, it was the one that affected him most deeply, together with seeing tanks either side of him blown up 'with his mates inside', adding that, in later life, he was 'deeply melancholy about man's inhumanity to man'.[72]

Only four of the twenty-one IWM interviewees referred to the Holocaust, war crimes or atrocities. One was an officer who was a member of the panel on a trial at the Volkswagen works, where 450 babies born to forced labourers were kept in a nursery and allowed to starve to death.[73] Another was a lawyer who worked as a prosecutor for the Judge Advocate General's department. Some of those he prosecuted were, in his view quite rightly, found guilty and condemned to death, such as a German official who had taken an Allied airman, who had landed by parachute, to his office and shot him, and an interrogator at Neuengamme concentration camp, who fitted a spike to a chair, operated by a pedal, to make those he questioned stand up more quickly, an idea he had taken from Dachau. Occasionally, though, he dealt with cases he was less sure about, such as six German civilians accused of ill-treating an RAF officer. 'They had done it', he said, but 'most people would have done the same after an air raid' and it could be difficult to understand that while the pilot was in an aeroplane they could shoot him, but if he landed by parachute, he was a POW and they must not touch him. On balance he considered 'it was fairly done'.[74]

Whereas most cases of war crimes were clear-cut, others were less so. With incomplete information, it could be difficult to know how victims met their fate. Another officer, based at Travemünde on the Baltic coast, spoke of a 'ghastly incident' in April or May 1945, shortly before the surrender, when a ship in the harbour, loaded with camp victims, was taken out to sea and sunk by the guards. At least, he said, that was one story. Another was that the ship had been sunk by a British aircraft and he was inclined to believe this second version. In June a large number of bodies were washed up on the beach and SS prisoners-of-war were made to haul out the bodies.[75] The officer was probably correct in his belief that the ship had been sunk by British aircraft. On 3 May 1945 the *Cap Arcona* and two other ships holding former inmates from Neuengamme concentration camp were attacked by the RAF on the mistaken assumption that they were troop transports. Around 7,000 prisoners were burnt, drowned or shot by SS guards while they were trying to escape.[76]

It is sometimes claimed that British and American soldiers who witnessed the liberation of concentration camps were provoked to acts of revenge. Richard Bessel, for example, referred to US forces after the liberation of Dachau, where 'Germans were gunned down while surrendering; captives were shot at the slightest provocation'.[77] He claimed that the liberation of Bergen Belsen had a similar effect on the British, taking as an example the British military commandant at Münster who was 'inclined initially to take a punitive attitude towards the German population due to [his] personal experiences of liberating the camps'.[78] For the individuals examined in this chapter, however, there is no evidence that initial feelings of hatred were translated into acts of revenge. A more common reaction was to make a distinction between those who had committed war crimes and the individuals they met face to face. One IWM interviewee described how they were always hearing rumours of SS atrocities, of their having shot prisoners, or murdered Americans, which made the British soldiers angry:

> But when you see a person face to face and he's unarmed you lose this anger and wildness, and just take them prisoner or whatever.[79]

The only two prisoners he took personally were 'a couple of lads of about 16' who 'came out of a wood with their hands up. They were just terrified'.[80]

Many influential British observers did not consider revenge a suitable response to war crimes and atrocities. The war journalist Leonard Mosley, who was present at the liberation of Belsen, reported that British soldiers, enraged by the piles of corpses, beat the SS guards and ordered them to collect the bodies 'to the accompaniment of lewd shouts and laughs' but added that it made him 'pensive to see British soldiers beating and kicking men and women, even under such provocation'.[81] Patrick Gordon-Walker, who recorded the first Jewish eve of Sabbath service held in Belsen, later broadcast on the BBC, responded similarly. He recorded in his diary that he was at first 'very angry with the Germans' but there was a need, he wrote, to 'restore our respect for death' and 'no human life should be taken away without due formality'. In his view, those responsible for the concentration camps should be punished, with the death penalty, but this had to be done by following proper legal processes, not through the same methods as the Nazis.[82]

According to a contemporary report on morale among the troops in April and May 1945, all British soldiers in Germany knew of the liberation of the camps, from reading newspapers or by word of mouth from colleagues, if not from their own experience, but this did not appear to affect their behaviour when carrying out their duties.[83] They combined a harsh view of Germans collectively with a pragmatic view of those they met as individuals. Michael Palliser, for example, said that although neither he nor anyone in his battalion personally discovered or visited any of the camps, another battalion in his regiment had and they heard accounts 'which were absolutely horrific'. When asked if this changed, or possibly reinforced, his attitude to the Germans, he replied that:

> I think it possibly reinforced it a bit. I'm not sure. I think that there was already a feeling that this had been a very barbaric regime, which was partly the result of whatever you like, wartime propaganda and so on, but I wouldn't say we were surprised. I think there was a tendency to say 'how typically German' in the mood of the time. I think that we were almost beyond being surprised by anything.[84]

This view of war crimes as 'typically German' was reflected in a similar comment from the officer on the war crimes panel at the Volkswagen works who, when asked why the babies had starved to death, replied that: 'It was just typical German ... [The Germans believed] they were Slav and there was nothing lower in life.'[85] When asked about the camps, he replied that he had not seen any himself, but knew others who had. He added, incongruously, that he went to Belsen once, to buy a dog from some Germans who had moved into the huts.[86] A second interviewee said that he passed through Belsen in June 1946, when leaving Germany, but it had been cleared and there were no inmates.[87]

The approach of trying to draw a line under the horrors of the past was perhaps best typified by an eight-page supplement on Belsen in the second issue of the *British Zone Review* on 13 October 1945. This was described as: 'An account, based on Official Reports, of the uncovering by the British Army of the Belsen Concentration Camp and of the action taken during the vital days to minimise the suffering of the 60,000 inmates.'

> The story of that greatest of all exhibitions of 'man's inhumanity to man' which was Belsen Concentration Camp is known throughout the world. Therefore it is not intended to repeat it here except very briefly, and then only as background for the story of what the British soldier did with the aid of British medical students and units of the British Red Cross to succour its tens of thousands of stricken inmates to prevent the spread in epidemic form of the disease and infection there found, and finally to wipe Belsen off the face of the earth.[88]

Belsen was therefore presented as something which was uniquely horrifying and 'known throughout the world', but which had occurred in the past, been dealt with and was now best 'wiped off the face of the earth'.

Over the course of the first six months of the occupation, without in any way minimizing the anger, shock and disgust with which British troops viewed war crimes and atrocities, other issues required their immediate attention and so were given higher priority. Those at the top of the British administration concentrated on the need to preserve law and order, prevent starvation and disease, maintain British influence, power and prestige, and reduce the cost of the occupation to the British taxpayer. The younger generation were not motivated by the same concerns as their seniors, though the consequences were similar. Through personal contacts, at work and in their leisure time, they became reconciled to their former enemies, cooperated willingly on the task of reconstruction and found no difficulty working with Germans they came to see as individuals and 'people like us.'

9

The English Army Officer Who Created the German News Magazine *Der Spiegel*

The story of John Chaloner, the English army officer who created the German weekly news magazine *Der Spiegel* (The Mirror), illustrates how the legacy of the British occupation could depend on young and inexperienced individuals, who were sometimes out of step with official policy. This was not atypical. Probably the best-known example is Ivan Hirst, the British officer who 'saved' the Volkswagen works from being dismantled,[1] but many other junior officers were given positions of great responsibility despite their youth, and were highly influential in their own fields of work. Howard was just nineteen years old when he was commissioned as an officer in August 1945 and sent to Germany. He was deeply committed to his work as Intelligence Officer for T-Force, believing that this was his opportunity to contribute to Britain's post-war economic recovery.[2] Thexton had a team of forty-five German staff working for him in his first position in the Reparations, Deliveries and Restitution division of the Control Commission, compiling lists of armaments factories and equipment in the British Zone, to be made available to the Allies as reparations.[3] Other young British men who played important and influential roles in occupied Germany include the intelligence officer Noel Annan, later Provost of Kings College Cambridge, and William Barnetson and Robert Maxwell, who both had similar jobs to Chaloner, as press officers in Hamburg and Berlin, and later owned or managed large publishing and media concerns in Britain.[4]

Chaloner's first task in 1945, as 'Press Chief' for British Military Government '30 Information Control Unit' in Hanover,[5] was to help set up newssheets under direct British control to replace the Nazi papers closed by the Allies.[6] From January 1946 he worked on establishing newspapers in the region, owned and managed by approved German licensees.[7] In March 1946, he decided to create a new magazine to be published by his information control unit in Hanover, using his official position and authority as a British officer to recruit staff and obtain

Figure 9.1 John Seymour Chaloner in 1947. © SPIEGEL VERLAG, Hamburg.

funding and supplies. Five issues of the magazine he founded, *Diese Woche* (This Week), appeared in November and December 1946. Chaloner was officially reprimanded for exceeding his responsibilities and told to have no further involvement with the magazine. His superiors at British Information Services Control headquarters objected to articles which criticized the British and Allied occupation authorities, but instead of closing the magazine, they allowed it to continue under a licence issued to its German editor, Rudolf Augstein, and *Diese Woche* was renamed as *Der Spiegel*.

The new magazine was an instant success. The highly regarded newspaper *Die Neue Zeitung* (The New Paper), published by the US occupation authorities, had to close in 1955 when funding was withdrawn,[8] but *Der Spiegel* survived as an independent publication with Augstein as editor and licence holder. Circulation rose from 50,000 copies per week in early 1947 to 110,000 in 1951 and 811,000 in 1966, far higher than other political weekly magazines in Germany.[9] By the end of the 1950s, its distinctive style was adopted as a model by much of the German press.[10] Its reputation and political influence grew to become, in the words of Peter Merseburger, Augstein's biographer, 'a paper of dissent and questioning without which democratic discourse would be unthinkable'.[11] The creation of the magazine by a young British officer was to prove as influential in securing a free and independent press in the future Federal Republic, as any other action taken by the British during the occupation in the field of print media.[12]

Information policy in the British Zone

British press and media policy in post-war Germany emerged from the murky world of wartime information, intelligence, propaganda and espionage services. During and immediately after the war, senior individuals involved in these fields moved seamlessly from one government department to another: the Foreign Office, the BBC, the Ministry for Economic Warfare, the Control Commission for Germany and the intelligence services.[13] The organization responsible for formulating British media and information policy for Germany was the Political Warfare Executive (PWE), which at first reported to three government departments – the Foreign Office, the Ministry of Information and the Ministry of Economic Warfare – before it was merged into the Foreign Office at the end of June 1945.[14] During the war, PWE and its Director General, Robert Bruce Lockhart, worked closely with the BBC European Service, which regularly broadcast news and information to Germany.[15] PWE also ran its own propaganda services, including a radio station, the *Sender der Europäischen Revolution* (Broadcaster of the European Revolution), managed by the Labour Party politician (and later minister) Richard Crossman, and operated by German socialist exiles.[16] PWE's black propaganda was managed by a former *Daily Express* journalist and fluent German speaker, Sefton Delmer, who used another group of German exiles and prisoners of war to set up radio stations that appeared to be run by German organizations such as army units. Programmes interleaved music and genuine news stories with propaganda, rumour and stories designed to mislead the enemy.[17]

Many of those who worked for PWE during the war were involved in press and broadcast media in Germany during the occupation, but the transition from wartime propaganda to news journalism was not always smooth. Disputes between former PWE employees were compounded by differences of opinion between some civilian PWE staff and Military Government army information units in the field. Foreign Office diplomats, exiled German socialists, army generals, newspaper journalists and writers all agreed on the need to fundamentally change, or at least reform the German press, but had different and often competing views regarding how this could best be achieved. This left plenty of scope for John Chaloner, a young press officer operating at local level, to devise and implement his own scheme to achieve the goal agreed by all, of establishing a free and democratic press in Germany.

The terminology used to describe the various organizations engaged in information services for Germany can be confusing, especially given the widespread contemporary use of acronyms. According to Michael Balfour, who joined PWE in 1941, transferred to the Control Commission in 1945, and was later one of the first historians of the occupation, PWE operated secretly during the war and used the cover name Political Intelligence Department (PID). The organization continued to exist for six months after the end of the war, still known as PID but now operating openly as a department within the Foreign Office, with some staff deployed to work with the British Control Commission in Germany.[18] A different organization with a similar acronym, the Psychological Warfare Division (PWD), was formed in 1944 as a division within SHAEF, the joint US and British Supreme Headquarters of the Allied Expeditionary Force. While PWD was mainly an American organization, some influential British individuals joined PWD for a time, including Balfour and Crossman.[19]

Before the end of the war, planning information policy for occupied Germany was largely driven by the United States and by PWD, while the British information and propaganda services focussed on supporting the armies in the field, and were reluctant to make any substantial commitment to initiatives that could not be implemented until after the war was won. A SHAEF PWD paper dated 24 April 1944, for example, recommended that there should be a 'fully integrated Psychological Warfare organisation' and a tripartite US, British and Soviet propaganda committee should be established to control information and propaganda policy.[20] In August, Brigadier McClure, the US head of PWD, submitted a plan, 'Operation Talisman', for a highly directed approach to the provision of information services in occupied Germany. News would be distributed from a central news agency and regional and local press would follow agreed directives. Existing German 'technical and operating' staff would do the work, under the direct control of Allied staff.[21] Although they agreed in principle, British officials were reluctant to make any firm commitments, and the plan was never implemented.[22]

When the war was over, British and US information teams went their separate ways. SHAEF was dissolved in July 1945. US officials transferred to the Information Services Control division of the US Military Government, to manage the press and media in the US Zone, while British officials who worked for PWD returned to their former departments.[23] All German newspapers were closed and replaced by newssheets or newspapers under direct Military Government control.[24] In the British Zone, newssheets were produced by local units attached to the army divisions, such as Chaloner's 30 Information Control Unit in Hanover, and coordinated centrally by PR/ISC, the Public Relations and Information Services Control division of the British Control Commission. By the end of 1945, 18 newssheets and papers were produced in the Zone under direct British control.[25] In the more highly organized and better-resourced US Zone, newspapers were published under direct US control, coordinated centrally by an Austro-Hungarian refugee, Hans Habe, and a team of German speaking exiles who had worked together at PWD. Articles written and proofed at their headquarters in Bad Nauheim, near Frankfurt, were taken to printing works in fifteen other towns and cities, some local news added, and the newspapers printed and distributed.[26] The United States also started the process of granting licences to Germans to publish newspapers and magazines earlier than the British, approving twenty-three licences between 31 July 1945 and the end of the year. The first licensed papers in the British Zone appeared in January 1946.[27]

Rather than collaborating in the provision of news, the United States and Britain established separate news agencies. At a time when communications were limited, travel was restricted and only the largest papers could afford to employ their own correspondents, newspapers throughout the world depended on centralized press agencies as their principal source of national and international news. The market was highly competitive, with the well-established British and French agencies, Reuters and Havas, facing increased pressure in the 1920s and 1930s from newer US agencies.[28] In Germany, the Nazis had effectively controlled the distribution of news through Goebbels' centralized *Deutsche Nachrichten Büro* (German News Office). This was abolished at the end of the war, but an alternative source of news had to be provided to support the new papers created by the Allies. Sefton Delmer, the former head of British wartime black propaganda, set up DPD, the *Deutsche Presse Dienst* (German Press Service) in Hamburg, with the assistance of colleagues, British and German, who had worked for him at PWE. The Americans established a rival agency, DANA, the *Deutsche Allgemeine Nachrichten Agentur* (United German News Agency) in Munich.[29]

Delmer hoped to follow the creation of a press agency with a model newspaper for the British Zone that would 'instil a new sense of democratic responsibility in the German people, one that would prevent it from swallowing uncritically the kind of charges Hitler used to bring against his enemies'.[30] Hans Habe and his team of German exiles had similar aims in the US Zone, where they created a highly successful newspaper, *Die Neue Zeitung*, branded on its front page masthead as 'An American newspaper for the German population'. The first issue appeared on 19 October 1945, printed in Munich on the same presses that had formerly been used to print the Nazi newspaper *Völkische Beobachter*. The paper was distributed in all four zones of Germany and sold over two million copies.[31] Delmer produced a dummy for a British zonal paper, dated 20 September, that would have competed with *Die Neue Zeitung*, but his plans were blocked and he was refused permission to go ahead. He resigned and returned to Britain.[32] A paper for the British Zone did eventually appear, but not until several months later, when the first issue of *Die Welt* was published on 2 April 1946.[33]

Delmer's greatest opponents, according to his memoirs, were British Military Government officials, whom he referred to (unreasonably) as *Gauleiters*, using the Nazi term for district officials. They told him in no uncertain terms that any centralized news service would come under the authority of the British military administration, not the Foreign Office or PWE/PID.[34] Delmer may have exaggerated, but at the highest level, the military authorities were deeply suspicious of the press and media. After Montgomery told his staff on 6 July 1945 that 'the Germans are hungry for information, we must give it to them' and 'very energetic action is required',[35] the director of PWE/PID, Robert Bruce Lockhart, attempted to explain to a senior official at the Foreign Office why the British had not yet succeeded in establishing more and better newspapers in their Zone. Montgomery, Lockhart wrote, had a 'long-standing antagonism' to SHAEF in general, and to PWD in particular, which was reflected in all sections of the British 21st Army Group.[36] As a result of Montgomery's attitude, he continued, there had been insufficient planning undertaken for the press and media in the British Zone of occupied Germany. Staff numbers were far lower at around 80, compared to 1,700 in the US Information Services Control division. Montgomery's chief of staff, General Weeks, Lockhart added, recognizing there was a problem, had been to see him a month earlier, on 9 June, and asked him to release General Bishop, at the time serving as deputy director of PWE, to be appointed as director of information services for the Control Commission in Germany. He agreed at once because he thought 'this was in the national interest'.[37]

Bishop was a professional soldier, not an expert in newspapers, the press or media. His role, both at PWE and as head of the Control Commission's PR/ISC division, was to maintain good relations with those in similar positions heading other divisions, make sure his staff did not step too far out of line and ensure, as far as he could, that instructions received from his superiors were implemented.

He wrote later that his main difficulty at PWE had been to persuade the highly intelligent and politically conscious individuals working for him that 'the job of the propagandist was to support the policies of the political and military authorities, and not to make these policies'.[38] Similar intermediary roles were undertaken by army brigadiers and generals in many parts of the Control Commission where military and civilian staff worked together.[39]

Bishop left his post as head of PR/ISC in May 1946, when he was appointed deputy chief of staff to Robertson. His successor and head of PR/ISC was Cecil Sprigge, a former journalist and a civilian. Sprigge resigned at the end of October 1947, after a review by Ivone Kirkpatrick, a senior Foreign Office official in London, concluded he was 'not up to the job'.[40] None of the senior officials in PR/ISC – Sprigge, his deputy Brigadier Gibson, or Michael Balfour, who was appointed head of the PR/ISC Information Services Control section in 1946[41] – appear to have been fully aware of Chaloner's plans to create a new magazine, before the first issues of *Diese Woche* were published in November and December 1946. In theory policy was determined by staff at headquarters, and implementation delegated to regional teams, such as John Chaloner's information control unit in Hanover. In practice Chaloner was lightly supervised, could ignore policy directives from headquarters, if he received them at all, and act on his own initiative.

Diese Woche, the precursor of *Der Spiegel*

Chaloner later claimed to have had responsibility for the whole of the British Zone, but his job as Press Chief for 30 Information Control Unit was limited to Hanover and what is now Lower Saxony. He established new papers in Lüneburg and Osnabrück, which involved not only identifying suitable German licensees, editors and journalists, untainted by a Nazi past, but also considerable effort to find printing machines that still worked and secure supplies of paper, ink and even string to tie the bundles of newspapers ready for delivery, all of which were in short supply in post-war Germany.[42]

In March 1946, when he was working in Osnabrück, Chaloner decided to create a new type of magazine that had never appeared in Germany before, modelled on the US weekly news magazine *Time* and the British *News Review*. With the help of two German secretaries, he put together a dummy, with the title *Diese Woche*, assembled from translations of articles and pictures taken from various British and German newspapers and magazines.[43] An official at PR/ISC headquarters reported, after a visit by one of his staff to 30 Information Control Unit, that:

> Captain Chaloner is waking into life a German version of 'Time' as a supplement to the newspapers, to fill out the background to the news and to provide a lighter political periodical. This will be up here soon in dummy form. Initially it will have to be run as an overt effort. Proposed circulation (zonal) 200,000 fortnightly with 16 pages. This will require 15 tons of paper or newsprint approximately.[44]

Chaloner's proposed circulation of 200,000 was far in excess of the 15,000 copies of the first issue of *Diese Woche* printed when the magazine finally appeared in November. An article in the *British Zone Review* reported that:

> Dummies were run off at Osnabrück in March last, but no newsprint was available even for a circulation of a few thousand. The project was accordingly put into cold storage until October, when hope was held out for sufficient newsprint to publish 15,000 weekly (zonal population 23 millions).[45]

At some point between April and September, Chaloner received authorization to go ahead. Exactly what was authorized and by whom is not known, but it would appear to have been limited to recruiting staff and producing further dummy copies, well short of permission to go ahead with a full production run and to sell and distribute copies across Germany.[46]

Although Chaloner had the original idea and created the first dummy issue, he had little involvement with the day-to-day running of the magazine, which he left to his two staff-sergeants, Henry Ormond and Harry Bohrer, both German-speaking Jewish exiles now working for the British army. Ormond acted as Publisher and Business Manager and Bohrer as Editor-in-Chief. Ormond had trained in Germany as a lawyer. He was arrested in 1938 and briefly imprisoned in Dachau, before being allowed to leave for Britain in August 1939.[47] Bohrer came originally from Prague, where he had attended a German-speaking school. He escaped to London before the war, his brother emigrated to Israel, but his sister and parents remained and were killed in the Holocaust.[48]

Bohrer recruited a team of German journalists to work on the magazine, including the future editor and owner of *Der Spiegel*, Rudolf Augstein, who Chaloner had employed some months earlier to work on the city's newssheet, the *Hannoverschen Nachrichtenblatt*.[49] They shared the same birthday; Augstein was exactly one year older than Chaloner. Although he had no previous experience of journalism, Bohrer was responsible for teaching his team of would-be writers, editors and journalists, that the apparently simple style of the new magazine was more difficult to write than the traditional heavyweight style of a serious German weekly or daily newspaper. He wrote later that they aimed to produce a paper that was lively, that said much in a few words, and that reported the news rather than providing comment and opinion.[50] Leo Brawand, the first economics editor of the magazine, recalled Augstein saying that they all respected Chaloner but '*Bohrer habe ich nicht nur gemocht, sondern beinahe geliebt*' (I didn't only like him, I almost loved him). Chaloner, in a later interview for *Der Spiegel*, when asked about Bohrer, confirmed this, saying: 'oh yes, they all loved Harry Bohrer'.[51] When Bohrer died in 1985, Augstein spoke at his funeral.[52]

Work on the new magazine started in earnest in October 1946. Offices for the new 'Publications Production Unit' were found on the sixth floor of the *Anzeiger Hochhaus*, one of the few buildings in Hanover to have escaped destruction during the war. Chaloner arranged for his team at *Diese Woche* to be sent a number of British and US publications, including several copies of the British weekly magazine *News Review*, which he told them to use as a model for their work. Other publications, which he requested from London, included *Time*, *Newsweek*, *Russia Today*, *Tribune*, *Life*, the *Spectator*, *Punch*, the *New Statesman and Nation* and a book of cartoons with work by well-known British cartoonists such as Zec, Giles, Vicki and Low.[53] Chaloner was busy with other things in October and November, making arrangements for a course in Lüneburg for the editors of German newspapers and dealing with paper shortages,[54] but kept in touch with progress and helped resolve problems as they occurred.

Paper, office equipment, supplies and transport for the new magazine were a constant problem. On 21 October, Ormond wrote to Chaloner asking for newsprint in the right size for the rotary printing machines and coal, bicycles and typewriters as, 'our typewriter position is desperate'. They had only two for the entire office, both on loan and one was only available in the afternoon. He also asked for three Volkswagen cars, office furniture and 'last not least we need money'.[55] Chaloner replied saying that 'paper supply is already on the way, size 63cm' and 'Don't forget to have a dress rehearsal actually on the rotary-machine to find any technical snags'.[56] Newsprint for the first three issues was provided direct from the UK, an extraordinary achievement given the drastic paper rationing in force in Britain as well as in Germany.[57] The three VWs could not be delivered for weeks, but on 8 November they collected forty bicycles, including fifteen diverted from their intended use by 30 Information Control Unit's research branch.[58]

Two pre-production dummy issues were produced on 25 October and 1 November. Chaloner sent his congratulations to Ormond in a letter dated

31 October, apologizing that 'pressure of work' had made it impossible for him to spend as much time on the magazine as he would have liked, and adding that:

> I know myself that this business of producing a magazine means not just an exciting new idea but real hard work, patience, a keenness that must not flag and a willingness to go on learning; all things that cannot be gained without sweat, blood and some tears. The fact that you have started from scratch and have always to compete against to-day's appalling shortages, doubles the meaning of your success.[59]

As this message shows, the mechanics of production and availability of supplies alone offered a tremendous challenge, which could only be overcome, as during the war itself, echoing Churchill's wartime exhortations, with 'sweat, blood and some tears'. Chaloner was interested in the layout and appearance of the magazine, the typeface and style of writing, and with motivating his staff, but he appeared to have little interest in the content, leaving this to Harry Bohrer and his team of German editors.

Although *Diese Woche* carried the imprint of a British Military Government unit, it did not set out to promote British views. In later years, in a filmed interview with *Der Spiegel* in 2006, when asked 'why he decided and how' to create the magazine, Chaloner said that, above all, he wanted to establish a paper that was independent of the government:

> It was to strongly develop the independence of the German press, so that there could be no question of it following the Hitler pattern, that it was somehow a government-owned organisation or publication.[60]

In Chaloner's view, the greatest danger to British interests came, not from a hostile press, but from hostile governments. If this meant that his magazine published articles that were critical of the British and Allied authorities, then so be it: 'that seemed to me the natural role of a so-called free press'.[61]

His superiors, however, did not entirely share his idealistic view of a free and independent press. Chaloner had gone ahead with printing the first issue, on 16 November 1946, without receiving formal authorization to do so. According to one story, shortly before they were due to go to press, he received a letter stating that certain conditions had to be met. He told his secretary, 'I have not read this letter' and later denied ever having received it.[62] In another account, his two staff-sergeants were in his office when he received an order to stop the printing. He told them to swear the telegram had arrived after he had left the office, and went down to the printing works, where he pressed the button to set the presses rolling.[63]

The first issue of *Diese Woche* included a number of stories which were critical of the British authorities and their Soviet former allies. The lead article was a graphic description, written by Augstein, of hunger and food shortages in Germany, especially in the Ruhr.[64] Another article described how a German refugee from the Soviet Zone had escaped from a train, full of German scientists and technicians being taken by force to Russia.[65] A third article described how soldiers in the Second Polish Corps in Italy, under the command of General Anders, did not wish to return home, quoting General Anders telling a press conference that many who had already done so had been transported across the Urals, to a large 'concentration camp' in Siberia.[66] All these stories, and others, were highly contentious, at a time when Britain and the Soviet Union were trading accusations with each other in the Allied Control Council meetings in Berlin.[67]

According to Leo Brawand's history of *Der Spiegel,* Augstein was called in by the British authorities to answer accusations that articles such as these provided ammunition to unrepentant Nazis. He was able to reply that he and his colleagues were doing no more than repeating stories which had previously appeared in British publications, which were already widely available in Germany and which were held up to them as models to follow in their work.[68] Chaloner was called in a few days later to answer similar accusations, of providing ammunition to former Nazis, and of having 'collaborated with the enemy' through giving excess freedom to, and working too closely with Augstein and the other German journalists.[69] On 29 November 1946, Sprigge confirmed the decisions he and his senior colleagues in PR/ISC had reached in the case. Chaloner was to be officially reproved for exceeding his responsibilities in going to press without authorization and should have 'nothing whatever to do with the paper from this moment'.[70] Another officer, Major Nick Huijsman, who was in charge of licensing publications in the British Zone, was told to take personal responsibility for *Diese Woche*, ensure it was run on 'the most cautious lines' and 'discover a group of Licensees to take over the paper'.[71]

Despite being instructed to have no further involvement with the paper, sometime between 11 and 13 December Chaloner was summoned again to meet Brigadier Gibson, deputy head of PR/ISC, to explain why another proposed magazine, *Das Andere Deutschland* (The Other Germany), had still not been published, due to a shortage of paper, ten months after Gibson had given instructions to go ahead.[72] According to Brawand, Chaloner had diverted the newsprint intended for *Das Andere Deutschland* to *Diese Woche.*[73] In a letter to Chaloner's immediate superior, an army colonel, Gibson wrote that the whole thing was 'very mysterious' and he had not quite got to the bottom of it, but they were 'under some pressure to publish [*Das Andere Deutschland*] from personages in England', presumably influential German émigrés and their political allies, who had long been keen to demonstrate that there was an 'other Germany' different from that of Hitler and the Nazis.[74]

Correspondence preserved in the archives between his superior officers shows that their attitude to the affair was not quite as portrayed later by Chaloner, who claimed he was 'sacked' from his job as Press Chief. They reacted to a young officer exceeding his responsibilities indulgently, more in sorrow than in anger, disappointed at his readiness to act on his own initiative, rather than, as they saw it, working with his (British) colleagues for the common good. Rather than criticizing him, Gibson wrote that 'Chaloner is a good, keen boy', and he would 'see what I can do about getting him taken on as a civilian on a year's contract',[75] though this never happened and Chaloner left his post in Hanover soon after the meeting. He was due to be demobilized from the army in January, so it is possible that rather than being 'sacked', he was not re-employed in the same position as a civilian, when he was due to leave the army.

Diese Woche continued to appear at weekly intervals, on 30 November, 7 December and 14 December with a Christmas double issue on 21 December,[76] and continued to include articles critical of the British and other Allies.[77] Chaloner's two staff-sergeants, Harry Bohrer and Henry Ormond, remained in post.[78] At some point, a decision was taken to transfer ownership and issue a preliminary licence to Rudolf Augstein. A report, probably from Ormond, dated 31 December 1946, stated that:

> With effect from 1 Jan 47, the periodical will be re-named 'DER SPIEGEL' published no longer by Publications Production Unit but as a purely German weekly, preliminary licence being given to Herr Augstein.[79]

The British authorities appeared to believe that, while criticism was not acceptable in an overt publication bearing the imprint of British Military Government, it could be tolerated in a licensed German paper.[80] The first issue of *Der Spiegel* was published on 4 January 1947. The name of the magazine was new but the format, style, offices, editors, journalists, writers and printers continued unchanged. A full licence was issued six months later, to Augstein and two colleagues,[81] after the British authorities had tried and failed to find at least one alternative licensee.[82]

Michael Balfour, who signed the preliminary licence as head of ISC, the Information Services Control branch of PR/ISC, wrote later that he had second thoughts the next day, but by then it was too late.[83] It appears that *Diese Woche* had acquired a momentum, which would have made it difficult to close, without obviously contradicting the principles of free speech and liberty of expression. Chaloner and his colleagues in 30 Information Control Unit had been working hard to promote the magazine well before the first issue of *Diese Woche* appeared. Five hundred copies of each of the two pre-production dummy issues, printed in October 1946, were widely circulated in order to generate advance orders, accompanied by what one British official referred to as an 'intensive publicity campaign' with the result that: 'Germany now awaits, with bated breath, the first issue of "Diese Woche".'[84]

On 9 December, after the first three issues had been published, Ormond reported that a total of 44,900 copies had been ordered from bookshops and other wholesale firms, well ahead of the number printed of 15,500.[85] A few days later, on 14 December, he reported that 'numerous applications for subscriptions were coming in, including some from the Rhineland, Westphalia, Schleswig Holstein, Hamburg, and the US and Russian zones' and the number of orders had increased further to 56,800.[86] In January Ormond successfully justified an increase in circulation to 50,000 copies[87] for the newly independent magazine, now renamed *Der Spiegel*, by appealing to Anglo-American rivalry:

> The Americans seem to be amazed that the British have, for once, put them in the shade, in the newspaper world.[88]

Equally significant, Ormond wrote in December, were letters received from 'people in all walks of life'.[89] One of these was from Heinz Norden, the Editor-in-Chief of *Heute* (Today), an illustrated magazine published by the US Military Government.[90] Norden complimented the editors of the new magazine, *Diese Woche,* which, he wrote, '*blaest wie ein frischer Wind durch das deutsche Zeitungswesen*' (blows like a fresh wind through the German newspaper world').[91]

Chaloner left Hanover and returned home in early 1947.[92] Bohrer and Ormond continued to be involved with the magazine for a further six months, until the full licence was granted to *Der Spiegel*.[93] In July 1947, three new press liaison officers were appointed, with the job of promoting the British point of view to the newly licensed German press. The officer responsible for *Der Spiegel* was Michael Thomas, formerly Ulrich Holländer, a half-Jewish refugee from Nazi Germany, who had fled to Britain in 1939 and returned to Germany in 1945 as an officer in the British army. He established an excellent relationship with Augstein and accompanied him and his first wife on a holiday to Italy in the summer of 1950.[94] By the mid-1950s the magazine had become a highly successful, established and influential part of the West German media.[95]

A free press, *Der Spiegel* and the legacy of occupation

Although the British were slower than the Americans to set up directly controlled newspapers immediately after the war, establish a licensed press or create a model newspaper for their Zone, by early 1949 a strong and independent press had been created in both zones. Forty-nine newspapers and weeklies were published under licence in the British Zone, with a total circulation of 10.1 million copies. In the US Zone fifty-six papers were published under licence in April 1949, but total circulation was lower than in the British Zone, at 6.43 million.[96] In 1949 the British press agency, DPD, merged with the French and US agencies to form the *Deutsche Presse Agentur* (DPA), the leading press agency in the Federal Republic.[97]

The story of John Chaloner and the creation of *Der Spiegel* illustrates how, in the absence of established institutional structures and clear lines of control, implementation could diverge from official policies. Chaloner's idealistic aim of promoting a free press, independent of government, succeeded in the case of *Der Spiegel* through his own efforts, those of his two Jewish staff-sergeants, and through the dedication and hard work of his team of young German journalists, despite opposition from senior occupation officials who objected to articles critical of the British and their Allies. Nevertheless, although Chaloner was officially reprimanded and told to have no further involvement with the magazine, the British authorities did not close *Diese Woche*. They allowed it to survive, licensed to Augstein and renamed as *Der Spiegel*. In this respect they were more willing to tolerate criticism than their equivalents in the US Zone. Heinz Norden, the editor of *Heute*, was sacked in 1947 for alleged communist sympathies and *Der Ruf*, a German magazine originally intended to represent the voice of the 'younger generation', was closed by the US authorities in April 1947.[98]

In later years, the British occupation authorities had a mixed relationship with *Der Spiegel*. In 1948, Lance Pope, the director of the Press Branch of PR/ISC, asked his regional officers to categorize the editors and principal journalists of the licensed press in the British Zone according to how favourable or unfavourable they were to the occupying powers. Six *Spiegel* editors and journalists, including Augstein, were among those listed in the first, most favourable, category as 'fundamentally pro-British' who 'will not be diverted from this conviction whatever has happened or may happen'. However, not everyone agreed with this assessment. On the copy of the report preserved in the archive, Augstein and his colleagues' names had been crossed out with a pencil and a question mark added.[99]

Der Spiegel could still be a thorn in the flesh for the authorities. In 1950, the British, French and US High Commissioners for Germany discussed a temporary ban on the magazine for reproducing a communist poster. At the time, this was forbidden in the western zones, after the Socialist Unity Party (SED) in East Germany declared at their congress in Berlin that there was no legal basis for the occupation of Germany by the Western Allies.[100] Brigadier Gibson, the same officer who, as deputy head of PR/ISC, had referred to Chaloner earlier as a 'good keen boy', told the commissioners, in his submission advocating a temporary ban, that *Der Spiegel* was:

> An independent and sensational publication which has no positive attitude to any serious question but devotes its columns to destructive criticism of activities and individuals, whether German or Allied. It is widely read by all classes – like [the popular British Sunday newspaper] the 'News of the World' and for the same reason in general.[101]

The commissioners decided not to ban the magazine but to issue a 'sharp warning'. Francois Poncet, the French chairman, explained their decision on the basis that although 'the feelings reflected by this mirror are generally very hostile to the Allies and the High Commission particularly … they do quite a lot of harm to the Communists also'.[102]

In 1962 in what has become known as the 'Spiegel Affair', the Chancellor of the Federal Republic, Konrad Adenauer and his Defence Minister, Franz Josef Strauss, tried to close the publication, after it revealed details of a NATO manoeuvre that included the use of tactical nuclear weapons. Augstein and the author of the article, Konrad Ahlers, were imprisoned pending charges.[103] Chaloner travelled to Germany, with his former colleagues Bohrer and Ormond, to support the magazine. In his interview with *Der Spiegel* in 2006, Chaloner described why he did this:

> They were threatening to close it and to kill it. And I wanted to be on the spot to point out that a) I had started the bloody thing, secondly that if they started to close down magazines because they were saying unpopular things about the government, that was nothing better than saying we're not going to have a real press freedom, it was going to be a government job.[104]

The magazine continued to appear; the attempt to close it failed after widespread public protests and the threatened resignation of Adenauer's liberal Free Democratic Party (FDP) coalition partners. Strauss was forced to resign, and the 'Spiegel Affair' is now regarded as one of the first major tests of post-war German democracy.[105]

John Chaloner stayed in touch with his former colleagues after he left Germany in 1947, but his relations with Augstein were ambivalent. After a year in Canada, Chaloner returned to England and set up his own company, Seymour Press, which grew to become one of the main UK distributors of foreign newspapers.[106] Despite his business success, and according to his sister, a sense of triumph in having achieved what he wanted when he founded *Der Spiegel*, despite knowing that 'the paper was far too liberal and progressive for The Old Guard Establishment to agree with',[107] he harboured a deep personal resentment against Augstein whose far greater fame and wealth he believed had been founded on his own efforts, for which he had never received adequate recognition or financial recompense. This did not prevent them working together at times; for example, the Seymour Press acted as the UK distributor for *Der Spiegel*, and they wrote to each other occasionally and exchanged cards on their mutual birthday.[108]

At other times the relationship was not as cordial. In 1950 Chaloner, Bohrer and Ormond arranged to meet Augstein to pursue a claim that each of them should receive a 10 per cent share in the capital of the business, based on an unwritten 'Gentleman's agreement' supposedly made shortly before Chaloner left Germany.[109] The claim was based on a moral obligation, rather than any formal business agreement. Other German newspaper and magazine publishers, such as Axel Springer, built highly successful businesses on licences granted by British press officers, without any expectation that they would be required to pay for this in future. Not surprisingly, the meeting with Augstein was unproductive. Ormond, who was then practising as a lawyer in Germany, specializing in restitution cases for Jewish property,[110] decided to waive his claim and it was agreed, in an exchange of letters, that Chaloner and Bohrer should each be repaid the relatively small sum of 3,000 DM for a loan made earlier, although when and how the loan had been made and what it was for were not specified.[111] Bohrer did not raise the matter again, but it continued to sour Chaloner's relationship with Augstein for many years. The dispute was finally resolved in the 1990s, when Chaloner wrote to *Der Spiegel* complaining that while Augstein was a wealthy man, he was now 'at the other end of the ladder'.[112] An agreement was reached by which Chaloner joined the *Spiegel*'s generous staff profit-sharing scheme, to which Augstein had donated 50 per cent of the business.[113] Payments to staff were based on length of service, so Chaloner, deemed to have joined in 1946, did very well from this, receiving a five-figure sum every year.[114] He died in February 2007, a few years after Augstein, who died in November 2002.

10

'Getting to Know the Germans'

During the war, the British had been encouraged to view Germans as collectively all alike, most famously by Vansittart:

> The *German* is often a moral creature; the *Germans* never; and it is the *Germans* who count. You will always think of *Germans* in the plural, if you are wise. That is their misfortune and their fault.[1]

Through making personal contact as the occupation progressed, the young men and one woman considered in Part Three of this book came to see Germans in the singular, not the plural. They learned to treat the people they met as individuals, rather than collectively as the enemy. Jan Thexton recalled later:

> My strongest memories really are just getting to know the Germans ... Because I wasn't a bit anti-German in any shape or form. I was brought up not to be anti-anything really.[2]

Although the British requisitioned houses and buildings, reserved hotels and theatres exclusively for their own use, ate in the mess, shopped in the NAAFI and arranged segregated film performances that excluded the local population, there was a high degree of contact between occupiers and occupied. This was not an occupation in which the victors were isolated from the local population.

When British soldiers and administrators met individual Germans, they generally found them cooperative and friendly. After the war, instead of facing armed men with weapons, the British encountered civilians, mostly old men, women and children. Some were clearly victims, who had lost their homes, belongings and families. British attitudes remained ambivalent, as shown by a debate in the letters pages of early issues of the *British Zone Review* on whether it was acceptable to 'feel sorry for the Germans'.[3] Wartime attitudes did not disappear overnight, but despite continued suspicion and mistrust, the occupation reinforced the similarities, rather than the differences between them. Reconciliation often depended on a shared interest of some kind, such as music or literature, working together, living nearby as neighbours or an attraction to someone of the opposite sex.[4] In some cases, encounters between occupiers and occupied were short-lived matters of convenience or necessity, such as casual prostitution, black market deals, instructions to subordinates at work, or attending a film, theatre or concert performance. Others developed into longer-term relationships, including marriage and friendships which lasted many years after the end of the occupation.

Singular or plural?

Treating people as individuals, rather than collectively as 'Germans', did not happen automatically, but required a conscious effort on both sides. Early attempts by the occupation authorities to regulate personal relationships, through the ban on any form of fraternization, including shaking hands or speaking to someone in the street, proved unenforceable and soon broke down. The ban was relaxed in July and September 1945, but some restrictions remained. Spending the night in a German house or hotel and the billeting of troops or Control Commission administrators with German families were forbidden until 1948.[5]

Some of the young men discussed in this chapter came into contact with Germans through their work, and were surprised to find they were working with, rather than against, their former enemies. A British naval officer, for example, who commanded a German minesweeping flotilla felt that this was 'an odd experience', as all he had to defend himself was a revolver, which would have been no help had they attempted to throw him overboard, so he got rid of it. He added:

> I have to say this. They work impeccably and are very fine seaman, and I had no problems of any kind at all. They seemed to accept me. I got on well with them. They were very correct ... We operated as if it were a British minesweeping flotilla except they were all Germans. Most incredible.[6]

Thexton assumed that good relations at work meant being willing to socialize with his colleagues outside work, even if this conflicted with official regulations:

> Fundamentally it was illegal more or less. But certainly you found that most people had some sort of association [with the Germans] ... One couldn't say: 'we're going to have a Christmas party, you can't come' if, say, you work with them every day of the week.[7]

A Russian interpreter remarked that relations with the Germans were, on the whole, 'very good and very friendly'.[8] A conscientious objector, who worked with ethnic German refugees from the areas ceded to Poland, when asked about non-fraternization, said that it did not affect them. His team's remit was to regenerate the local German welfare organizations, such as *Evangelische Hilfswerk*, *Caritas* and the Red Cross, and to feed supplies through these organizations. They made friends wherever they could, he said, and he made an enormous number of friends, adding that it was an 'exhilarating period' in his life.[9]

As an officer in the army of occupation, Michael Palliser had little contact with German civilians. Yet despite a 'dislike of everything German', which he attributed to his and his fellow officers' wartime experiences and prejudices, he remembered their having polite, even friendly, relations with individuals, such as the owners of the house they requisitioned for their officers' mess in Bad Godesberg.[10] Despite official regulations prohibiting billeting with German families, the previous occupiers, an aristocratic war widow and her sister, were permitted to move upstairs to the servants' quarters. On one occasion the war widow offered to travel to Cologne to buy a 'spare part' for the British officers and came back in despair, quite unaware of how badly damaged the city was:

> She had had no idea of what had happened to Cologne, although she was living in Bad Godesberg which is, what, fifteen miles or something. That seemed to me quite extraordinary. It showed they had lived an extremely restricted life, if you like, during the war in Germany. It was an extraordinary thing. Of course she hadn't found the spare part because whichever shops she tried to go to had all been destroyed. She was very shocked by it. She was a nice person.[11]

Many German civilians went out of their way to be friendly with the occupying forces, with several IWM interviewees commenting that the Germans they met were favourably disposed to the British, if only because they were not the Russians.[12] Some British soldiers reciprocated and made a conscious effort to be civil and polite, sometimes friendly, to the Germans they met, since that was their understanding of normal social behaviour. An RAF ground crew member in Berlin, for example, when asked about his feelings towards the enemy, described how he felt sorry for an old man working in his billet whose wife suffered from polio. It may have been against the non-fraternization rules, he added, but 'if you've got a person working in your billet you've got to talk to them. How the hell can you get him to do anything if you don't talk to him?'[13]

Some of the IWM interviewees were surprised at the lack of resistance. A de-nazification officer said that part of his job was to keep an eye out for any sign of opposition, but there was none, and no trace of the Nazi 'werewolf' movement they had anticipated. He thought the Germans were 'just so weary of the whole business'.[14] An NCO in Berlin commented that it was strange meeting German civilians. He had been led to believe that resistance would spring up very quickly, but it never happened, adding: 'Some of the Germans treated us as if we were the victorious army and they were pleased to see us.'[15] His main spare time activity was attending the State Opera, where every Sunday there were performances by the major German orchestras or the ballet. He saw the film *Henry V* for the first time with German subtitles in a German cinema: 'It was as relaxed as that'.[16]

Despite generally favourable attitudes, some suspicions remained. Many of the British occupiers employed German servants, at home or in the officers' mess or clubs, or encountered German tradespeople when they needed goods or services. A woman IWM interviewee, in Germany with her husband, revealed that her feelings were mixed towards the Germans who worked for them. Although she admired the way the Germans 'coped with their difficulties', she had not forgotten what had happened during the war. She and her husband were 'very nice to German people', she said:

> We gave them little jobs. You went to the hairdressers and you paid them the money you had to pay them, and you gave them some cigarettes, which were worth a lot.[17]

But she implied that the Germans were not suitably grateful. They 'accepted their defeat wonderfully but did not quite come clean … deep down they weren't really sorry'. When asked if Germans had a hard time at the end of the war, she agreed, but added defensively that the British 'had a hard time too' and still shared what they had with the Germans. She repeated the point, as if she felt it was in doubt and needed to be emphasized: 'I think we were all very nice to the people who worked for us.'[18]

Friends and lovers

Personal relationships in occupied Germany between male occupiers and female occupied are often discussed in physical terms, as prostitution and casual sex, liaisons and marriages of convenience[19] or, occasionally, as love at first sight followed by marriage.[20] A few occurrences of rape by British soldiers were reported as the war came to close in May 1945, together with incidents of looting and plundering, but these were controlled by the Military Police, and there were no mass rapes as occurred in the Soviet Zone, or to a much lesser extent in the French and US Zones.[21] In some cases, including three of the four young officers considered in this study, relationships between British men and German women developed from casual acquaintances, or socializing with neighbours or colleagues at work, to lasting friendships, sexual partnerships or marriage.[22] Their experiences demonstrate the importance of social constraints, moral judgements and a code of accepted behaviour, understood by both sides, in addition to physical attraction and sexual exploitation.

Personal relationships between British men and German women were widely accepted by most of the young men discussed in this chapter. Relations with German women were generally described as part of a return to normal civilian life, conducted in accordance with accepted standards of morality: going out with friends, sightseeing, parties, the cinema, getting to know people at work, meeting the family or the prospect of marriage. Although IWM interviewees were reluctant to talk in detail about personal and intimate matters, admitting their own relationships with reluctance or apologies, they expressed no sense of disapproval of social or sexual relationships with the defeated enemy.[23]

Among the more senior commissioned officers the position may have been different. When Thexton asked his commanding officer for his permission to marry (as required by the official regulations), the officer tried to dissuade him, saying, 'Look I'd much sooner you married a wog, than marry a German'[24] (thereby revealing that his racial and ethnic prejudices were not confined to Germans). On the other hand, an NCO in Berlin said that 'the officers were just the same as the other ranks regarding fraternisation'.[25] Another IWM interviewee described the hypocrisy of more senior officers, who outwardly disapproved of their men's fraternization, but had German girlfriends.[26] Thexton recalled accompanying an intelligence officer who 'used to go out at night and tap into all the telephone calls', including 'very senior officers ringing up their popsies and so on, which was totally forbidden at the time'.[27]

According to Michael Howard, when interviewed for the IWM sound archive in 2008, all the men and NCOs in his Intelligence Section 'settled in' with German girls and at least two of them eventually married their girlfriends, but he claimed that 'it was different for officers', though attitudes varied and there were exceptions. Two officers in his unit, he continued, from a different regiment, had German girlfriends and no one raised any formal objections. They all, however, 'had ambitions' of education or future careers, which would have made it 'extremely foolish' to 'acquire a German bride', so none thought of this as a possibility.[28]

In a written memoir published two years later, Howard revealed rather more of his own relationship with the daughter of the local doctor. His later account, comprising his 'letters home from the ruins of Nazi Germany' reproduced

Figure 10.1 Michael Howard in 1947. Photo courtesy Michael Howard.

verbatim, with an accompanying commentary, suggests that perhaps it was not so different for officers, if they were as young as he was, just nineteen years old when he first arrived in Germany in February 1946.[29] The story combines elements of a holiday romance, in a strange but generally friendly country, with changing perceptions of the former enemy.

The doctor, who owned the house in which Howard and other officers were billeted, had to move out but was allowed to keep three consulting rooms on the ground floor so he could continue his practice, and the doctor's family retained use of the garden. Howard wrote to his mother in July 1946:

> One of the Mess gardens has been most beautifully kept and you can lie there and forget the rest of Germany. The family who used to live in the house have kept it up to scratch: it is the doctor's house – he is a nice fellow and interesting to talk to ... The younger daughter aged 19 also would like to be a doctor, she doesn't think she will ever qualify as she is not good enough at the subjects that matter. I quite often meet them in the garden and natter to them, and I have been asked round to feed with them: that I had to refuse.[30]

This letter must, as he said in his commentary: 'have rung alarm bells in my mother's mind; the very idea that I might have social rather than, say, master/slave relations with German civilians must have set them off, not to mention the suspicion that social might easily develop into sexual relations, as indeed they might'.[31] A month later he wrote to his mother to reassure her that she had nothing to worry about while explaining that he had become bored with the all-male company and conversation in the officers' mess and found he had more in common with 'a pleasant and intelligent German than a stupid and uncongenial Englishman'.[32]

The relationship continued and a few months later, in January 1947, Howard sent his parents photos of the doctor's daughter, taken with a camera he had acquired in Germany. In the accompanying letter, as he commented later, he was 'at pains to reassure my parents that there was no romantic attachment, when it must have been plain to them that one was developing nevertheless'.[33] He emphasized the practical and social constraints upon them, such as his family's assumptions regarding acceptable behaviour within their social class, the need to achieve financial security before marriage, the 'unacceptable stigma in the society' in which his family moved of marrying a German, that 'pregnancy would mean marriage' and 'at once be interpreted as a naked attempt at entrapment'.[34] We were not, he wrote, 'in the grip of an entirely uncontrollable passion'.[35]

Soon after this exchange of letters, a new colonel was appointed to command the unit. As the colonel brought his (English) wife and family with him to Germany, he needed a larger house and decided to take the doctor's house for himself, ejecting the British officers from their mess, and the doctor from his consulting rooms. Howard's sympathies were now fully on the side of the German doctor and his family against his own colonel, whose behaviour he considered morally unacceptable. As he explained to his mother:

> [The colonel] was quite incapable of understanding that in a country where there are only 230,000 houses for 6 million inhabitants, it literally is morally wrong for two people to occupy a 32 room house ... The Colonel was so childish as to ask me to try and prove that the doctor had been an ardent Nazi. When I told him that I knew the old boy quite well, and was quite certain that he had not been one, he was a bit taken aback ... The stupidity of it – no wonder the people get a bad impression of us.[36]

The matter spread to involve local politicians and trade unions in the town. Opposition to the colonel's attempt to requisition the doctor's house antagonized relations between the British and Germans, which had already started to deteriorate due to local protests at the continued low level of food rations. The dispute was eventually resolved by designating the house as offices for the Intelligence Section, to which Howard belonged, rather than living quarters for the colonel, allowing the doctor to keep his consulting rooms, while the colonel found another house in a town eighteen miles away. This was, according to Howard, 'a blessing in disguise'.[37] His judgement on the colonel, whom he considered had 'learnt to dispense entirely with a moral sense of any sort', was devastating:

> Trying to explain to him why something is 'right', or 'wrong' instead of 'a good thing' or 'a bad thing' is like trying to explain the colour of a sunset to a man who has been blind for fifteen years, and isn't interested in sunsets.[38]

Margret, the doctor's daughter, gained a place to read medicine at the University of Bonn and moved there in early October 1947. Shortly before he left Germany, Howard went to visit her. They exchanged fond farewells with 'much sighing, some tears, many promises, promises to write, and promises to meet again', but neither would be 'deflected from our immediate aims, she to qualify as a doctor and I to get my degree and find financial independence'. They stayed in touch, as friends, for over sixty years.[39]

Husbands and wives

Some personal relationships between British men and German women resulted in marriage. In total around 10,000 'war brides' left Germany and emigrated to the UK to be with their husbands between 1947 and 1950.[40] These figures were slightly lower than the number of German war brides who went to the United States, although estimates vary.[41] Some war brides have published their memoirs which describe extraordinary personal histories, meeting their future husbands, emigrating to a strange and unfamiliar country, and eventually settling in and being accepted by their new families, but it is difficult to know how typical their experiences were.[42] Fourteen war brides were interviewed by Inge Weber-Newth and Dieter Steinert, as part of a study of German immigration to Britain between 1947 and 1951.[43] In a later article, Weber-Newth presented a generally negative picture of their experiences, both in Germany and Britain, quoting a German charity, *Caritas*, that only a small number were content, and stating that the interviews showed that unfavourable perceptions of their status as war brides 'remained a burden for many decades'.[44]

While acknowledging that 'the spectrum of relationships was diverse', Weber-Newth placed post-war occupation marriages in a context of social and cultural dislocation at the end of the war, claiming that 'Allied troops were not generally welcomed... during the first few weeks a harsh regime was practised and the occupiers took what they saw as their rights as a victor', and corruption, sex and prostitution were inevitable in the circumstances.[45] The reasons the women interviewed for the study gave for marrying were generally practical, such as hope for improved material conditions, the higher status and better appearance of Allied soldiers, a desire to have a family and children and a concern that otherwise they might not be able to marry,[46] given the gender imbalance in post-war Germany.[47]

Isobel Schropper has conducted similar research among Austrian war brides. She discovered that the situation was similar in many ways but, despite a generally negative reaction in Austria to women who associated with British soldiers, significant barriers to marriage imposed by the British authorities and original expectations not being met when they arrived in Britain, the eighteen war brides she interviewed generally displayed more positive attitudes:

> Irrespectively of how difficult it was to deal with cultural differences, all the interviewees expressed pride in having overcome them and in having established their place in the families of their husbands.[48]

Given the similarities in the situation in Germany and Austria and the small samples considered, it is difficult to generalize from these results and claim that Austrian war brides were more content in Britain. It is more likely that both studies reflected individual differences among those interviewed. Some German and Austrian war brides settled in Britain and remained married for the rest of their lives. Others, unsurprisingly, found it difficult to cope with cultural differences and unmet expectations and returned home, separated or divorced.

Historical research on German and Austrian war brides has generally been conducted with wives rather than husbands, either because the research was conducted as part of a wider study of migration,[49] or because women were more likely to retain links with German or Austrian religious or cultural organizations, which made it possible to identify them later, but not husbands in cases where they had separated or divorced. However, some conclusions can be drawn from contemporary records. British men were under very little practical or material pressure to marry. They often encountered antagonism from some members of the local German population and concerns or disapproval from parents or other family members on both sides. Even if their girlfriends became pregnant, members of the occupying forces were under no legal obligation to marry the mother or provide financial support for illegitimate children.[50] It has to be assumed, therefore, that those who married did so for romantic reasons, to keep the woman they loved, because they were encouraged or persuaded to do so by their girlfriends, or because it was in accordance with their moral and social understanding of correct behaviour, or a combination of all these reasons.

Official regulations at first prohibited and then strongly discouraged marriage.[51] Non-fraternization rules were relaxed in September 1945, but marriage with 'ex-enemy aliens' was forbidden in the British Zone until 31 July 1946, when a government spokesman announced in the House of Lords that it would be permitted, subject to certain criteria.[52] These criteria were onerous, imposing numerous bureaucratic and legal obstacles, before a British man who had decided to marry a German woman received permission to do so. Approval in each case was required from commanding officers. No marriage was permitted until six months after the date of application, during which time the man was required to return to the UK on leave, presumably intended as a cooling-off period.[53] Similar regulations and guidelines, issued by the British Control Commission for Austria, specified that it was 'the duty of the Commanding Officers to try and dissuade members of the forces from marriage overseas', both for security reasons and in their own interest, by making them aware of cultural differences which could cause difficulties. In addition the regulations specified that the proposed marriage had to be discussed with a religious chaplain, and the husband had to ensure that suitable accommodation would be available in Britain.[54] A 'list of certain categories of women considered politically undesirable for marriage' was compiled by the British authorities though not openly circulated.[55] Prospective wives had to have a medical examination and receive a certificate of good health from a British medical officer, together with a certificate of good character signed by the *Oberbürgermeister* (town mayor) or other suitable German official.[56]

Thexton had great difficulty obtaining authorization from his commander in Germany, a brigadier, who denied any knowledge of a change in the regulations. Thexton went home to enlist the support of his MP, who agreed to help. On his return to Germany he found a big notice on his desk: 'Here is your authority to get married. God help you.' Having obtained authorization from his British commander, he still had to obtain permission from the German authorities before he and his wife could be married in a German registry office. When interviewed in 2007, he said that he had written an official notice of the correct procedure, which was circulated in the British Zone. He was told later that 'three thousand other couples married in that year [1947–8] … based upon what I'd negotiated with the Germans'.[57]

Marriage with a former enemy alien was the ultimate symbol of acceptance and reconciliation, especially as this automatically meant that the spouse acquired British nationality and the right to live in Britain. Personal relationships, both sexual and non-sexual, between British men and German women were common and widespread, but marriage was different, as it implied a long-term commitment on both sides. It is worth noting that, for a relatively small but significant number of British men in occupied Germany, such as Thexton, meeting and arranging to marry their future wives was a deliberate decision that affected their future lives as much if not more than anything they did during and after the war. Rather than providing evidence of 'the breakdown of moral and cultural norms' in a society 'confronted with destruction, death and the flight of women and children for survival', as claimed by Weber-Newth,[58] the history of the 10,000 German and Austrian war brides who married British servicemen and members of the Control Commission shows the strength and persistence of social convention and moral standards. In the field of personal relationships between men and women, British and German individuals still applied and expected similar standards of social and personal behaviour.

People like us?

In contrast to their view of German civilians, the four young officers and twenty-one IWM interviewees considered here increasingly perceived Russian soldiers, and Russian, Polish and other Eastern European Displaced Persons (DPs), unfavourably in terms of national stereotypes, despite the Soviet Union having fought on the same side as Britain in the war and the DPs having suffered as forced labourers under German rule. Extensive contacts with German civilians, at work, as neighbours, domestic servants, friends, lovers and potential marriage partners, resulted in their being perceived as individuals and 'people like us'. Lack of contact with Russian soldiers and Eastern European DPs contributed to their being perceived by the British occupiers as socially and culturally different.

One IWM interviewee described the Russians in Berlin as 'fine fighting soldiers' but a 'very different sort of people from what we were'.[59] Similarly, initial sympathy for DPs as victims of Nazism was replaced with a perception of them as a problem. Although this view was often based on hearsay and rumour, there was no lack of circumstantial evidence to reinforce numerous stories the British heard from the Germans they met, and repeated among themselves, of Russian soldiers and DPs looting, raping, stealing and murdering.[60] These post-war perceptions contributed to the development of an anti-communist Cold War mentality, as they reinforced long-standing suspicions of Soviet intentions, and more recent concerns about new communist regimes in Poland and Eastern Europe.

Russian soldiers

In the closing stages of the war in Europe, it appeared to some British military units in Germany that their movements were directed as much against a potential Russian threat, as against German military opposition which had already collapsed. Michael Palliser, for example, described how, when his battalion of Churchill tanks was dispersed around the countryside north of Hamburg, hoping to be sent to Denmark, which had a reputation of being something of a 'land of milk and honey', another brigade 'came zooming through us one day, to our indignation, and zoomed on up to Denmark' in order to get there before the Russians. [61]

This was not an isolated occurrence. In the final days of the war, a number of British units raced to reach positions ahead of the Russians. In his history of T-Force, Sean Longden described how one unit, under the command of Major Tony Hibbert, was ordered on 1 May, shortly before VE Day, to advance urgently to the naval port of Kiel on the Baltic.[62] Hibbert later made enquiries as to where his orders had originated and discovered that, a month earlier, on 4 April 1945, a radio signal from the Japanese embassy in Stockholm to Tokyo had been intercepted, stating that the Russians intended to occupy Denmark. As a result, on 1 May, the same day that Hibbert was ordered to advance to Kiel, the Royal Navy received orders to enter Copenhagen harbour, which it did on 4 May, and British troops advanced to Wismar on the Baltic coast, twenty miles inside the area agreed as forming the Soviet Zone, arriving on 2 May just before the Russians.[63]

Throughout the Cold War, the idea that the British and Americans could, or should, have combined with Germany, their wartime enemy, against the Soviet Union, their former ally, was commonplace in West Germany, while British government officials were anxious to deny they had ever been sympathetic to the idea. When interviewed in 2010, Michael Palliser explained that in his view, tensions between the Allies at the end of the war could never have developed into open conflict, as British troops would have refused to fight with the Germans against the Soviet Union.[64] But if, as Palliser suggested, the attitude of the great majority of British troops towards their Russian Allies was favourable during and immediately after the war, the situation changed quickly. When asked when he first became aware of increasing suspicion of the Russians, Palliser replied:

> I think that within, I would say, two or three months it was quite clear that there were tensions. The Russians were making life more difficult and one kept getting stories of how they treated returning prisoners-of-war and there was a build-up of distrust of the Russians, which in a way … I was in Berlin a year after, '46 rather than '45 … there was undoubtedly a very powerful feeling of distrust of the Russians.[65]

The IWM interviewees who spoke of their encounters with Russian soldiers told a similar story, of a short period of friendly relations, followed by tensions soon after the war, consolidating over the next twelve months into a deep sense of suspicion and mistrust.[66]

There was more contact between British and Russian soldiers in Berlin than elsewhere, but it was limited, hence the British saw and heard evidence of the behaviour of Russian soldiers, as dirty, drunk, looting and raping, without having sufficient personal contact to appreciate the Russian point of view. Four of the IWM interviewees were members of an advance party of British servicemen who went to Berlin in July 1945.[67] The stories they told reflected the German population's perception of the Russians and highlighted behaviour both British and Germans considered socially, culturally and morally reprehensible.

One IWM interviewee was the British officer responsible for security in the *Tiergarten*, the principal black market district of Berlin. He had been told that if they could work with the Russians in Berlin they could do so in the rest of Germany and Europe, but they never did. People would rush in to say that Russians were looting. On one occasion a man came in stark naked claiming that the Russians had stolen his clothes. They had to employ 1,000 Germans for a week, he continued, to clean the barracks they took over from the Russians. In the garages where they stayed there was a dead body in the cellar. All washbasins had been used as toilets.[68] One evening he saw a large number of Russian soldiers, men and women, with their ponies loaded with loot, singing songs which may have come from Central Asia: 'There was something ominous about it all.' Asked about the attitude of the Russian troops to the British, he said that on the whole it was very good. They wanted schnapps, and it didn't matter if it was real or petrol. Personally he had few connections with the Russians but when he came across them he found them very helpful.[69]

An NCO told a similar story: 'The Russians behaved appallingly.' All the stories of soldiers with watches up their arms were quite true. He saw that dozens of times. Also 'pulling standard lamps out of a house and wondering why they wouldn't work.' Leaving a cinema one night, he walked straight into rifle fire where British troops were firing at Russians. When they first arrived in Berlin the troops were meant to stay in the Olympic Stadium, but it was uninhabitable. Two Olympic pools had been used as latrines. Statues had their heads knocked off and cupboards were reduced to matchwood. For the first two to three weeks, the British soldiers slept in lorries at the back of the stadium. In general, he said: 'It must have been terrible for the Germans – without a doubt... Like the Vikings, plunder, pillage and rape.' Asked about the attitude of the Russians to the British troops he replied that it was cautious. The ordinary soldiers didn't mix with each other and there was no organized contact.[70]

Most British people in Germany had little contact with Russian soldiers. After an initial period of friendly relations, they adopted the stereotypes prevalent at the time among the German population, as these views were generally in accordance with their own preconceptions and were confirmed by the negative experiences of those who did encounter Russian troops, especially in Berlin.

Displaced Persons

At the end of the war there were around 10.8 million DPs in the area of the former German Reich, plus occupied parts of France and Belgium,[71] but this number reduced rapidly over the next twelve months.[72] At the end of September 1945, there were between 1.2 and 1.4 million DPs in the western zones,[73] including 825,000 Poles, 100,000 Ukrainians and 188,000 from the Baltic States. Around 600,000 DPs were accommodated in each of the US and British Zones and 100,000 in the French Zone.[74] Numbers then declined more gradually in the British Zone to 365,872 in June 1946,[75] and 217,725 in August 1947.[76]

Official policy and planning for DPs conducted during the war by SHAEF was based on the assumption that liberated DPs would wish to return home as soon as possible, but would be amenable to staying in temporary 'Assembly Centres' for a short period while travel arrangements were made.[77] Once Displaced Persons were accommodated in camps, the British occupiers had little contact with them, except when required to resolve a dispute or conflict. From September 1945, most DPs in the British Zone were Poles who refused to return following reports of poor living conditions in Poland under communist rule. Some feared enlistment in the Polish army or of being treated as collaborators. Others, originally from the east of the country, which was transferred to the Soviet Union after the war, did not wish to return to their former homes, now under foreign rule and no longer part of Poland.[78] As discussed in Chapter 8, there were relatively few Jewish DPs in the British Zone, no more than 20,000 throughout the occupation period. In the US Zone numbers were far higher, increasing rapidly from around 36,000 in January 1946 to a peak of around 250,000, due to an influx of Jews facing renewed persecution in Eastern Europe after the end of the war, and hoping to emigrate to Palestine.[79]

In a pioneering study, Wolfgang Jacobmeyer claimed that the perception of DPs by American and British occupation forces was misinformed and based on inaccurate stereotypes.[80] In a study of crime statistics for Bremen from May to November 1945, he showed that the crime rate among the DP population, 2.03 per cent including minor offences, was roughly similar to that among the German populations of other major cities over the same period. It was much higher than in 1928, but comparing post-war crime rates with a pre-war norm was not appropriate. Most crimes in Germany in 1945 and 1946, Jacobmeyer argued, whether committed by DPs or the local population, were associated with attempts to obtain food and were therefore a consequence of the economic conditions at the time, not evidence of an increase in criminality.[81] However, figures for Bremen may not be typical of the rest of the country. Records of crimes tried at the British Military Government High Court in Hamburg, 22 June 1945 to 31 March 1947, tend to support the anecdotal evidence from contemporary observers of a high crime rate among DPs. Over 25 per cent of those accused were Polish, Russian or Eastern European. Of the nine people sentenced to death, for armed robbery, murder or the unlawful possession of firearms, eight were Polish and one German.[82]

Of those considered in this chapter, three of the four young officers and five of the twenty-one IWM interviewees spoke of contacts with DPs, in all cases referring to them as potential sources of trouble, but not without sympathy. Initially the predominant image was of the constant movement of people, both Germans and other nationalities, as if, as one commentator described it, a giant ant-heap had been disturbed.[83] Michael Palliser referred to it as 'part of the normal scene … the feeling of the lost tribe almost'.[84]

Michael Howard described how one of his colleagues, a British officer, was killed by a 'marauding band of DPs'. His colleague was taking his German girlfriend home when they were flagged down by a German woman, who told them that 'drunken Polish DPs were ransacking the farm where she lived'. The British officer drove to the farm but was shot dead. His girlfriend managed to get into the driving seat of the car and return to the town. The DPs were later captured by a platoon of British soldiers, tried and condemned to death by firing squad.[85] Howard was not unsympathetic towards DPs as individuals, though critical of the Soviet and Polish governments, whom he blamed for the DPs' unwillingness to go home. He explained that Western Europeans – mainly Belgians, Dutch and French – returned home very quickly, as did Russian DPs, although those who had been captured in the fighting were 'seen as cowards, collaborators and traitors' by the Soviet government and 'many were eliminated on return'. By the end of 1946, he wrote, the great majority of those remaining were Poles and 'the DP problem had effectively become a Polish DP problem'.[86]

The US soldier and commentator Saul Padover suggested that Germans blamed Eastern European DPs whenever a crime had been committed. US soldiers believed them, though everyone plundered at that time, including US soldiers and German civilians. Padover added that Goebbels would be 'laughing up his sleeve' at this 'final triumph of his propaganda'.[87] This explanation is not satisfactory, as, initially at least, British (and US) soldiers had no reason to believe the Germans rather than the DPs; everything they had been told during the war encouraged them to see DPs favourably, as representatives of Allied nations and victims of the Germans who deserved their sympathy. British officers responsible for maintaining order were not as naïve as Padover suggested. In the absence of any functioning German police at the end of the war, the occupation forces investigated and resolved many cases themselves and were not necessarily dependent on second hand reports from the local population.

Jacobmeyer suggested a different explanation for the US and British Allies placing an exaggerated emphasis on crime committed by DPs: that they were disappointed at the lack of gratitude shown by DPs for their liberation and surprised that they of all people should resort to crime.[88] This explanation is not satisfactory either. The occupation forces may at times have felt that DPs were not suitably grateful for their liberation, but they were not surprised if oppressed slave labourers took revenge against their former German masters, and doing so did not necessarily make them criminals. General Templer, for example, described the chaos of 'The Early Days' in an article in the *British Zone Review*:

> Over this grim scene there swarmed a milling mass of displaced persons, drunk with liberation and in some cases alcohol, looting, raping and killing. Considering the history of the past five years, this was not surprising.[89]

Rather than a lack of gratitude, the British occupiers found the reluctance among some DPs to return home surprising and unsettling. When British reports spoke of criminality among DPs, it was often qualified by reference to 'Poles and Russians',[90] who had stayed in Germany instead of returning home. The British had assumed that liberated slave labourers from countries invaded and occupied by the Germans would wish to return home as soon as possible, as many did. Although the reluctance of some DPs to return home was understandable, it raised difficult questions. Britain had entered the war to defend the independence of Poland. Was a country truly liberated if people who had lived there before the war did not want to return? Or were some DPs reluctant to return because they were collaborators, who had volunteered to work in Germany rather than being forced to do so, in which case did they deserve favourable treatment as victims of Nazi oppression?

In contrast with the German population, personal contacts with Russian soldiers and Displaced Persons were very limited and, from September 1945, nearly always in circumstances of conflict. Jacobmeyer has written of the alienation of DPs from the German population once they were gathered together in camps and claimed this contributed to a perception of them as 'the enemy'.[91] It appears that a similar process applied to the British occupiers. When British forces entered the camps and encountered DPs directly, it was generally in difficult circumstances of resolving disputes, or investigating allegations of theft, looting or murder.[92] The policy of internment in camps and the lack of direct personal contact led to a collective, and often incorrect, perception of Russian soldiers and those DPs who remained after September 1945 as drunken, criminal troublemakers, who did not observe accepted standards of behaviour and had no respect for 'civilised' values, such as respect for life and property, personal cleanliness and self-control.

By the end of 1946, the remaining DPs in the British Zone were mostly Poles who were unwilling to return home to a country now under communist control. Most of the DPs 'left behind' in Germany were eventually able to emigrate to the United States, Great Britain, Australia or Canada, although there were still 100,000 DPs living in Germany in 1950, including 64,000 in camps in the British Zone, when their status was officially changed from 'Displaced Persons' to '*Heimatlosen Ausländer*' (Homeless Foreigners).[93] The fate of Eastern European DPs in Germany reinforced emerging Cold War attitudes among British occupiers, who came to see post-war governments in Warsaw and Moscow, not as gallant Allies who had helped win the war, but as intolerant, totalitarian regimes that oppressed their own people. In contrast, 'getting to know the Germans', at work, socially, as friends, partners and lovers, helped occupiers and occupied appreciate what they had in common, rather than what divided them, and so contributed to reconciliation between former enemies.

11

Conclusion

This book focuses on the transition from war to peace, exploring what twelve influential British individuals aimed to achieve in occupied Germany, and why, and how this changed over time. Through examining subjective issues of motivation and agency, placing the selected individuals within the historical context, and discovering the limitations and constraints on their scope for action, it aims to explain why British policies changed rapidly in the first three years after the end of the war, from the 'Four D's' agreed at Potsdam, to a more positive policy, which I have described as the 'Three R's' of physical and economic Reconstruction, political Renewal and personal Reconciliation.

Diversity

A biographical approach highlights the diversity of aims and intentions among British people in Germany, which varied according to their age and experience, roles and responsibilities, and political and religious beliefs. This diversity helps to explain some of the apparent contradictions in British policy towards Germany, which reflected differences within British society at home: army generals such as Montgomery, Robertson and Bishop justifying pragmatic measures by exhortations to 'save the soul of Germany'; Ingrams, a former colonial official, promoting a British model of local democracy, and encountering opposition to his proposed reforms from some of his British colleagues; Albu, a committed international socialist, attempting to persuade General Templer, an army general and Irish landowner, of the need for a 'positive socialist policy'. Generalized descriptions of British policy and actions, which do not account for diversity of attitudes and behaviours, are at best an oversimplification and at worst a distortion. As Mary Fulbrook has noted, to describe patterns of behaviour in dichotomous terms 'misses the complexities surrounding different degrees of constraints and a related sense of agency'.[1] The occupation cannot be characterized simply as 'pragmatic' or 'idealistic', 'reconstructing' or 'dismantling' German industry, or as 'isolated from' or 'integrated with' the local population. The reality was more complex.

While Montgomery, Robertson, Bishop and their senior colleagues accepted and implemented the Potsdam decisions to disarm, demilitarize and de-nazify Germany, they perceived these tasks as relatively straightforward, compared with the far more difficult work of creating order out of chaos and promoting an economically viable, stable democracy. A policy of economic reconstruction, to be followed by political renewal, was outlined as early as September 1945 in a new Directive of Military Government, prepared by Montgomery, Robertson and their colleagues at the highest level of Military Government, at a time when the Foreign Office had no formal responsibility for internal affairs within the British Zone and the new Labour government had only recently assumed office. In 1946 the Foreign Office played a significant part in accelerating the process of devolution of power to local German administrations, but the process had been foreshadowed in Montgomery's memos a year earlier, and Ingrams and his colleagues in the Administration and Local Government branch had already started to implement a policy of devolution of power before the end of 1945, with the creation of nominated representative councils, licensing of political parties and preparations for democratic elections.

The three army generals, Montgomery, Robertson and Bishop, were concerned to restore order from chaos, prevent unrest and, more generally, preserve the established social order, as this was in their own interest as members of a professional British establishment that had gained its wealth and social position from public service at home and in the Empire: in the army, in government positions, in business or through inheriting landed estates. They justified a policy of reconstruction through reference to the need to 'rebuild civilisation' after the destruction of war, missionary ideals of 'saving the soul of Germany', and paternalistic notions of imperial trusteeship, caring for a nation until the inhabitants were, in their view, mature enough to take responsibility for government. After leaving Germany, they were able to present a self-congratulatory account of humane and benign British policies, which had contributed to a peaceful and economically prosperous Federal Republic of (West) Germany. Sholto Douglas was the exception among this group. He hated his time in Germany, was pragmatic rather than idealistic and troubled by personal issues, such as being instructed to confirm the death penalty on Goering, and allegations of corruption made in the British press.

The partial and self-congratulatory account of the army generals can be qualified by examining the histories of other British individuals, who also played an important and influential role in occupied Germany. The four civilian administrators were a diverse group with little in common, despite all working in different ways to promote their conception of democracy in Germany. Ingrams' background was similar to that of the army generals. He was influenced by his religious beliefs and experience of imperial administration. Despite some early success in establishing nominated representative councils, his attempt to model political renewal in Germany on antiquated notions of British 'parish pump' democracy encountered strong resistance from leading German politicians and some of his British colleagues. The two committed international socialists, Albu and Flanders, left Germany at the end of 1947, disappointed that their achievements had not matched early hopes of establishing a 'positive socialist policy' in Germany. Their socialist colleague, Berry, was apparently more successful in Hamburg, though his aims were more modest. Influenced by his experience as a district administrator during the occupation of the Rhineland after the First World War, he supported the newly elected SPD administration in Hamburg led by the former exile Max Brauer, promoted the interests of the city, established good working relations between British and German officials, and in so doing defused potential conflicts and preserved British interests, which he perceived as similar to those of the city: stability, economic reconstruction, personal reconciliation, and the maintenance of good relations with the city's business and political elite. As Frances Rosenfeld has shown, both sides were proud of this at the time, but reconciliation was achieved at the cost of ignoring difficult issues, such as the city's Nazi past, and its destruction by Allied bombing.[2]

The four young men with no adult experience but war were concerned above all for their own welfare and personal future. They were not motivated by religious beliefs or ideals of service to the British Empire, and appeared unaware of exhortations from the generals at the top of the administration to 'rebuild civilisation' or 'save the soul of Germany'. Nevertheless, all four were conscientious, worked long hours when required and did not question the aims of the occupation, or the policies of economic reconstruction, political renewal and personal reconciliation. As shown by the example of John Chaloner and the creation of *Der Spiegel*, those lower down the hierarchy were sometimes able to act on their own initiative, even when this ran counter to official policy. Inevitably, as young men, they had more intimate personal relations with Germans than their senior officers. Contacts of all kinds, at work and socially, including friendships and sexual relations with German women, and in Thexton's case, marriage, led them to see Germans as 'people like us', rather than in terms of the stereotypes prevalent during the war.

Partial truths

Many earlier claims by historians regarding British policy in occupied Germany appear to be partial truths that reflect some aspects of the situation, but not all. For example, some historians have argued that the principal motivation underlying British policy was security: the need to disarm Germany and memories of the failure of appeasement after the First World War.[3] Although this was true of many in Britain, security concerns were not especially prominent among the twelve individuals discussed here. Unlike those based in Britain, they could see for themselves the scale of destruction in the German cities, the lack of resistance to the occupation among the great majority of the German population, and the willingness of the Germans they worked with to cooperate in achieving mutual aims of economic reconstruction and political renewal. A second partial truth, later denied by many senior British figures, who felt that the criticism it implied of their personal motivation was inaccurate and unjust,[4] was that the British aimed to exploit the occupation for economic reasons, and help British industries gain a commercial advantage at the expense of their German competitors. Despite later denials, there was some truth in these allegations, but the British Zone proved to be an economic liability, not an asset that could be exploited. While some individuals tried to exploit the situation to their personal advantage, the most important economic factor affecting British policy and actions was the perceived need to reduce the cost of the occupation. The need to reduce costs reinforced a policy of promoting German economic revival, to generate exports of manufactured goods to pay for the import of raw materials, especially food, subsidised by the British taxpayer.

The post-war period was experienced by most Germans as a time of great hardship, not surprisingly so in view of widespread hunger, outbreaks of disease, overcrowded accommodation and an uncertain future, but this was not, as some Germans claimed at the time, the result of deliberate British policy. The British tried to ameliorate the worst effects of war and twelve years of Nazi rule, through securing imports of wheat, repairing the transport infrastructure and reviving the economy. The lessons Robertson and Berry drew from their personal experience of the Rhineland occupation were not only that appeasement had failed in the 1930s, but also that they had failed to support German democrats in the 1920s, and that, through inflicting unnecessarily harsh terms in the peace settlement of 1919, the British and their Allies had helped create the economic and social conditions which made it possible for Hitler to seize power in 1933. As Military Governors, Robertson and Montgomery emphasized the positive aspects of their policy of promoting reconstruction and giving Germans 'hope for the future', rather than the negative aspects of disarmament, de-nazification and economic controls.

The reactions of the twelve individuals discussed in this book to the Holocaust and other atrocities committed by Germans were similarly complex. According to Mass Observation reports, British attitudes towards Germany reached a low point at the end of the Second World War, following press reports of the liberation of the concentration camps,[5] but this was not typical of British soldiers in Germany and did not prevent them from having good relations with the local inhabitants. British soldiers made a distinction between Germans collectively, and those individuals they met face-to-face. Palliser reported that he and his fellow officers were not surprised by reports of 'horrific atrocities'. They considered this 'typically German' and 'were almost beyond being surprised by anything', but they still had friendly, but not intimate, relations with a German war widow and her sister, who lived in the house where they were billeted. Chaloner was the only one of the twelve who was present at the liberation of a concentration camp. According to his sister, the experience affected him deeply, but he never spoke of it, except in private family conversations, and indirectly in a later novel. The experience did not prevent him, or his two Jewish staff-sergeants, Bohrer and Ormond, from working closely with a team of young German journalists to create *Der Spiegel*. Some British soldiers were motivated, at times, by a desire for revenge, but this was not typical and was officially discouraged. A more common response, typified by Montgomery, was to generalize the issues of war crimes and the Holocaust and speak of the need to 'restore civilisation', or refer, as did the *British Zone Review* in October 1945 and Chaloner later in private conversations with his sister, to 'man's inhumanity to man'.

Shared assumptions

Despite diversity among those considered in this book, a number of assumptions were shared by all. The most significant of these was the aim of preventing another war. This was rarely stated explicitly but always assumed. 'Winning the

Peace' meant that, this time, there would be no more war. As Robertson said in a speech to Control Commission staff in July 1947:

> What is our object in being here? It is often forgotten and often misunderstood. We are not here to exact retribution from a beaten enemy. We are not here for the good of the Germans and in order to build up their country for them. Both of those are things which to a certain extent we may have to do as a means to the end, but neither of them is our object. Our object here in Germany is to create such conditions as shall be conducive for peace in Germany and Europe and hence the world. That is our object: and everything we do shall be directed towards that end, and nothing else.[6]

A second assumption was that the war had been caused by German aggression, and that it was essential to prevent the Nazi Party and former Nazis from achieving political power again. But there was no consensus about how this could best be achieved. Socialists such as Albu and Flanders held very different views from senior officers such as Montgomery, Robertson and Bishop. The socialist view was that the Nazi Party had achieved power through the support of the armed forces, landowners and industrialists, and it was necessary to remove their political influence in Germany through demilitarization, land reform and the socialization of industry. However, many of the most senior members of British Military Government were landowners, or had worked in business, and could not be expected to subscribe to these views. Montgomery's family held land in Ireland. Robertson had managed a factory for Dunlop in South Africa. They found it easier to think in terms of a population led astray by their leaders, or a group of evil men who had to be removed from power. Once this had been done, they hoped the German people would learn to live in peace with their neighbours.

Perhaps surprisingly, in view of the wartime alliance with the Soviet Union and the Soviet contribution to winning the war, an anti-Russian, anti-communist consensus was shared by all, regardless of their political principles. British concerns over a military threat from Russia and an ideological threat from communism, which dated back to the nineteenth century and the Bolshevik revolution of 1917, were reinforced by developments in occupied Germany. Over time, four distinct issues contributed to the prevalent and near-universal Cold War mentality of the 1950s and 1960s. Firstly, long-standing concerns about Russia as a possible threat to the British Empire, expressed most clearly by Montgomery. Secondly, a fear of communism among the professional middle classes, typified by Bishop, as a social and political ideology that could spread, like a disease, across Europe. The two socialists, Albu and Flanders, did not share this view but were equally opposed to Russian communism for a third set of reasons, which dated back to the conflicts between socialists and communists in Germany in the 1920s and 1930s. These came to a head in the Fusion campaign in Berlin in early 1946, when Albu compared communist 'totalitarian' tactics with those of the Nazis. Fourthly, changing perceptions of Russian soldiers and Polish DPs reinforced anti-Russian and anti-communist prejudices. Accounts by British personnel, including by Palliser, Howard and IWM interviewees, show that DPs were viewed sympathetically by many British personnel who came into contact with them, but at the same time they were perceived to be culturally different and not 'people like us'. Alternatively, as part of a different but complementary narrative, DPs were described as 'gallant allies' whose reluctance to return home confirmed a negative view of life under communism in Poland and the Soviet Union. By the end of the period examined, 'winning the peace' had come to mean resisting Russian communism, as much as preventing a revival of Nazism within Germany.

A further assumption shared by all was that, as the occupying power, the British had an obligation to maintain the basic functions of government in their zone of occupation and care for the welfare of the inhabitants. This meant they had to preserve life, prevent hunger and disease, maintain law and order and provide opportunities for employment, thereby preventing idleness and resulting discontent. These paternalistic notions were expressed most explicitly by those who had worked in the Empire, such as Montgomery, Robertson, Bishop and Ingrams. Similar ideals, together with a sense of duty and personal obligation, were promoted in the English public schools and may have influenced those who had not worked in the Empire.[7] All but two of the twelve individuals received a public school education.[8]

All twelve assumed that Britain was and would continue to be a great power in Europe and in the world.[9] They gave no indication that they thought they were representatives of a power in decline. Although they understood that Britain lacked economic resources, this was to be expected after a long and difficult war. Even Albu, who before the war had voted for an anti-imperialist candidate and advocated the creation of a socialist community of nations, had been brought up on the adventure stories of Kipling, G.A. Henty and Captain Marryat.[10] The attitudes I have described as 'echoes of Empire' and 'missionary idealism' were most prevalent among the older generation of army officers, such as Montgomery, Robertson and Bishop, and former colonial administrators such as Ingrams. In their cases, direct parallels can be observed between their experiences in the Empire and policy and practices in occupied Germany.

Imperial attitudes were less apparent among the socialist civilian administrators, Albu, Flanders and Berry, or the younger generation of officers, although Palliser, Thexton and Howard all had fathers who had worked overseas, in the navy, in Bermuda and Fiji.

All assumed that Britain should not have to bear the cost of the occupation. Early idealistic notions that the British would stay in Germany for twenty-five years and do whatever was necessary to prevent another war were soon superseded by the requirement imposed from London that the cost to the British taxpayer had to be reduced. From early 1946 onwards, all those considered here accepted that British involvement in Germany would be temporary and had to be progressively scaled back. This implied that new social and political structures could not be imposed against the will of the Germans, as any reforms could be reversed once the British left. Even Ingrams accepted that he had to obtain agreement from the 'German Working Party' to his proposed changes to electoral procedure. Once Ordinance 57 devolved responsibility to local German administrations, British scope to implement any structural change was further reduced. British policy was limited to giving the Germans space to make their own decisions and reform their own institutions, while the British retained the power of veto, offering guidance and advice, but not imposing an alien model of government upon reluctant Germans.

British aims and intentions in occupied Germany

The principal claim made in this book is that, despite apparent contradictions in British policy and despite the diverse backgrounds, age and experience, political, moral and religious beliefs among the 'governing elite', the most significant British aims in occupied Germany can be summarized as the three R's, of physical and economic Reconstruction, political Renewal and personal Reconciliation. Although they justified it in different ways, all twelve individuals responded pragmatically to the chaos and destruction they saw around them and endorsed a policy of economic reconstruction and political renewal, promoted by Montgomery and his colleagues at the top of Military Government in the first six months of the occupation. Only a minority wanted to change fundamentally the structure of German social and political institutions. All, including those who had hoped for a revolution within Germany to overthrow Hitler, now considered it essential to keep the peace, maintain law and order, control disease, rebuild the economic infrastructure and provide employment, as they believed a stable, peaceful and democratic Germany was in Britain's national interest and in their own interest as members of a professional middle class. They worked to restore what they understood to be representative and responsible government by Germans, initially at local level and later regionally.

A deliberate policy of personal reconciliation followed later, in 1947, after numerous individual encounters at all levels between British and Germans had started to build trust and mutual respect. Examples given in this book include the tribute paid by the leading CDU politician, Karl Arnold, to Bishop in a letter shortly before Christmas 1949 (see Chapter 3), the close working relationship between Berry and Brauer (see Chapter 7), the connections Albu and Flanders had with their German socialist colleagues in *Neu Beginnen* and the ISK (see Chapter 6), Chaloner's recruitment of a team of young German journalists to create *Der Spiegel* (see Chapter 9), Howard's relationship with the daughter of the doctor in whose house he was billeted and the 10,000 British men, including Thexton, who met and married their wives in Germany (see Chapter 10). The policy of personal reconciliation received official endorsement with the formation of officially approved Anglo-German discussion groups and cultural centres, and from May 1947 in official directives and instructions.

The twelve individuals justified a policy of Reconstruction, Renewal and Reconciliation in different ways, on the basis of the 'mental baggage' each brought with them. The older generation drew on their personal religious beliefs, referring to the need to 'rebuild civilisation' or 'save the soul of Germany', and their understanding of the British Empire as a force for good in the world. Those with personal experience of the occupation of the Rhineland after the First World War wrote of the need to support democratic politicians and prevent a recurrence of economic and social conditions which had favoured the rise of extreme political parties, both Nazis and communists. Socialists argued that only a 'positive socialist policy' could prevent a return to fascism. Some members of the younger generation were motivated by the ideals for which they had fought the war, or from principles acquired at school or from their families. At the same time, they and others were concerned for the future, trying to rebuild their careers or personal lives after six years of war.

Since the end of the war and the occupation, both Britain and Germany have been politically stable and economically prosperous, so it could be argued that the goal of 'winning the peace' was achieved. On the other hand, many people in both countries are still coming to terms with the past; in Germany with memories of death, violence, the Holocaust, loss of their homes, and forty years of division between a capitalist West and communist East. In Britain, although the ruptures were less, some still have difficulty coming to terms with the end of Empire and a diminished global role. It is hoped that this book can contribute to a better understanding of British aims in occupied Germany and assist further research on how Germany emerged from Nazi dictatorship, war and foreign occupation, and the distinctive role of the British in helping or, on occasions, hindering this process. In so doing it can help us understand better the legacies of competing ideologies, oppressive governments, violent wars, and the subsequent defeat, occupation and rule of one country by another, which continue to cast their long shadows on the world today.

Appendix

Dramatis Personae: The Twelve Principal Individuals

Note: Roles performed in occupied Germany are shown in **bold**.

Military Governors and army generals

Field Marshal Bernard Montgomery, 1887–1976

Born in London in 1887. His father was vicar of St Mark's, Kennington, in South London, and Bishop of Tasmania before returning to Britain as Secretary of the Christian missionary Society for the Propagation of the Gospel. Educated at St Paul's School, London, and the Royal Military Academy, Sandhurst. Commissioned as an officer in 1908, served in India, and in France in the First World War, where he was wounded. Stationed between the wars in the Rhineland, Ireland, Egypt, India and Palestine and served as an instructor at the army Staff College. Promoted Major General in 1938. At the start of the Second World War he took part in the retreat and evacuation at Dunkirk. Transferred to North Africa in 1942, he commanded the 8th Army at the Battle of El Alamein – the first decisive Allied victory in the war – followed by the retreat of German forces and the invasion of Sicily in 1943. Appointed Commander-in-Chief of all Allied ground forces for the invasion of Normandy in 1944. After his replacement as Commander-in-Chief by General Eisenhower, he commanded the mainly British and Canadian 21st Army Group in its advance through France, Belgium and the Netherlands into Germany. Accepted the unconditional surrender of all German armed forces in Northwest Europe on 4 May 1945, shortly before VE Day on 8 May. **Appointed Military Governor of the British Zone of Germany and Commander-in-Chief of all British armed forces in Germany from 22 May 1945 to 1 May 1946.** Created Viscount Montgomery of Alamein in the 1946 New Year Honours. Chief of the Imperial General Staff, 1946–8. Chairman, Western European Union commanders-in-chief committee, 1948–51, and deputy supreme commander to Eisenhower, NATO Allied command in Europe, before retiring in 1958, and writing his memoirs, which proved highly controversial. Died 1976.

General Brian Robertson, 1896–1974

Born in India in 1896. His father, Sir William Robertson, rose from the ranks to Field Marshal, Chief of the Imperial General Staff, 1915–8, and Commander-in-Chief of the British Army of the Rhine, 1919–20. Educated at Charterhouse and the Royal Military Academy, Woolwich. Commissioned in the Royal Engineers, 1914, served in France in the First World War, and then in India. Attended the army Staff College, 1926–7. Member of the British delegation at the Geneva disarmament talks, 1932–3. Managing Director, Dunlop, South Africa, 1935–40. Enlisted in the South African Defence Force and served in the Second World War as Quartermaster General for the 8th Army under Montgomery and Chief Administrative Officer to General Alexander in Italy. **Appointed Deputy Military Governor and Chief of Staff to Montgomery in Germany, from July 1945 to May 1946, and to Sholto Douglas, from May 1946 to November 1947. Military Governor of the British Zone and Commander-in-Chief of all British armed forces in Germany, from November 1947 to September 1949. British High Commissioner to the Federal Republic of Germany, from September 1949 to June 1950.** Commander-in-Chief of Middle East land forces, 1950–3. Chairman, British Transport Commission, 1953–61. Succeeded his father in the baronetcy in 1933. Created Baron Robertson of Oakridge in 1961. Died 1974.

Major General Alec Bishop, 1897–1984

Born in Devon in 1897. Educated at Plymouth College and the Royal Military Academy, Sandhurst. Commissioned as an officer in 1916. Served in Mesopotamia (Iraq) in the First World War, where he was wounded. After the war served for six years in India. Attended the army Staff College, 1926–7. Joined the Colonial Office, 1931. During the Second World War served as a staff officer at the War Office in London. Appointed Major General, Director of Quartering in 1944 and Deputy Director of the Political Warfare Executive (PWE) in March 1945. **Moved to Germany in July 1945 as Director of PR/ISC (Public Relations and Information Services Control) for the Control Commission for Germany. Appointed Deputy Chief of Staff to Brian Robertson, 1946–8, and Regional Commissioner for North Rhine-Westphalia, 1948–50.** Assistant Secretary at the Commonwealth Relations Office, 1951–7. British Deputy High

Commissioner in Calcutta, 1957–62. Appointed High Commissioner for Cyprus in 1964 but retired due to ill health in 1965. Died 1984.

Marshal of the Royal Air Force Sholto Douglas, 1893–1969

Born in Oxford in 1893. His father, Robert Langton Douglas, was assistant chaplain at Merton College, but left the church, remarried, became a successful art critic and dealer and emigrated to the United States in 1940. Educated at Tonbridge School and Lincoln College, Oxford. Commissioned in the artillery in 1914, joined the Royal Flying Corps and qualified as a pilot in 1915. Ended the First World War with the rank of Lieutenant Colonel. Rejoined the RAF in 1920 after a short break as a civil aviation pilot. Attended the Air Staff College and the Imperial Defence College where he served as an instructor. Posted to Egypt, 1929–32, and the Sudan as area commander. From January 1936 he held senior positions in the Air Ministry, succeeding Hugh Dowding as Head of Fighter Command in November 1940. Appointed Head of Middle East Command in December 1942 and Head of Coastal Command in January 1944. **From August 1945 to January 1946 he was Commander-in-Chief, British Air Forces of Occupation (BAFO). On 1 May 1946 he succeeded Montgomery as Military Governor of the British Zone and Commander-in-Chief of all British armed forces in Germany**. Left Germany in November 1947 and was created Baron Douglas of Kirtleside in the 1948 New Year Honours. Chairman of British European Airways (BEA) from March 1949 until he retired in 1964. Died 1969.

Civilian administrators

Harold Ingrams, 1897–1973

Born in Shrewsbury in 1897. Educated at Shrewsbury School where his father was an assistant master. Commissioned in the King's Shropshire light infantry in 1914. Served in France and Belgium in the First World War where he was wounded. Joined the Colonial Service after the war and appointed assistant district commissioner in Zanzibar, 1919–27. Assistant colonial secretary in Mauritius, 1927–33. Appointed as a political officer in Aden in 1934 and served in senor positions in Aden and South Arabia until 1945. Published *Arabia and the Isles* in 1942. **Seconded from the Colonial Service to the Control Commission for Germany as Head of the Administration and Local Government (ALG) branch from July 1945 to August 1946.** Appointed Chief Commissioner of the

Northern Territories of the Gold Coast (Ghana) in 1947, but left a year later and retired from the Colonial Service in 1948. His account of travelling overland to take up the position was published in 1949 as *Seven across the Sahara.* Continued to work for the Colonial Office in various advisory roles until 1968. Died 1973.

Austen Albu, 1903–94

Born 1903. His father and mother ran a dress fabrics and fashion business, founded in London by his maternal grandfather. Educated at Tonbridge School and the City and Guilds College, London. Worked as an engineer in Newcastle and Coventry, 1924–6. Successfully applied for a position as Works Manager for Aladdin and spent a year in the United States, 1930–1. On returning to Britain, managed a new factory for Aladdin in West London. Joined the Fabian Society and Socialist League and in 1933 was elected chairman of his local constituency Labour Party in Uxbridge. Formed the Socialist Clarity Group with Patrick Gordon-Walker in 1937. **Appointed in February 1946 by John Hynd, Minister for Germany, on a temporary three-month contract as Head of the German Political Department, in the Political Division of the Control Commission for Germany. Promoted by Robertson, in May 1946, to Deputy Chairman, Governmental Sub-Commission.** Left Germany in November 1947. Elected Labour Party MP for Edmonton in a by-election in November 1948 and continued to represent the constituency until he retired in February 1974. Died 1994.

Allan Flanders, 1910–73

Born in Watford in 1910. Educated at Latymer Upper School, Hammersmith, and from 1929 to 1932 at the *Walkemühle*, the training school of the German socialist organization, the *Internationaler Sozialistischer Kampfbund* (ISK). From 1933 to 1943 he worked in various jobs in Sheffield and London, including as a door-to-door salesman and technical draughtsman, while acting as the leading member of the ISK's British section, the Socialist Vanguard Group. In 1943 he applied and was accepted for a position as Research Assistant at the Trades Union Congress (TUC). **Appointed by John Hynd, Minister for Germany, to succeed Austen Albu in May 1946 as Head of the German Political Department, in the Political Division of the Control Commission for Germany.** Returned to Britain at the end of 1947, and studied industrial relations in the United States. Appointed in 1949 as senior lecturer in Industrial Relations at Oxford University, where he, Hugh Clegg and Alan Fox were leading members of the Oxford

School of Industrial Relations. Elected Fellow of Nuffield College, Oxford, in 1964. Visiting Professor in Industrial Relations at the University of Manchester Institute of Science and Technology, 1969–71, and Reader in Industrial Relations at Warwick University, 1971–3. Died 1973.

Vaughan Berry, 1891–1979

Born in 1891 in Madras, India, where his father was a stockbroker. His father died when he was four years old, shortly after the family returned to Britain. Educated at a charity school, the Royal Asylum of St Anne's, Redhill, Surrey, the City of London School and Cambridge University, where he studied French and German. Served in the First World War as an officer in Salonika, Ireland and France, where he was wounded. Transferred to the Intelligence Corps after the end of the war and was posted to Germany. Appointed District Officer for the Inter-Allied Control Commission of the Rhineland from 1920 to 1925 for the town of Benrath, near Düsseldorf, and subsequently also for Solingen, in the Ruhr. Manager at the Union Discount Company of London, 1925–40. In January 1932 he founded the XYZ Club, a group of Labour Party members and sympathizers working in the City of London, including Douglas Jay, Francis Williams and Christopher Mayhew. During the Second World War he served as Chairman of the local Manpower Board in Reading, Berkshire, and at the Board of Trade in London. Returned to the Union Discount Company in 1945 but retired at the end of the year. **Recommended in May 1946 by John Hynd, Minister for Germany, as one of five Regional Commissioners in Germany. Appointed Regional Commissioner for Westphalia from May 1946 to September 1946 and Regional Commissioner for Hamburg from September 1946 to May 1949.** British representative on the International Authority of the Ruhr from June 1949 to September 1950. Knighted in 1949. Died 1979.

Young men with no adult experience but war

Jan Thexton, 1920–2008

Born 1920 in Plymouth. His father was a non-commissioned officer in the army. Spent his early childhood in Bermuda. Returned to Britain in the late 1920s. School not known. Worked briefly in an accountant's office after leaving school, before volunteering as a territorial for the Middlesex Yeomanry (signals). Called up in 1939 to help prepare for mobilization. Fought in the Second World War with an armoured tank division in North Africa, 1941–3. Returned to Britain to prepare for the invasion of Normandy. Fought with the army across France, Belgium and the Netherlands and into Germany. His rank at the end of the war was sergeant. **Part of the British army of occupation from May 1945 to May 1946 based in Hanover. After demobilization he returned to Germany as part of the Control Commission. Worked for twenty years in Germany, from 1946 to 1966, in the Control Commission Reparations Branch, in the Mandatory Requirements Office and subsequently as a liaison officer at the British Embassy.** After returning to Britain he was a civil servant at the Ministry of Defence, ending his career as director of a branch helping to promote British arms sales to Europe, Turkey, Iran, Israel and Pakistan. Died 2008.

Michael Palliser, 1922–2012

Born in 1922 in Reigate, Surrey. His father was a naval officer and his mother the daughter of a naval engineer. As his parents were often overseas, he spent much of his early childhood with his grandparents at Wokingham in Berkshire. Educated at Wellington College and Merton College, Oxford. He joined the Coldstream Guards and after initial training and six months at Sandhurst was commissioned in 1942 as an officer in an armoured tank battalion. After a further two years stationed in Britain, he fought with the army in Normandy, across France, Belgium and the Netherlands and into Germany. **Promoted to the rank of captain in 1944. Part of the British army of occupation in Schleswig Holstein, Berlin and Bad Godesberg, near Bonn, from the end of the war until he was demobilized in January 1947.** Joined the Foreign Office after returning to Britain. After various diplomatic postings he was appointed Private Secretary to the Prime Minister, Harold Wilson, in 1966, Minister at the British Embassy in Paris in 1969, head of the UK delegation to the European Community in Brussels in 1971 and, following British accession, UK Ambassador and Permanent Representative to the European Communities in 1973. Appointed Permanent Under-Secretary at the Foreign and Commonwealth Office and Head of the Diplomatic Service 1975–82. Knighted KCMG in 1973 and GCMG in 1977. Died 2012.

John Chaloner, 1924–2007

Born in 1924 in London. Both his parents were writers and journalists. Educated at the Beltane School, Wimbledon, and at Sandhurst. Commissioned as an officer in the Westminster Dragoons. Fought in the Second World War as a tank commander in the invasion of Normandy and subsequent campaigns across Northwest Europe into Germany. **At the end of the war he was a captain in the British army of occupation. Applied and was accepted for a position as Press Officer, 30 Information Control Unit, from July 1945 to the end of 1946. Promoted to the rank of major in 1946.** Established German newspapers in Hanover, Lüneburg and Osnabrück. Created *Diese Woche,* the precursor of the German weekly news magazine *Der Spiegel* in October and November 1946. After returning to Britain in early 1947, he formed a company, Seymour Press, which distributed foreign publications in the United Kingdom. Also published six novels and wrote and illustrated a series of books for children. Bought and ran a dairy farm in Sussex. Publishing adviser to the Institute of Directors and Confederation of British Industry on their in-house journals. Died 2007.

Michael Howard, 1926–

Born in 1926 in Fiji where his father was a colonial administrator. Left Fiji aged eight to attend boarding school in England. Educated at Rugby School. Volunteered for the army in 1943 but not called up until 1944. Commissioned as an officer in the Rifle Brigade in August 1945. Posted to Germany in February 1946. **Appointed as Intelligence officer for T-Force from April 1946 to December 1947. T-Force was a secret unit assisting the British Intelligence Objective Sub-Committee (BIOS) investigate German scientific and technical abilities and 'evacuate' selected German scientists and technicians to Britain. Promoted to the rank of Captain in 1947.** After returning to Britain he completed a shortened two-year degree at Cambridge University, 1948–9. Subsequently employed by W.R. Grace, a large US-based international manufacturing and trading company, and pursued a career in business. Published *Otherwise Occupied* in 2010, a memoir of his work for T-Force and his life as a young British army officer in occupied Germany.

Notes

Chapter 1

1 Bernard Montgomery, *The Memoirs of Field-Marshal the Viscount Montgomery of Alamein, K.G.* (London: Collins, 1958), p. 341.

2 E.g. *British Zone Review*, Vol. 1, No. 6, 8 December 1945, p. 2; Vol. 1, No. 18, 25 May 1946, p. 3.

3 E.g. Montgomery wrote in his memoirs published in 1958 (p. 341), 'I often wonder if we have won the peace. In fact I do not think we have', but did not elaborate further.

4 The first reference to the 'Four D's' was in 1948 by Carl Friedrich, Professor of Government at Harvard University, Director of the US Civil Affairs Training School, and Special Adviser on Governmental Affairs to the US Military Governor of Germany from 1946 to 1949. See Carl Friedrich, 'Military Government and Democratization', in Carl Friedrich (ed.), *American Experiences in Military Government in World War II* (New York, 1948), cited in Ulrich Reusch, *Deutsches Berufsbeamtentum und Britische Besatzung 1943–1947* (Stuttgart: Klett-Cotta, 1985), p. 61. More recent historians have used slightly different sets of four words, starting with the letter 'D', to describe Allied policies agreed at Potsdam, referring to 'Disarmament' instead of 'Demilitarization', and 'Decentralization' or 'Decartelization' instead of 'Deindustrialization'. For more details see the online blog post: http://howitreallywas.typepad.com/how_it_really_was/2009/11/the-4-ds-of-the-potsdam-agreement-1945.html (accessed 8 March 2016).

5 Alan Kramer, *The West German Economy, 1945–1955* (Oxford: Berg Publishers Ltd, 1991), p. 12. The British Zone was the largest of the four zones, with a population in 1946 of approximately. 23 million, compared to 17 million in each of the US and Soviet Zones, 5 million in the much smaller French Zone and 3.2 million in Berlin.

6 Eric Hobsbawm, *Age of Extremes* (London: Abacus, 1995).

7 E.g. Konrad H. Jarausch, *After Hitler: Recivilizing Germans, 1945–1995* (New York: Oxford University Press, 2006); Ulrich Herbert, 'Liberalisierung als Lernprozeß. Die Bundesrepublik in der deutschen Geschichte – eine Skizze', in Ulrich Herbert (ed.), *Wandlungsprozesse in Westdeutschland: Belastung, Integration, Liberalisierung 1945–1980* (Göttingen: Wallstein Verlag, 2002); Richard Bessel, *Germany 1945: From War to Peace* (London, New York, Sydney and Toronto: Simon & Schuster, 2009).

8 E.g. Axel Schildt, 'The Long Shadows of the Second World War: The Impact of Experiences and Memories of War on West German Society', *German Historical Institute London Bulletin*, Vol. XXIX, No. 1, May 2007, pp. 28–49; Jeffrey Herf, *Divided Memory: The Nazi Past in the Two Germanys* (Cambridge, MA and London: Harvard University Press, 1997); Richard Bessel and Dirk Schumann (eds), *Life after Death: Approaches to a Cultural and Social History of Europe during the 1940s and 1950s* (Cambridge: Cambridge University Press, 2003); Frank Biess and Robert G. Moeller (eds), *Histories of the Aftermath: The Legacies of the Second World War on Europe* (New York and Oxford: Berghahn Books, 2010).

9 Although the occupation of Germany is rarely considered in histories of the British Empire, themes such as ruling strategies, cooperation and conflict, and relations with the local population clearly apply to both. See, for example, John Darwin, *Unfinished Empire: The Global Expansion of Britain* (London: Allen Lane, 2012) and Clive Dewey, *Anglo-Indian Attitudes: The Mind of the Indian Civil Service* (London and Rio Grande: The Hambledon Press, 1993).

10 Michael Balfour and John Mair, *Four Power Control in Germany and Austria 1945–1946* (Oxford: Survey of International Affairs 1939–1946, Oxford University Press, 1956); Frank Donnison, *Civil Affairs and Military Government. North-West Europe 1944–1946* (London: HMSO, 1961).

11 Robert G. Moeller, 'Writing the History of West Germany', in Robert G. Moeller (ed.), *West Germany under Construction: Politics, Society and Culture in the Adenauer Era* (Ann Arbor: The University of Michigan Press, 1997).

12 Josef Foschepoth, 'British Interest in the Division of Germany after the Second World War', *Journal of Contemporary History*, Vol. 21, 1986, pp. 391–411; Anne Deighton, *The Impossible Peace: Britain, the Division of Germany and the Origins of the Cold War* (Oxford: Clarendon Press, 1990); John E. Farquharson, 'From Unity to Division: What Prompted Britain to Change Its Policy in Germany in 1946', *European History Quarterly*, Vol. 26, 1996, pp. 81–123.

13 For an overview of the extensive historiography on Montgomery see Colin Baxter, *Field Marshal Bernard Law Montgomery 1887–1976: A Selected Bibliography* (Westport, CT and London: Greenwood Press, 1999). Other senior British officers, diplomats and administrators who have written memoirs or been the subject of biographies include Brian Robertson, Sholto Douglas, Brian Horrocks, Alec Bishop, Gerald Templer, Alec Cairncross, William Strang, Yvone Kirkpatrick, Gordon Macready, Noel Annan and Robert Birley.

14 E.g. Brian Robertson, Lord Robertson of Oakridge, 'A Miracle? Potsdam 1945 – Western Germany 1965', *International Affairs*, Vol. 41, No. 3, 1965, pp. 401–410.

15 E.g. Günter Trittel, 'Von der "Verwaltung des Mangels" zur "Verhinderung der Neuordnung". Ein Uberblick über die Hauptprobleme der Wirtschaftspolitik in der Britischen Zone', in Claus Scharf and Hans-Jürgen Schröder (eds), *Die Deutschlandpolitik Grossbritanniens und die Britische Zone* (Wiesbaden: Franz Steiner

Verlag, 1979). For criticism of the occupation in the British press and Parliament see Jochen Thies, '"What Is Going on in Germany?" Britische Militärverwaltung in Deutschland 1945–6', in Scharf and Schröder (eds), *Die Deutschlandpolitik Grossbritanniens und die Britische Zone*; Matthew Frank, 'The New Morality – Victor Gollancz, "Save Europe Now" and the German Refugee Crisis, 1945–46', *Twentieth Century British History*, Vol. 17, No. 2, 2006, pp. 230–256. For contemporary criticism of the occupation by Germans see Barbara Marshall, 'German attitudes to British Military Government 1945–1947', *Journal of Contemporary History*, Vol. 15, 1980, pp. 655–684; Josef Foschepoth, 'German Reaction to Defeat and Occupation', in Moeller (ed.), *West Germany under Construction.*

16 Lothar Kettenacker, 'British Post-War Planning for Germany: Haunted by the Past', in Ulrike Jordan (ed.), *Conditions of Surrender, Britons and Germans Witness the End of the War* (London and New York: I.B. Tauris Publishers, 1997).

17 John E. Farquharson, 'The British Occupation of Germany, 1945–1946: A Badly Managed Disaster Area?' *German History*, Vol. 11, No. 3, 1993, pp. 316–338.

18 See, for example, articles in the section on 'Neuanfang oder Restauration: Neuordnungsversuche in der britischen Besatzungszone', in Josef Foschepoth and Rolf Steininger (eds), *Britische Deutschland- und Besatzungspolitik* (Paderborn: Ferdinand Schöningh, 1985).

19 Reinhold Wagnleitner, *Coca-Colonization and the Cold War: The Cultural Mission of the United States in Austria after the Second World War* (Chapel Hill and London: The University of North Carolina Press, 1994), English edition, translated by Diana M. Wolf. See also Uta G. Poiger, 'Rock 'n' Roll, Female Sexuality and the Cold War Battle over German Identities', in Robert G. Moeller (ed.), *West Germany under Construction*, p. 381; Ralph Willett, *The Americanisation of Germany 1945–1949* (London and New York: Routledge, 1989). See also the collection of articles on 'Americanization', by Boehling, Gienow-Hecht, Goedde, Kroes and Poiger in *Diplomatic History*, Vol. 23, No. 1 (Winter 1999).

20 E.g. Petra Goedde, *GIs and Germans: Culture, Gender and Foreign Relations 1945–49* (New Haven and London: Yale University Press, 2003); Christina von Hodenberg, *Konsens und Krise: Eine Geschichte der westdeutschen Medienöffentlichkeit 1945–1973* (Göttingen: Wallstein Verlag, 2006).

21 Josef Foschepoth, 'German Reaction to Defeat and Occupation', p. 87.

22 Moeller, 'Writing the History of West Germany', p. 5; James M. Diehl, 'Change and Continuity in the Treatment of German *Kriegsopfer*', in Moeller (ed.), *West Germany under Construction*; Curt Garner, 'Public Service Personnel in West Germany in the 1950s: Controversial Policy Decisions and Their Effects of Social Composition, Gender Structure, and the Role of Former Nazis', in Moeller (ed.), *West Germany under Construction*; Martin Broszat, Klaus-Dietmar Henke and Hans Woller (eds), *Von Stalingrad zur Währungsreform: Zur Sozialgeschichte des Umbruchs in Deutschland* (Munich: R. Oldenbourg Verlag, 1988).

23 Moeller, 'Writing the History of West Germany', p. 2.

24 Ian D. Turner (ed.), *Reconstruction in Post-War Germany: British Occupation Policy and the Western Zones 1945–1955* (Oxford: Berg Publishers Ltd, 1989); Adolf Birke and Eva Mayring (eds), *Britische Besatzung in Deutschland: Aktienerschliessung und Forschungsfelder* (London: German Historical Institute, 1992); Alec Cairncross, *The Price of War: British Policy on German Reparations 1941–49* (Oxford: Basil Blackwell, 1986); Kramer, *The West German Economy, 1945–1955*; Jill Jones, 'Eradicating Nazism from the British Zone of Germany: Early Policy and Practice', *German History*, Vol. 8, No. 2, 1990, pp. 145–162; Nicholas Pronay and Keith Wilson (eds), *The Political Re-education of Germany and Her Allies after World War II* (London and Sydney: Croom Helm, 1985); Michael Ahrens, *Die Briten in Hamburg: Besatzerleben 1945–1958* (Munich and Hamburg: Dölling und Gallitz Verlag, 2011); Gisela Schwarze, *Eine Region im demokratischen Aufbau: Der Regierungsbezirk Münster 1945–6* (Düsseldorf: Schwann, 1984).

25 Lothar Kettenacker, *Krieg zur Friedenssicherung: Die Deutschlandplanung der britischen Regierung während des zweiten Weltkrieges* (Gottingen: Vandenhoeck & Ruprecht, 1989), pp. 11, 517.

26 Ian Turner, 'British Policy Towards German Industry, 1945–9: Reconstruction, Restriction or Exploitation?' in Turner (ed.), *Reconstruction in Post-War Germany.*

27 Ian D. Turner, 'British Occupation Policy and its Effects on the Town of Wolfsburg and the Volkswagenwerk, 1945–1949' (PhD Diss: Manchester UMIST, 1984), p. 730.

28 Pronay and Wilson (eds), *The Political Re-education of Germany*, p. 1.

29 Bessel, *Germany 1945: From War to Peace*, p. 288.

30 Frances Rosenfeld, 'The Anglo-German Encounter in Occupied Hamburg, 1945–50' (PhD Diss: Columbia University, 2006), p. 291.

31 John Gimbel, *The American Occupation of Germany: Politics and the Military, 1945–1949* (Stanford, CA: Stanford University Press, 1968); F. Roy Willis, *The French in Germany: 1945–1949* (Stanford, CA: Stanford University Press, 1962); Norman Naimark, *The Russians in Germany: A History of the Soviet Zone of Occupation, 1945–1949* (Cambridge, MA and London: The Belknap Press of Harvard University Press, 1995).

32 Apart from three popular rather than academic histories: Douglas Botting, *In the Ruins of the Reich* (London: George Allen & Unwin, 1985); Giles MacDonagh, *After the Reich* (London: John Murray (Publishers), 2007); Frederick Taylor, *Exorcising Hitler: The Occupation and Denazification of Germany* (London: Bloomsbury, 2011). Although published over twenty years ago, the best single volume summary of British academic research on the occupation is still the compilation, Turner (ed.), *Reconstruction in Post-War Germany.*

33 A biographical approach, researching a number of individuals, has not been used previously as an historical method for studying the British occupation of Germany, though it has a long tradition in other areas, from classical and medieval

collections of 'lives' to feminist and social historians researching those 'marginal to the historical mainstream'. See Krista Cowman, 'Collective Biography', in Simon Gunn and Lucy Faire (eds), *Research Methods for History* (Edinburgh: Edinburgh University Press, 2012). Cowman used the term 'Collective Biography' to describe historical works (such as this book) which set the 'lived experiences' of two or more individuals within their historical context, rather than 'prosopography', large-scale statistical surveys of defined groups of people, as used in the social sciences.

34 Thexton's school is not known. All the others except Chaloner (who went to a 'progressive' Montessori school) attended well-established leading English public schools.

35 Its full name was the Control Commission for Germany (British Element), abbreviated to CCG or CCG (BE), reflecting the original intention to have a single Allied Control Commission, which would issue directives and control central German authorities, responsible for the administration of the whole country. This was never implemented, due to French opposition to the establishment of central German administrations, and later disagreements among the Allies.

36 The best-known example is Ivan Hirst, 'The Englishman who saved Hitler's Beetle', BBC News, 30 July 2003. Available online: http://news.bbc.co.uk/1/hi/magazine/3104469.stm (accessed 8 March 2016).

37 The Allied Museum, Berlin, *The Windsor Park Seminar. Berlin: The British Perspective 1945–1990*, 1–2 September 2009.

38 The interviews with Palliser and Thexton have been lodged with the IWM Sound Archive (IWM SA), accession numbers 32236/4 (Michael Palliser) and 30895 (J.M.G. Thexton).

39 The principal sources used for Howard and Chaloner were: Interview with Michael Howard, IWM SA accession number 31405; Michael Howard, *Otherwise Occupied: Letters Home from the Ruins of Nazi Germany* (Tiverton, Devon: Old Street Publishing, 2010); Der Spiegel private business archive, recorded interviews with John Chaloner, 21 October 2003 and 2 November 2006; Leo Brawand, *Der Spiegel – ein Besatzungskind: Wie die Pressefreiheit nach Deutschland kam* (Hamburg: EVA Europäische Verlagsanstalt, 2007).

40 The Imperial War Museum Sound Archive (IWM SA) was started in 1972 with the aim of collecting experiences of conflict of all kinds. It is now one of the largest collections of its type in the world, comprising over 50,000 hours of recorded material. Interviews from the archive were selected which met the following criteria: British people who served in Germany in an official capacity in the armed services or Control Commission for at least one year between 1945 and 1948 and were aged between 18 and 32 at the end of the war. All selected interviews were conducted by IWM full-time or trained freelance staff between 1988 and 2008, following a consistent open and non-prescriptive life history approach.

41 Paul Thompson, *The Voice of the Past* (Oxford and New York: Oxford University Press, 1988), p. 137.

42 On the fallibility of memory see Gabriele Rosenthal, *Erlebte und erzählte Lebensgeschichte: Gestalt und Struktur biographischer Selbsbeschreibungen* (Frankfurt and New York: Campus, 1995); Alistair Thomson, 'Life Stories and Historical Analysis', in Gunn and Faire (eds), *Research Methods for History*; Alessandro Portelli, 'What Makes Oral History Different', in Robert Perks and Alistair Thomson (eds), *The Oral History Reader* (London and New York: Routledge, 1998). As Alessandro Portelli noted, the subjectivity of the speaker is an advantage for oral history, conveying emotional content, feeling and attitudes as much as facts.

43 Mary Fulbrook, *Dissonant Lives: Generations and Violence Through the German Dictatorships* (Oxford: Oxford University Press, 2011), p. 5.

44 For example, I expected to find that memoirs and oral history interviews created from the 1950s onwards would be influenced by the prevalent Cold War mentality of the time, and would therefore display a greater hostility towards communism and the Soviet Union than earlier written records. This was not the case. Many documents in the National Archives from 1945 to 1948 showed similar anti-Soviet attitudes, suggesting that these predated the Cold War.

45 Victor Sebastyen, *1946: The Making of the Modern World* (London: Pan Macmillan, 2014), p. xvii.

Chapter 2

1 Montgomery, *The Memoirs of Field-Marshal the Viscount Montgomery of Alamein, K.G.*, p. 345.

2 Imperial War Museum (IWM) Montgomery papers (BLM and LMD), BLM 85, 'Notes on the Occupation of Germany', Part 1.

3 Nigel Hamilton, *Monty: The Field-Marshal 1944–1976* (London: Hamish Hamilton, 1986), p. 541.

4 Ibid.

5 John Ramsden, *Don't Mention the War: The British and the Germans since 1890* (London: Little Brown, 2006), chapter 6, 'Putting poor Germany on its feet again', pp. 212–253. For contemporary references to 'putting Germany on its feet again' see Michael Balfour, 'In Retrospect: Britain's Policy of "Re-education"', in Nicholas Pronay and Keith Wilson (eds), *The Political Re-education of Germany and Her Allies after World War II* (London and Sydney: Croom Helm, 1985), p. 140; W. Friedmann, *The Allied Military Government of Germany* (London: Stevens & Sons Limited, 1947), pp. 31–32; M.E. Pelly and H.J. Yasamee (eds) assisted by G. Bennett,

Documents on British Policy Overseas, Series 1, Volume 5, Germany and Western Europe, 11 August–31 December 1945 (London: Her Majesty's Stationary Office, 1990), pp. 273–279, 'Report of a Meeting between Mr Attlee and a Deputation led by Sir William Beveridge, on refugees', 25 October 1945.

6 Ramsden, *Don't Mention the War*, p. 245.

7 Farquharson, 'From Unity to Division', pp. 81–123.

8 Anne Deighton argued that the key turning point was the Paris Foreign Ministers' conference in the spring of 1946, when the British and the United States agreed to merge their zones to form a single economic unit. Konrad Adenauer placed it a year later, when the United States first announced the European economic recovery programme (Marshall Plan), after the failure of the Moscow conference in April 1947. See Anne Deighton, 'Cold-War Diplomacy: British Policy Towards Germany's Role in Europe, 1945–9', in Ian D. Turner (ed.), *Reconstruction in Post-War Germany: British Occupation Policy and the Western Zones 1945–1955* (Oxford: Berg Publishers Ltd, 1989); Konrad Adenauer, *Memoirs 1945–53*, translated by Beate Ruhm von Oppen (London: Weidenfeld and Nicolson, 1966), chapter 6, 'The Turning Point'.

9 Ian Turner and Alan Kramer also argue that British Military Government policy and practice were 'reconstructionist' from the start of the occupation. See Turner (ed.), *Reconstruction in Post-War Germany*, p. 8; Kramer, *The West German Economy*, p. 223.

10 Lieutenant-General Sir Brian Horrocks, *A Full Life* (London: Leo Cooper 1974), p. 284; Nigel Hamilton, 'Montgomery, Bernard Law [Monty], first Viscount Montgomery of Alamein (1887–1976)', in *Oxford Dictionary of National Biography* (Oxford University Press, 2004); online edition, May 2011 (henceforward Hamilton, 'Montgomery', *DNB*): http://www.oxforddnb.com/view/article/31460 (accessed 15 March 2016).

11 Hamilton, 'Montgomery', *DNB*; Alan Moorehead, *Montgomery* (London: Hamish Hamilton, 1946); Alun Chalfont, *Montgomery of Alamein* (London: Weidenfeld and Nicolson, 1976); Baxter, *Field Marshal Bernard Law Montgomery 1887–1976*.

12 Montgomery was born in 1887, Robertson in 1896 and Bishop in 1897.

13 IWM Bishop papers (AB) AB1, Alec Bishop, 'Look Back with Pleasure' (Beckley, Sussex: unpublished typescript, 1971), p. 3.

14 Victor Bonham-Carter, *Soldier True: The Life and Times of Field-Marshal Sir William Robertson* (London: Frederick Muller Limited, 1963).

15 *Who's Who 1983* (London: A&C Black, 1983), p. 198.

16 David Garnett, *The Secret History of PWE: The Political Warfare Executive 1939–1945* (London: St Ermin's Press, 2002), p. 431; FO 898/401, memo from RHBL (Bruce Lockhart) to Harvey, 10 July 1945 and attached 'minute on our difficulties over our information services in Germany'.

17 Bishop, 'Look Back with Pleasure', p. 88; FO 898/401, note from RHBL (Bruce Lockhart) to Oliver Harvey, 10 July 1945, attaching a 'minute on our difficulties over our information services in Germany'.

18 Oral History Interview with General Lord Robertson of Oakridge, 11 August 1970 by Theodore A. Wilson (Harry S. Truman Library & Museum). Available online: www.trumanlibrary.org/oralhist/robertsn.htm (accessed 8 March 2016). Robertson's account of his transfer to Germany is confirmed by papers in The National Archives (TNA) WO 258/83.

19 Ibid.

20 Kettenacker, *Krieg zur Friedenssicherung*; Kettenacker, 'British Post-War Planning for Germany'.

21 See, for example, the article by Bishop, 'Re-educating Germany', *British Zone Review*, Vol. 1, No. 6, 8 December 1945, pp. 3–4, initialled W.H.A.B. At the end of the article he wrote: 'We cannot, therefore, afford to fail in this intangible, difficult, but intellectually exciting task on which Information Services Control has embarked. During the war years we have learnt that nothing is impossible, though perhaps an "impossible task" may take a little longer to accomplish.'

22 George Clare, *Berlin Days* (London: Macmillan, 1989), p. 16; Yvone Kirkpatrick, *The Inner Circle* (London: Macmillan, 1959), pp. 190–191; Noel Annan, *Changing Enemies: The Defeat and Regeneration of Germany* (London: HarperCollins, 1995), p. 148; William Strang, *Home and Abroad* (London: Andre Deutsch, 1956), p. 226; Ethel Mannin, *German Journey* (London: Jarrolds Publishers (London) Ltd, 1948), pp. 17–19; W. Byford-Jones, *Berlin Twilight* (London: Hutchinson, 1947), p. 19; Arthur Geoffrey Dickens, *Lübeck Diary* (London: Victor Gollancz Ltd, 1947), p. 18, p. 27; Fenner Brockway, *German Diary* (London: Victor Gollancz Ltd, 1946); Alec Cairncross, *A Country to Play with: Level of Industry Negotiations in Berlin 1945–46* (Gerrards Cross: Colin Smythe Limited, 1987). See also 'Passing Comment', *British Zone Review*, Vol. 1, No. 20, 22 June 1946, p. 1.

23 Gimbel, *The American Occupation of Germany*, p. 6; Lucius D. Clay, *Decision in Germany* (London: William Heinemann Ltd, 1950), p. 21.

24 Bishop, 'Look Back with Pleasure', p. 88.

25 The *British Zone Review* published 'articles and views which have been approved by the responsible authority'. Its objects were to disseminate information to Control Commission and armed forces staff in Germany and to governmental and other bodies at home, on the 'problems, aims, work and achievements of the British element of the Control Commission'. See FO 1056/535, British Zone Review policy, 'Standing Instructions for the preparation and publication of the British Zone Review', 23 July 1945.

26 'The Early Days', *British Zone Review*, Vol. 1, No. 4, November 1945, p. 1, initialled G.W.R.T.

27 Donnison, *Civil Affairs and Military Government, North-West Europe, 1944–46.*

28 BLM 86, 'Notes on the Occupation of Germany', Part 2, p. 8.

29 BLM 85/15, 'Notes on the Present Situation', 6 July 1945; *British Zone Review,* Vol. 1, No. 1, p. 2.

30 *British Zone Review,* Vol. 1, No. 1, 29 September 1945, p. 13; ibid., Vol. 1, No. 4, 10 November 1945, p. 7.

31 'Quo Vadis?' *British Zone Review*, Vol. 1, No. 3, 27 October 1945, p. 1.

32 'The Year of Genesis', *British Zone Review*, Vol. 1, No. 8, 5 January 1946, p. 1.

33 BLM 87/23, memorandum to the Permanent Secretary, COGA, 19 December 1945.

34 Robertson, Truman presidential library interview; IWM AB3, speech by Bishop at the Anglo-German Association dinner, 2 November 1954. See also Horrocks, *A Full Life*. Revised and extended edition, p. 268. First published by William Collins, 1960. Horrocks was one of Montgomery's three Corps Commanders.

35 FO 1005/739, 'Infm Control Policy Directive No. 1', 12 May 1945.

36 BLM 85/10.

37 FO 1005/739, 'Infm Control Policy Directive No. 3', 27 May 1945.

38 FO 1005/739, 'Infm Control Policy Directive No. 4', 8 June 1945.

39 BLM 86/4, LMD 143/6-7.

40 FO 1005/739. Information Control Policy Directive no. 9, issued on 18 July 1945, stated that: 'Attitude of all output should now be more positive. Every fact should be emphasised which may inspire hope for the future in Germany.' See also FO 1056/25, memorandum headed 'Reconstruction of Germany' from A.G. Neville, 12 July 1945 and related documents in the file. These show Montgomery gave instructions to Bishop, who arrived in Germany on 10 July, Neville and information services staff, to give maximum publicity to steps taken by the British Military Government to improve the provision of food, transport, 'industries' and the postal services.

41 BLM 164/2, copy of telegram from Churchill to Montgomery, undated. Montgomery's reply was sent on 5 June 1945.

42 Jessica Reinisch, 'Public Health in Germany under Soviet and Allied Occupation, 1943–1947' (London: PhD Diss, 2004), p. 389.

43 TNA, 'Spotlights on history', 'The Blockade of Germany', available online: http://www.nationalarchives.gov.uk/pathways/firstworldwar/spotlights/blockade.htm (accessed 8 March 2016).

44 Donnison, *Civil Affairs, North-West Europe,* p. xiii; John Cloake, *Templer: Tiger of Malaya: The Life of Field Marshal Sir Gerald Templer* (London: Harrap, 1985), p. 149.

45 Kramer, *The West German Economy*, pp. 74–76.

46 Günter J. Trittel, *Hunger und Politik: Die Ernährungskrise in der Bizone (1945–1949)* (Frankfurt and New York: Campus Verlag, 1990); John E. Farquharson, *The Western Allies and the Politics of Food, Agrarian Management in Postwar Germany* (Oxford: Berg Publishers Ltd, 1985); Michael Wildt, *Der Traum vom Sattwerden; Hunger*

und Protest, Schwarzmarkt und Selbsthilfe in Hamburg 1945–1948 (Hamburg: VSA Verlag, 1986).

47 Kramer, *The West German Economy*, pp. 79, 97; FO 1030/303, memo from Robertson to Street, 26 March 1946, headed 'Coal'.

48 'Less Food, Less Coal', *British Zone Review*, Vol. 1, No. 15, 13 April 1946, p. 1.

49 Ian Turner, 'Das Volkswagenwerk – ein deutsches Unternehmen unter britische Kontrolle', in Josef Foschepoth and Rolf Steininger (eds), *Britische Deutschland- und Besatzungspolitik* (Paderborn: Ferdinand Schöningh, 1985), p. 299.

50 Farquharson, *The Western Allies and the Politics of Food*.

51 Pelly and Yasamee, *Documents on British Policy Overseas*, pp. 242–245, 'Urgent request for wheat allocations'.

52 Ibid., note 7.

53 BLM 170/10, message from Montgomery to Hynd, 26 February 1946.

54 FO 1030/303, letter from Robertson to Street, 5 May 1946.

55 Dickens, *Lübeck Diary*, pp. 336, 342; Rainer Schulze, 'A Difficult Interlude: Relations between British Military Government and the German Population and their Effects for the Constitution of a Democratic Society', in Alan Bance (ed.), *The Cultural Legacy of the British Occupation in Germany* (Stuttgart: Verlag Hans-Dieter Heinz, Akademischer Verlag Stuttgart, 1997).

56 Kramer, *The West German Economy*, pp. 73–84.

57 Jessica Reinisch, *The Perils of Peace: The Public Health Crisis in Occupied Germany* (Oxford: Oxford University Press, 2013), pp. 296–299.

58 Ibid.

59 IWM BLM 86/19, address to the Newspaper Society, 2 October 1945.

60 Farquharson, *The Western Allies and the Politics of Food*, p. 90, citing a speech by Ernest Bevin, HC Deb 26 October 1945 vol. 414 c2375; Mary Fulbrook, *Dissonant Lives: Generations and Violence Through the German Dictatorships* (Oxford: Oxford University Press, 2011), p. 60, citing Richard Bessel, *Germany after the First World War* (Oxford: Clarendon Press, 1993), p. 39.

61 HC Deb. 26 October 1945 vol. 414 cc2351-54.

62 'Will Germany Starve this Winter: The Problem of Feeding the British Zone', *British Zone Review*, Vol. 1, No. 1, 29 September 1945, p. 3.

63 Bishop, 'Look Back with Pleasure', p. 89.

64 Antoine Capet, '"The Creeds of the Devil" Churchill between the Two Totalitarianisms, 1917–1945', *Finest Hour Online*, 31 August 2009. Available online: http://www.winstonchurchill.org/support/the-churchill-centre/publications/finest-hour-online/725-the-creeds-of-the-devil-churchill-between-the-two-totalitarianisms-1917-1945 (accessed 8 March 2016).

65 Winston Churchill, *The World Crisis*, 6 vols. (London: Thornton Butterworth, 1923–31; abridged edition, London: Penguin, 2007), Vol. IV, *The Aftermath*, quoted in Capet, 'The Creeds of the Devil'.

66 Joseph M. Conlon, 'The Historical Impact of Epidemic Typhus'. Available online: http://entomology.montana.edu/historybug/TYPHUS-Conlon.pdf (accessed 8 March 2016). Epidemic typhus should not be confused with the serious, but rarely fatal disease, typhoid fever.

67 Reinisch, *The Perils of Peace*, p. 291. Some of the most serious outbreaks of typhus occurred in concentration camps before they were liberated, including Bergen-Belsen, where thousands of inmates died of the disease.

68 Capet, 'The Creeds of the Devil'.

69 BLM 85/7, speech in reply to receiving the Freedom of the City of Antwerp, 7 June 1945.

70 Capet, 'The Creeds of the Devil'; David Reynolds, *In Command of History: Churchill Fighting and Writing the Second World War* (London: Allen Lane, 2004), pp. 476–477. See also BLM 162, 'The Truth about the Telegram'. In a speech at Woodford in 1954, Churchill said he had sent Montgomery a telegram in May 1945 ordering him to 'stack' weapons previously used by the German armies, in case they were needed 'to fight the Russians with German help'. The speech aroused controversy in the press and in Parliament and Churchill was obliged to retract the claim, after no such telegram could be found in the archives. In a handwritten note for the file, dated June 1959, Montgomery stated that there never was any telegram, as he received verbal, not written, orders from Churchill to do this, but subsequently decided, on his own initiative, to destroy the weapons after receiving no further instructions from London.

71 BLM 164/3, telegram from Montgomery to Churchill, 5 June 1945.

72 BLM 86/3, 'Notes of Corps Commanders Conference', 2 August 1945.

73 BLM 88/13, 'Notes on the German situation', 1 May 1946.

74 Ulrich Reusch, 'Die Londoner Institutionen der britischen Deutschlandpolitik 1943–48. Eine behördengeschichtliche Untersuchung', *Historisches Jahrbuch*, Vol. 100, 1980, pp. 379–380.

75 FO 371/46973, C5121-2, 'Prime Minister's meeting on machinery for Control Commission'.

76 Reusch, 'Die Londoner Institutionen', pp. 381–382, 387.

77 FO 371/46973, C5121-2, 'Prime Minister's meeting on machinery for Control Commission'.

78 Reusch, 'Die Londoner Institutionen', pp. 381–385; Ulrich Reusch, 'Das Porträt: John Burns Hynd (1902–1971)', *Geschichte im Westen*, Vol. 1, No. 1, 1986.

79 Reusch, 'Die Londoner Institutionen', pp. 395–396.

80 BLM 170, 'Control Commission, important memoranda'.

81 FO 371/46735, C5132, 'F M Montgomery's Messages to Germans', minute by Cadogan, 11 August 1945.

82 Ibid.

83 Reusch, 'Die Londoner Institutionen', p. 406.

84 BLM 165/5, 'Germany and Austria in the post-surrender period. Policy directive for the Allied Commanders in Chief.' Montgomery's copy is numbered 797.
85 BLM 85/15, 'Notes on the Present Situation', 6 July 1945.
86 The SHAEF handbook was issued in December 1944, but covered only the immediate pre- and post-surrender period. SHAEF was dissolved in July 1945.
87 IWM BLM 85/15, 'Notes on the Present Situation', 14 July 1946.
88 FO 1050/806, 'Draft Directive from Chief of Staff (British Zone)', 21 July 1945.
89 Ibid.
90 WO 258/83.
91 For example, headings such as 'Shortage of Food' and 'Inadequate Transportation facilities' were changed to a more neutral 'Food' and 'Transportation Facilities'.
92 FO 1050/1040, 'Directive on Military Government from Chief of Staff (British Zone)', 10 September 1945.
93 FO 371/46735, C5962.
94 For a contemporary assessment by British officials of the status of the SHAEF handbook, JCS 1067 and directives prepared by the United States and UK before the end of the war, see FO 371/46730, C1047, 'Directive to Supreme Commander Allied Expeditionary Force regarding the Military Occupation of Germany in the interim post-defeat period' and 'C1071 – Allied Policy for the Occupation and Military Government of Germany'. On the status of occupation planning documents generally, see also Donnison, *Civil Affairs, North-West Europe*, chapter 11, 'Supreme Commander's Plans for Germany'; Balfour and Mair, *Four Power Control in Germany and Austria 1945–1946*, pp. 22–24; Reusch, *Deutsches Berufsbeamtentum*, pp. 121ff; Ulrich Schneider, 'Nach dem Sieg: Besatzungspolitik und Militärregierung' in Josef Foschepoth and Rolf Steininger (eds), *Britische Deutschland- und Besatzungspolitik* (Paderborn: Ferdinand Schöningh, 1985).
95 Gimbel, *The American Occupation of Germany*, p. 167.

Chapter 3

1 Montgomery, 'Introductory Message by the Commander-in-Chief British Zone', *British Zone Review*, Vol. 1, No. 1, 29 September 1945, p. 1.
2 E.g. Reinisch, *The Perils of Peace*, p. 295.
3 Bishop, 'Can We Re-educate Germany?' *British Zone Review*, Vol. 1, No. 6, 8 December 1945, pp. 3–4, initialled W.H.A.B.
4 Oral History Interview with General Lord Robertson of Oakridge, 11 August 1970 by Theodore A. Wilson (Harry S. Truman Library & Museum). Available online: www.trumanlibrary.org/oralhist/robertsn.htm (accessed 8 March 2016); Montgomery, *The Memoirs of Field-Marshal the Viscount Montgomery of Alamein, K.G.*, p. 399.

5 Montgomery, BLM 88/7, memorandum on 'The Problem in Germany', 1 February 1946.

6 Bishop, 'Ave Atque Vale', *British Zone Review*, Vol. 1, No. 17, 11 May 1946, initialled W.H.A.B.

7 Robertson, FO 1030/328, DMG press conference, 29 April 1947.

8 David G. Williamson, *The British in Germany 1918–1930: The Reluctant Occupiers* (New York and Oxford: Berg, 1991); Margaret Pawley, *The Watch on the Rhine* (London and New York: I.B. Tauris, 2007). See also contemporary British accounts of the Rhineland occupation: Violet Markham, *A Woman's Watch on the Rhine* (London: Hodder and Stoughton, 1921); G.E.R. Gedye, *The Revolver Republic: France's Bid for the Rhine* (London: J.W. Arrowsmith Limited, 1930); 'Apex', *The Uneasy Triangle: Four Years of the Occupation* (London: John Murray, 1931); B.T. Reynolds, *Prelude to Hitler* (London: Jonathan Cape, 1933); Ferdinand Tuohy, *Occupied: 1918–1930: A Postscript to the Western Front* (London: Thornton Butterworth, 1931); Katharine Tynan, *Life in the Occupied Area* (London: Hutchinson, 1925).

9 BLM 87/2, 'Notes on the post-war army', 7 October 1945. See also George Murray, 'The British Contribution', in Arthur Hearnden (ed.), *The British in Germany: Educational Reconstruction after 1945* (London: Hamish Hamilton, 1978), p. 65; Annan, *Changing Enemies*, p. 155.

10 BLM 85/10, 'The Field Marshal's letters on Non Fraternisation'.

11 'Experiences of Rhineland Occupation 1919–1925', *British Zone Review*, Vol. 1, No. 2, 13 October 1945, p. 5; 'Lessons of History', *British Zone Review*, Vol. 1, No. 5, 24 November 1945, pp. 1–2; 'Why Weimar Failed', *British Zone Review*, Vol. 1, No. 7, 22 December 1945, pp. 4–5.

12 Robertson, 'A Miracle? Potsdam 1945 – Western Germany 1965', pp. 401–410; J.H. Morgan, *Assize of Arms: Being the Story of the Disarmament of Germany and Her Rearmament (1919–1939)* (London: Methuen, 1945).

13 The reports of the parliamentary group were published with an introduction for a general audience as: Anthony Weymouth, *Germany: Disease and Treatment* (London: Hutchinson, 1945).

14 Williamson, *The British in Germany*, p. 348.

15 A leading exponent of this view was the influential journalist G.E.R. Gedye. His account was published as *The Revolver Republic*.

16 Violet Markham, *Return Passage* (London: Oxford University Press, 1953), p. 159. See also 'Apex', *The Uneasy Triangle*; Reynolds, *Prelude to Hitler*; Tynan, *Life in the Occupied Area*.

17 Markham, *A Woman's Watch on the Rhine*, pp. 26, 66, 207–208, 220, 257, 298.

18 Robertson, 'A Miracle? Potsdam 1945 – Western Germany 1965'.

19 FO 608/129, 'Peace Conference files (British delegation) 1919', folios 422–458, 'Bolshevism in Germany', report by Lt. Gibson, Irish Guards, of a visit to Germany from 1 to 24 February [1919].

20 Ibid., folios 403–412, 'Conditions in Germany', memo by Mr Powicke, 26 February 1919, with attached report by Colonel Cornwall summarizing the observations of the officers.

21 BLM 164/3, telegram from Montgomery to Churchill, 5 June 1945.

22 Darwin, *Unfinished Empire*, p. 11; D.C. Watt, *Britain Looks to Germany: A Study of British Opinion and Policy towards Germany since 1945* (London: Oswald Wolff, 1965), p. 73.

23 Annan, *Changing Enemies*, p. 157; Friedmann, *The Allied Military Government of Germany*, p. 46.

24 Darwin, *Unfinished Empire*, p. 204.

25 Ibid., pp. 2, 343, 365.

26 BLM 86/11, speech on receiving the Freedom of the City of Londonderry, 15 September 1945.

27 Bishop, 'Look Back with Pleasure', p. i.

28 Ibid., p. 30.

29 IWM catalogue entry for the papers of Major General Sir Alec Bishop.

30 David Williamson, *A Most Diplomatic General: The Life of General Lord Robertson of Oakridge* (London and Washington: Brasseys, 1996), p. 33.

31 Ibid., pp. 33–34, 46.

32 WO 258/83.

33 FO 1030/329, 'Verbatim notes of speech by Deputy Military Governor to Staff', 31 July 1947, quoted in Williamson, *A Most Diplomatic General*, p. 105.

34 Darwin, *Unfinished Empire*, pp. 342, 400.

35 Ibid., p. 2.

36 Bishop, 'Look Back with Pleasure', p. 58.

37 Bernard Porter, *The Lion's Share* (Harlow: Longman Group Limited, 1975), second edition 1984, p. 312; Bishop, 'Look Back with Pleasure', p. 44.

38 Montgomery, 'Introductory Message by the Commander-in-Chief British Zone', p. 1.

39 Copy given to me by my father who played a part in the D-Day landings. Also available online: http://www.kansasheritage.org/abilene/ikespeech.html (accessed 8 March 2016).

40 Letter from Col. J. Hennessey, 'Open Letter Bag', *British Zone Review*, Vol. 1, No. 4, 10 November 1945, p. 18.

41 Robert Birley, *The German Problem and the Responsibility of Britain. The Burge Lecture* (London: SCM Press, 1947), p. 5.

42 Matthew Grimley, 'Civil Society and the Clerisy: Christian Elites and National Culture, c.1930–1950', in Jose Harris (ed.), *Civil Society in British History: Ideas, Identities, Institutions* (Oxford: Oxford University Press, 2003), pp. 231–247; Walter James, *A Short Account of Amy Buller and the Founding of St. Catherine's, Cumberland Lodge* (Privately printed, 1979), pp. 44–45; S.P. MacKenzie, *Politics*

and Military Morale: Current-Affairs and Citizenship in the British Army, 1914–1950 (Oxford: Clarendon Press, 1992), p. 68.

43 Sir Walter Moberly, *The Crisis in the University* (London: SCM Press Ltd, 1949), p. 20.

44 Amy Buller, *Darkness over Germany* (London, New York and Toronto: Longmans, Green and Co, 1943), p. 150.

45 James, *A Short Account of Amy Buller.*

46 Buller, *Darkness over Germany*, pp. 193, 196.

47 Birley, *The German Problem and the Responsibility of Britain.*

48 BLM 159, BLM 161.

49 Goronwy Rees, *Sketches in Autobiography: 'A Bundle of Sensations' and 'A Chapter of Accidents' with 'A Winter in Berlin', a Further Autobiographical Essay* (Cardiff: University of Wales Press, 2001), edited with introduction and notes by John Harris. *A Bundle of Sensations* was first published by Chatto & Windus, London, 1960 and two extracts were serialized in *The Sunday Times* on 22 and 29 May 1960 as 'Monty' and the 'Drama of Dieppe'. According to John Harris: 'Reviewers of *A Bundle of Sensations* were much taken by Rees' pages on Monty and Nigel Hamilton [Montgomery's biographer] agrees: "Anyone who ever served or worked with Montgomery will testify to the accuracy of this portrait."'

50 *Bishop Montgomery: A Memoir* (London: The Society for the Propagation of the Gospel in Foreign Parts, 1933), initialled M.M. (Maud Montgomery), available online: http://anglicanhistory.org/england/hhmontgomery1933/ (accessed 8 March 2016).

51 Hamilton, 'Montgomery', *DNB.*

52 Bishop, 'Look Back with Pleasure', p. 165.

53 Bessel, *Germany 1945: From War to Peace*, p. 316.

54 Christopher Probst, 'Protestant Responses to Martin Luther's "Judenschriften" in Germany, 1929–1945' (London: PhD Diss, 2008).

55 E.g. AB2, letter from Bishop to Dr Stoltenhoff, General Superintendent of the German Evangelical Church, 5 January 1949.

56 BLM 86/3, notes of Corps Commanders Conference, 2 August 1945; FO 1030/322, notes of Corps Commanders' Conference, 14 December 1945.

57 Williamson, *A Most Diplomatic General*, p. 4. Charterhouse is a leading English Public School. Networks of public school 'old boys' persisted well into adult life and crossed generations. Robertson sent his son to Charterhouse, as well as having been a pupil there. Robert Birley, education advisor to Robertson in Germany, was headmaster of Charterhouse before the war, and headmaster of Eton afterwards.

58 Robert Graves, *Goodbye to All That* (Harmondsworth: Penguin Books, 1960), first published by Jonathan Cape 1929, pp. 37, 53–54.

59 'The Year of Genesis', *British Zone Review*, p. 1, initialled B.H.R.

60 AB12, 'Press statement by the Military Governor' [Robertson], 22 December 1947.

61 Horace, *Odes*, iii, 1.

62 'The Year of Genesis', *British Zone Review.*
63 The German terms *Land* and its plural *Länder* refer to the self-governing regions in Germany, which together now comprise the Federal Republic of Germany. Before regional government was rationalized by the Allies during the occupation, former provinces of Prussia, such as 'North Rhine province', were administered differently at local level from former (pre-1871) independent German states, such as Bavaria.
64 In order to facilitate comparisons with other individuals and groups discussed in this book, Bishop, Montgomery and Robertson could be considered as typifying a composite 'ideal type' of benevolent senior British army officer in Germany, sharing a classical education at English public schools, and motivated by sincerely held Christian beliefs. Categorizing them in this way reflects their self-image and the ideals they aspired to and does not imply any ethical endorsement or moral judgement. The concept of an 'ideal type' as a logical construction and aid to understanding derives from Max Weber. According to Weber, ideal types are concepts created by historians to help describe and explain real historical events. In Weber's view it is impossible to understand the real world without creating some kind of theoretical constructs, but this should not be done implicitly (thereby concealing the historian's interpretation and possible bias) but explicitly, through defining precise, specific and logically consistent ideal types, based on evidence, but not necessarily identical to anything found in its entirety in the real world. See Max Weber, 'Die Objektivität sozialwissenschaftlicher und sozialpolitischer Erkenntnis', in Johannes Winckelmann (ed.), *Gesammelte Aufsätze zur Wissenschaftslehre* (Tübingen, 1988).
65 Bishop, 'Ave Atque Vale', initialled W.H.A.B. The quote is from Catullus, '*Atque in perpetuum, frater, ave atque vale*', which the *Oxford Dictionary of Quotations* translates as 'And so, my brother, hail, and farewell evermore!'
66 Ibid.
67 AB2, letter from Karl Arnold, 22 December 1949, my translation from the original German.
68 AB3, speech by Bishop at the opening of *Die Brücke* in Cologne, 4 May 1950.
69 Ibid.

Chapter 4

1 BLM 170/21, letter to Attlee, 2 May 1946.
2 Robertson, 'A Miracle? Potsdam 1945 – Western Germany 1965', pp. 401–410.
3 Sholto Douglas with Robert Wright, *Years of Command: The Second Volume of the Autobiography of Sholto Douglas, Marshal of the Royal Air Force Lord Douglas of Kirtleside G.C.B. M.C. D.F.S.* (London: Collins, 1966), pp. 362, 350.
4 Ian D. Turner, 'The Apparatus of Occupation Rule', in Ian D. Turner (ed.), *Reconstruction in Post-War Germany: British Occupation Policy and the Western*

Zones 1945–1955 (Oxford: Berg Publishers Ltd, 1989), p. 360. See also 'Profile General Robertson', *The Observer*, 8 December 1946.

5 Sholto Douglas, *Years of Combat: The First Volume of the Autobiography of Sholto Douglas, Marshal of the Royal Air Force Lord Douglas of Kirtleside G.C.B. M.C. D.F.S.* (London: Collins, 1963), pp. 17–26; Vincent Orange, 'Douglas, (William) Sholto, Baron Douglas of Kirtleside (1893–1969)', *Oxford Dictionary of National Biography* (Oxford University Press, 2004); online edition, January 2011 (henceforward Orange, 'Douglas', *DNB*): http://www.oxforddnb.com/view/article/32876 (accessed 15 March 2016).

6 Douglas, *Years of Combat*, pp. 92–93.

7 Douglas, *Years of Command*, p. 11.

8 Orange, 'Douglas', *DNB*.

9 Douglas, *Years of Command*; Orange, 'Douglas', *DNB*.

10 Ibid.

11 Douglas, *Years of Command*, p. 307.

12 Ibid., p. 281.

13 Ibid.

14 Ibid., p. 285.

15 Ibid., pp. 305–306. In December 1945 Douglas wrote to his father: 'I don't think you appreciate what an unpleasant life we lead in Germany at the present time... I won't enlarge on this, but I loathe [underlined] being here. We live in an atmosphere of misery and starvation.'

16 Ibid., p. 308.

17 Douglas, *Years of Command*, pp. 308–310.

18 FO 1030/323, handwritten letter from Montgomery to Robertson, 27 January 1946.

19 Orange, 'Douglas', *DNB*; Douglas, *Years of Combat*, pp. 26–37.

20 Douglas, *Years of Command*, p. 321.

21 Ibid., pp. 323–324.

22 On Germans blaming the British for the cut in food rations see Schulze, 'A Difficult Interlude', pp. 67–109. See also Dickens, *Lübeck Diary*, pp. 336, 342.

23 Wildt, *Der Traum vom Sattwerden*, pp. 37ff; Trittel, *Hunger und Politik*, pp. 251ff.

24 Kramer, *The West German Economy, 1945–1955*, p. 76; Trittel, *Hunger und Politik*, p. 216.

25 Douglas, *Years of Command*, p. 287.

26 Montgomery, *The Memoirs of Field-Marshal the Viscount Montgomery of Alamein, K.G.*, p. 399; Oral History Interview with General Lord Robertson of Oakridge, 11 August 1970 by Theodore A. Wilson (Harry S. Truman Library & Museum). Available online: www.trumanlibrary.org/oralhist/robertsn.htm (accessed 8 March 2016).

27 FO 1039/669, 'Speech by Marshal of the Royal Air Force, Sir William Sholto Douglas... at the opening of the Exhibition, "Germany under Control" in London on 7th June 1946'.

28 Ibid., speech by Douglas at the Exhibition opening, 7 June 1946.

29 FO 945/533, 'Speech by Mr. John Hynd, M.P.'. Another copy is in FO 1039/669.

30 Hugh Dalton, *High Tide and After* (London: Frederick Muller Ltd, 1962), pp. 111–113.
31 FO 1030/307, letter from Robertson to Corps Commanders, 1 May 1946. See also TNA CAB 129/9, Cabinet memo by Bevin on 'Policy towards Germany', 3 May 1946, which stated that £80 million was the net cost of civil administration and food imports, after deducting proceeds from German exports. The cost of the 'military establishment', including pay and allowances of the occupation troops, was a further £65 million.
32 Dalton, *High Tide and After*, pp. 111–113.
33 Deighton, 'Cold-War Diplomacy', pp. 15–34.
34 Ibid.
35 FO 1030/170, Commander-in-Chief's lecture to the Imperial Defence College, 12 June 1947.
36 Ibid.
37 Ibid.
38 Deighton, 'Cold-War Diplomacy', p. 29.
39 HC Deb 10 May 1946 vol. 422 c1417.
40 FO 936/743, letter from Hollis (for Chiefs of Staff) to Hynd, 14 May 1946.
41 FO 1030/308, statement by Ralph C. Tarlton, 17 June 1946.
42 FO 936/743, 12 page report dated 16 October 1946, by T.E. Harris, Public Safety Branch, CID, on 'Alleged Illicit Dealings by Military Government Officers'.
43 FO 936/743, letter from Robertson to Jenkins, 31 October 1946.
44 FO 936/743, memo from Hynd to Prime Minister, 9 December 1946.
45 For a highly critical overview of alleged corruption in the British Zone see Patricia Meehan, *A Strange Enemy People* (London: Peter Owen Publishers, 2001), pp. 113–132.
46 FO 936/743, comment on the COGA departmental minute sheet initialled M.D. Deputy Secretary [Maurice Dean], 29 November 1946.
47 Meehan, *A Strange Enemy People*, p. 119; FO 1032/1370, letter from Tyler to Chief of Staff, 26 January 1949, 'Claim by Princess Feodora of Schaumburg-Lippe'.
48 Meehan, *A Strange Enemy People*, p. 119; FO 1067/192-3, 'Deficiencies at Villa Hugel'.
49 FO 936/741, report on 'Illegal trading in Germany', by A.W. Bechter, 17 July 1946.
50 Ibid., pp. 6–8.
51 FO 936/741, report by Superintendent Thorp, Metropolitan Police CID, 27 September 1946.
52 FO 936/741, letter from Robertson to Dean, 10 January 1947 and attached 'Interim liquidation report'.
53 FO 936/741, 'Operation "Sparkler" Final Report', 15 April 1947.
54 Paul Chambers, 'Post-War German Finances', *International Affairs*, Vol. 24, No. 3, July 1948, pp. 364–377.

55 Ibid. See also *Daily Mirror,* p. 2, 'Viewpoint', 11 July 1946.

56 Illegal black and 'grey' market trading was widespread in Britain, as well as Germany, for at least ten years after the war, due to shortages of supplies, rationing and price controls. See Mark Roodhouse, *Black Market Britain, 1939–1955* (Oxford: Oxford University Press, 2013). For a contemporary account of British and US participation in the black market in Berlin see W. Byford-Jones, *Berlin Twilight* (London: Hutchinson, 1947), pp. 35–37. See also an interesting fictional account, which conveys the mood of the time, based on the author's experiences as a sergeant in the Intelligence Corps: Colin MacInnes, *To the Victors the Spoils* (London: Alison and Busby, 1986), first published in 1950.

57 HC Deb 9 April 1946 vol. 421 c1818.

58 Ibid., c1849.

59 HC Deb 10 May 1946 vol. 422 cc1350-447; HC Deb 29 July 1946 vol. 426 cc526-640.

60 HC Deb 29 July 1946 vol. 426 cc529-530.

61 For example from James Hudson, (Ealing), HC Deb 9 April 1946 vol. 421 c1959.

62 HC Deb 22 October 1946 vol. 427 cc1487-1623; HC Deb 14 November 1946 vol. 430 cc238-371; HC Deb 5 February 1947 vol. 432 cc1775-916.

63 *Daily Mirror,* p. 2, 8 July 1946.

64 Ibid.

65 *Daily Mirror*, p. 1, 'Bevin Tells Russia: Germany Costing Britain Too Much', 11 July 1946; *Daily Mirror*, p. 1, 'Bevin Insists "We can't borrow more to aid Germany"', 12 July 1946.

66 FO 371/55578, press cutting from the *Manchester Guardian*, 21 September 1946; Thies, 'What Is Going on in Germany?' p. 42.

67 Richard Greenhough, 'Spotlight on a Prince's Fabulous Castle', *Daily Mail,* p. 1, 8 July 1947.

68 Ibid.

69 Douglas, *Years of Command,* p. 356.

70 Ibid.

71 FO 936/653, T. Hayward, Assistant Inspector General, Public Safety Branch, final report on 'Property of Prince Wolrad of Schaumburg-Lippe missing from Schloss Buckeburg', 30 June 1948.

72 Ibid.

73 Ibid.

74 Ibid.

75 FO 1032/1461, interim report by Inspector Hayward, headed 'HQ Special Enquiry Bureau, Public Safety branch', 30 December 1947.

76 Ibid.

77 Ibid.

78 FO 1032/1371, letter from Coningham to Douglas, 30 July 1947.
79 Vincent Orange, *Coningham: A Biography of Air Marshal Sir Arthur Coningham KCB, KBE, DSO, MC, DFC, AFC* (London: Methuen, 1990), p. 250.
80 FO 1032/1461, letter from de Putron to Robertson, 10 February 1948.
81 FO 1032/1461, letter from Westropp, who was dealing with the case for Robertson, to de Putron, 27 February 1948.
82 FO 1032/1371, memo from Petterson, Regional Economic Officer to Lingham, Acting Regional Commissioner, 13 July 1947, enclosing 'Report on the Estate of Prince Wolrad at Schaumburg-Lippe as at 7 July 1947', by E.S. Hawarth, Property Control Branch; FO 1032/1370, memo from Goff to Parker, 8 July 1947 'Prince Wolrad's Estate in Schaumburg-Lippe'.
83 FO 936/653, Hayward, final report, 30 June 1948.
84 FO 1032/1371, 'Report on the Estate of Prince Wolrad at Schaumburg-Lippe as at 7 July 1947'.
85 FO 1030/151, receipt for 72 items of silverware and furniture 'taken' [crossed out and replaced by hand with 'requisitioned'] by Lady Douglas on 25 September 1946. Also receipts for a painting from *Schloss Bückeburg,* and a receipt for pictures from *Villa Hugel.*
86 Douglas, *Years of Command*, p. 318.
87 FO 1030/151, letter from Brigadier A/Q to HQ BAOR and others on 'Military Governor's residence', 9 May 1946.
88 FO 1030/171, note expressing satisfaction for the hard work done by the sappers on the swimming pool at Ostenwalde, 23 June 1947.
89 FO 1030/151; FO 1030/171.
90 FO 1030/151, letter from Chambers to Douglas, 7 October 1946.
91 FO 1032/1461. Hayward's interim report, 30 December 1947 alleged that in January 1947, Air/Cdr Constantine was discovered to have flown to the UK with 900lbs of luggage, leaving the same quantity to follow in a freight plane. Silver from Bückeburg was recovered from these items.
92 FO 936/653, note from Lord Henderson to Strang, 31 July 1948.
93 Lady Douglas, for example, issued an official receipt for the 72 items she requested from Bückeburg on 25 September 1946.
94 FO 1046/201, 'Report for Director, Property Control Branch relative to claim for compensation for missing items', by E.S. Haworth, 2 March 1949.
95 FO 1032/1461, letter from Robertson to O'Rorke, Inspector General, Public Safety, 2 January 1948.
96 Douglas, *Years of Command*, pp. 329ff.
97 See for example Henry E. Collins, *Mining Memories and Musings: Autobiography of a Mining Engineer* (Ashire Publishing Ltd, 1985), pp. 39ff. Collins was a professional mining engineer and Director of Coal Production in the British Zone from 1945 to 1947. He wrote in relation to the proposed de-nazification of

'lower grade' former Nazis in managerial positions in the industry: 'In November 1945, I was consulted on a list of persons to be arrested as important Nazis. I was horrified to see a number of names of key men in the coal industry ... I was able to have the names erased from the list because the persons concerned were vital to the recovery of coal production.'

98 Douglas, *Years of Command*, p. 325.

99 Douglas, *Years of Combat*, pp. 111ff.

100 Douglas, *Years of Command*, p. 154.

101 Ibid., pp. 24–26.

102 Ibid., p. 154.

103 Ibid., p. 48.

104 Douglas, *Years of Combat*, pp. 141–142.

105 Ibid., p. 326.

106 Douglas, *Years of Command*, p. 330.

107 Horrocks, *A Full Life*, p. 185.

108 AB2, three letters from Kesselring to Bishop, dated 1948 and 1950.

109 Douglas, *Years of Command*, p. 337. Douglas's account in his memoirs is supported by FO 800/466, exchange of telegrams with Bevin, 5–8 October 1946; FO 1060/1388, correspondence between Douglas and Hynd, August–October 1946.

110 Douglas, *Years of Command*, p. 344.

111 Ibid., p. 347.

112 Ibid., p. 359.

113 Ibid., p. 360.

114 AB1, Bishop, 'Look Back with Pleasure', p. 127.

115 Lord Pakenham, *Born to Believe* (London: Jonathan Cape, 1953), pp. 177–178.

116 Douglas, *Years of Command*, pp. 330, 343.

117 Ibid., p. 362.

118 See for example letters from Douglas on housing conditions in the Zone in FO 1030/188, to Deputy Military Governor (Robertson), 3 July 1946, Service chiefs, 5 October 1946 and McCreery, 17 November 1946.

119 FO 936/425, handwritten letter from Douglas to Bevin, 15 May 1947.

120 Ibid., memo from Bevin to Attlee, 20 June 1947.

121 Ibid., memo from Bevin to Prime Minister, 6 October 1947.

122 Orange, 'Douglas', *DNB*.

123 HC Deb 05 February 1947 vol. 432 cc1775-916, opening speech by the Conservative spokesman, Richard Law, in the Adjournment debate on Germany.

124 FO 1030/329, 'Verbatim notes of speech by Deputy Military Governor to Staff', 31 July 1947.

125 Bishop, 'Can We Re-educate Germany?' pp. 3–4, initialled W.H.A.B.

126 Robertson, FO 1030/328, DMG press conference, 29 April 1947.

127 At its peak in 1946 the total number of British personnel in the Control Commission was around 26,000. Although this was criticized at the time for being too high, it was small compared to the total population of the British Zone of around 23 million.

Chapter 5

1 E.g. Wolfgang Rudzio, *Die Neuordnung des Kommunalwesens in der Britischen Zone* (Stuttgart: Deutsche Verlags-Anstalt, 1968); Reusch, *Deutsches Berufsbeamtentum.*

2 Leonard St Clair Ingrams was a banker, employed during the war as a government official in various departments including propaganda, economic warfare and the secret services. He later worked for the Economics Division of the Control Commission in Germany. See Garnett, *The Secret History of PWE*, pp. 14, 41–42; Sefton Delmer, *Black Boomerang: An Autobiography, Vol. 2* (London: Secker and Warburg, 1962), pp. 25, 36–37; Monika Dickhaus, 'The Foster-Mother of "The Bank that Rules Europe"', in Alan Bance (ed.), *The Cultural Legacy of the British Occupation in Germany* (Stuttgart: Verlag Hans-Dieter Heinz, Akademischer Verlag Stuttgart, 1997).

3 Harold Ingrams, *Arabia and the Isles* (London: John Murray, 1966), third edition, first published in 1942, pp. 321–322.

4 Roger T. Stearn, 'Ingrams, (William) Harold (1897–1973)', in *Oxford Dictionary of National Biography* (Oxford University Press, 2004); online edition, January 2014 (henceforward Stearn, 'Ingrams', *DNB*): http://www.oxforddnb.com/view/article/46523 (accessed 15 March 2016).

5 G. Rex Smith, '"Ingrams Peace", Ḥaḍramawt, 1937–40. Some Contemporary Documents', *Journal of the Royal Asiatic Society*, Vol. 12, No. 1, April, 2002, pp. 1–30.

6 Stearn, 'Ingrams', *DNB*.

7 Churchill Archives Centre, Ingrams papers (henceforward IGMS) 6/5, confidential memo, 'The anomalous position of the Branch', 20 July 1946.

8 Harold Ingrams, *Seven across the Sahara* (London: John Murray, 1949), p. 2.

9 FO 1050/806; 1050/181; 1050/160; 1050/1040; IGMS 2/2; 3/5; 3/7; 4/5.

10 IGMS 5/8.

11 Rudzio, *Die Neuordnung des Kommunalwesens,* pp. 44–45.

12 Bernard Crick, 'Robson, William Alexander (1895–1980)', in *Oxford Dictionary of National Biography* (Oxford University Press, 2004); online edition, May 2010: http://www.oxforddnb.com/view/article/31622 (accessed 15 March 2016).

13 Robson published his views on local government reform in Germany in two articles: W.A. Robson, 'Local Government in Occupied Germany', *The Political*

Quarterly, Vol. XIV, No. 4, October–December 1945, pp. 277–287; William A. Robson, 'Local Government in Germany: A Background to Municipal Elections', *The Times*, 11 September 1946, p. 5.

14 Rudzio published his study in 1968, before official papers were released. Reusch, *Deutsches Berufsbeamtentum*, published in 1985, includes extensive reference to Ingrams and his colleagues in ALG branch, for example, pp. 145–166.

15 IGMS 4/1, 'Papers on Electoral Procedure', letter from P. Balfour, 2 February 1946. See also IGMS 3/3, extracts of press articles and intelligence summaries relating to the government of occupied Germany; IGMS 3/4, minutes of the first meeting of the Allied Control Authority Government Structure subcommittee, held in Berlin on 19 December 1945.

16 Robson, 'Local Government in Occupied Germany'.

17 IGMS 1/1, lecture on 'Regional and Local Government in Germany: Now and the Future', February 1946. See also J.M. Cobban, 'Reviving Local Government', *British Zone Review*, Vol. 1, No. 6, 8 December 1945, p. 8, in which he wrote: 'Adm and LG branch has its eye fixed on the Parish Pump rather than on the County Hall.'

18 Harold Ingrams, 'Building Democracy in Germany', *The Quarterly Review*, No. 572, April 1947, p. 209.

19 IGMS 1/1, draft notes dated Jan 1946 for a lecture on 'Regional and local govt under the Nazis'.

20 Ingrams, *Seven across the Sahara*, p. 16.

21 Ibid., p. 85.

22 IGMS 6/5, 'Note for file'. An identical copy of the note dated 24 July is in IGMS 2/1 and an undated handwritten version in IGMS 4/7. Ingrams' copy of the directives is in IGMS 1/8, 'Policy Directives for Allied C-in-Cs'.

23 IGMS 1/8. The reference in the directives to promoting the 'decentralisation of the political structure and the development of local responsibility' is in a draft appendix to Directive no. 1: Appendix A 'Draft Directive on Treatment of Germany in the Initial Post-Defeat Period', UK re-draft of US draft directive.

24 IGMS 6/5, 'Note for file'.

25 IGMS 2/1, letter from Ingrams to Balfour, 19 February 1946, with a one page paper entitled 'On Promoting Democracy in Germany'.

26 IGMS 2/1, 'On Promoting Democracy in Germany'.

27 The first edition of the directive, issued on 15 September 1945, is in FO 1050/423, 'Military Government Directive on Administrative, Local and Regional Government and the Public Services: Part 1 Democratisation and Decentralisation of Local and Regional Government'. The second edition dated 1 February 1946, with Ingrams' foreword, is in Churchill Archives Centre, Albu papers (henceforward AP), Box 10.

28 IGMS 3/7, lecture given by Ingrams during November 1945; IGMS 1/1, lecture on 'Regional and Local Government in Germany: Now and the Future', February 1946.

29 Sidney and Beatrice Webb, *The Parish and the County* (London: Frank Cass, 1963), first published in 1906, p. 48.
30 Callum G. Brown, *The Death of Christian Britain: Understanding Secularisation 1800–2000* (London and New York: Routledge, 2001), pp. 16–17.
31 Ibid.
32 FO 1050/806, memo from P. Balfour, Major-General, Chief I.A.& C. Division, 2 August 1945, on 'Draft Directive from Chief of Staff (BZ)'.
33 FO 1050/806.
34 See for example FO 1050/806, memo from Ingrams, to Working Party members, 6 August 1945, on 'Mil Gov Instr No. 21 – Assemblies of Germans'.
35 FO 1050/806, memo from W.H. Ingrams, 10 August 1945 and attached paper headed 'Working Party on Democratic Development: some considerations on points arising in connection with measures for development of democracy in the BZ'.
36 Ibid., p. 1.
37 Ibid.
38 Ibid.
39 Ibid., p. 2.
40 Ibid., p. 1.
41 Ibid., pp. 2–13.
42 Ibid., p. 2.
43 Ibid., pp. 3–13.
44 IGMS 2/1, letter from Ingrams to Seel, 17 July 1945.
45 Ibid.
46 FO 1050/1040, 'Directive on Military Government from Chief of Staff (British Zone)', 10 September 1945, pp. 11–15.
47 IGMS 1/4. Ordinance no. 8 regulated public discussions, Ordinance no. 9 permitted non-political meetings such as theatrical events, concerts, circuses and carnivals, Ordinance no. 10 concerned applications for permits for a political meeting, Ordinance no. 11 applications for public processions and Ordinance no. 12 regulated the formation of political parties.
48 FO 1050/423, 'Military Government Directive on Administrative, Local and Regional Government and the Public Services. Part I: Democratisation and Decentralisation of Local and Regional Government', 15 September 1945.
49 Ibid., p. 6.
50 Ibid., p. 7.
51 Ibid., p. 31.
52 'Quo Vadis?' *British Zone Review*, Vol. 1, No. 3, 27 October 1946, p. 1.
53 IGMS 2/1, memo from TND/FG on 'Progress of Nominated Representative Councils', 9 May 1946.

54 IGMS 1/7, minutes of the first meeting of the working party on electoral procedure.

55 Ibid.

56 IGMS 3/5, 'Papers of the Second Meeting of the German Working Party', 31 January–2 February 1946.

57 Ibid.

58 Ibid., FO 1049/2114, 'Confidential Report on Chancellor on the Duchy of Lancaster's Tour', 25 January 1946, sent to Strang by Noel Annan (Lieutenant-Colonel, Political Division). The report noted under the heading 'electoral procedure' that Hynd considered that 'the views of the German Working Committee on this subject should prevail'.

59 FO 1056/27, 'Minutes of the first weekly meeting between Political Division and A. & L.G. Branch' held on 6 February 1946. See also IGMS 4/1, 'Note of conversation with Macassey', 6 February 1946.

60 AP 13/2, diary entry for 3 February 1946.

61 AP 13/2, diary entry for 4 February 1946; FO 1056/27, 'Minutes of the first weekly meeting between Political Division and A. & L.G. Branch', 6 February 1946.

62 IGMS 3/7, papers for 3rd meeting of working party for electoral procedure.

63 Ibid.

64 AP15, Austen Albu, 'Back Bench Technocrat', unpublished autobiography, chapter III, pp. 6–7; FO 371/55611, C2327, 'German Local Elections in the British Zone', notes of meeting held on 16 February 1946.

65 Ingrams, 'Building Democracy in Germany', pp. 217–218; Raymond Ebsworth, *Restoring Democracy in Germany: The British Contribution* (London: Stevens & Sons Limited, 1960), p. 65.

66 AP15, Austen Albu, 'Back Bench Technocrat', chapter III, p. 6; See also FO 371/55611 'German Local Elections in the British Zone'. A minute in the file by an FO official tends to confirm Albu's claim that that the new system was his idea.

67 Reusch, *Deutsches Berufsbeamtentum*, pp. 197–239.

68 Ibid. pp. 252–253.

69 Before regional elections were held in the British Zone, in October 1946, the heads of German regional governments and members of the consultative group were British nominees.

70 Michael Thomas, *Deutschland, England über alles: Rückkehr als Besatzungsoffizier* (Berlin: Siedler Verlag, 1984).

71 FO 1050/149, 'Comments on Conference of Oberprasidenten etc in Hamburg on 29th Oct 45: By Capt M.A. Thomas'.

72 FO 1050/149, 'Address to the Oberpräsidenten Landes [*sic*] – and Ministerpräsidenten by the D.C.O.S. (Exec.) at Detmold on 19 Nov. 45'.

73 FO 1050/149, 'Notes on the conference of the heads of the Lander and Provinces of the British Zone held at Detmold, November 19/20, By Capt M.A. Thomas'.

74 Reusch, *Deutsches Berufsbeamtentum*, p. 88, citing, inter alia, William Harbutt Dawson, *Municipal Life and Government in Germany* (London, 1914), pp. viii, ix, 113–115.

75 Harold Laski, *Studies in the Problem of Sovereignty* (New Haven, CT, 1917), cited in Jose Harris, 'From Richard Hooker to Harold Laski: Changing Perceptions of Civil Society in British Political Thought, Late Sixteenth to Early Twentieth Centuries', in Jose Harris (ed.), *Civil Society in British History: Ideas, Identities, Institutions* (Oxford: Oxford University Press, 2003), p. 35.

76 Robson, 'Local Government in Germany', p. 284.

77 FO 938/248, letter from Sander to Hynd, 28 February 1946.

78 Ebsworth, *Restoring Democracy in* Germany, p. 128; Reusch, *Deutsches Berufsbeamtentum*, pp. 358ff.

79 For a full discussion of Ingrams' plans to reform the German Civil Service and the outcome, see Reusch, *Deutsches Berufsbeamtentum*. For a British account by a former member of ALG branch, see Ebsworth, *Restoring Democracy in Germany*.

80 Ebsworth, *Restoring Democracy in Germany*, pp. 100–105.

81 IGMS 6/5, confidential Memo on 'The anomalous position of the Branch', 20 July 1946.

82 Ibid.

83 Ingrams, 'Building Democracy in Germany', p. 222.

84 IGMS 2/1, 'On Promoting Democracy in Germany'. Ingrams did not claim the British were racially superior. The difference between British and Germans, in his view, was due to nurture rather than nature – the favourable physical environment of 'Island Britain' contrasted with 'the plains of Germany'. The idea that the physical environment and prevailing climate of a country influence the character of the people living there was not original or unique to Ingrams, and can be traced back at least to Montesquieu in the eighteenth century.

85 E.g. IGMS 4/1, 'Note of conversation with Macassey', 6 February 1946. Macassey was a Home Office official who told Ingrams that Hynd favoured the system of proportional representation used by the National Union of Railwaymen. Ingrams noted that Macassey added that the system was 'most complicated and involves about 12 counts' and 'the Germans weren't capable of working it'.

86 IGMS 6/5, 'Memorandum on Relations with Germans', 29 September 1945.

87 IGMS 5/6, notes of meeting held on 19 July 1946.

88 IGMS 3/5, 'Papers of the second meeting of the German Working Party', 31 January–2 February 1946; IGMS 2/1, letter to Philip Balfour, 20 September 1945 on 'Developments in Hamburg'.

89 IGMS 2/2 'Introduction by Germany [*sic*] Working Party on Electoral Procedure' in notes of the 1st meeting of the German Working Party on Electoral Procedure, 10–12 January 1946.

90 Ebsworth, *Restoring Democracy in Germany*, pp. 113–114.
91 E.g. Jarausch, *After Hitler*.
92 Herbert, 'Liberalisierung als Lernprozeß'.

Chapter 6

1 For Albu's appointment by Hynd see Churchill Archives Centre, Albu papers (henceforward AP) AP15, Albu, 'Back Bench Technocrat', unpublished autobiography, chapter II, p. 33. For Flanders' appointment by Hynd see Mary Saran, *Never Give Up* (London: Oswald Wolff, 1976), p. 95; and Modern Records Centre, Socialist Vanguard Group papers (henceforward SVG), MSS.173/3/4, report of SVG executive meeting on 18 December 1945. John Kelly, *Ethical Socialism and the Trade Unions: Allan Flanders and the British Industrial Relations Reform* (New York and Abingdon: Routledge, 2010), p. 44 and Denis Healey, *The Time of My Life* (London: Michael Joseph, 1989), p. 88, are incorrect in stating that Flanders was appointed by Ernest Bevin.
2 Hynd and Flanders were both active in the Fabian Society in Sheffield during the war. Hynd was also associated with the Socialist Clarity Group, founded by Albu and Patrick Gordon-Walker after the Socialist League, led by Stafford Cripps, was disaffiliated from the Labour Party. See AP 7/2, letters from Hynd to Albu, 5 and 29 January 1940.
3 Reusch, 'Das Porträt'; Reusch, *Deutsches Berufsbeamtentum*, pp. 101, 259. Hynd was a self-taught railway official who spoke several languages fluently, including German. He was elected MP for Sheffield Attercliffe in a by-election in 1944. Apart from his contacts with German exiles, he had no experience which would have made him a suitable candidate as Minister for Germany. For his links with German exiles see Churchill College Archives, Hynd papers, 3/4, 'Personal correspondence about Germany or with Germans 1944–70'; Ludwig Eiber, *Die Sozialdemokratie in der Emigration* (Bonn: J H W Dietz Nachfolger, 1998), pp. XLV, CXV, 655, 745, 840; Mark Minion, 'Left, Right or European? Labour and Europe in the 1940s: The Case of the Socialist Vanguard Group', *European Review of History: Revue européenne d'histoire*, Vol. 7, No. 2, July 2010, p. 246.
4 The group was originally known as the 'Org' and operated secretly within both the SDP and KPD. The name *Neu Beginnen* came from the title of a pamphlet written in 1933 by the group's leader, Walter Löwenheim, under the pseudonym 'Miles'. Some members were former communists who had joined the KP-O (Communist Party-Opposition), a group formed in 1929 which opposed the subservience of the KPD to Moscow. *Neu Beginnen* split in 1935. One half, led by Löwenheim, believed resistance within Germany was not possible and ceased to be politically active. Löwenheim emigrated to Britain. The other half, led by Karl Frank and Richard

Löwenthal, continued to be active for a short period within Germany, before they were discovered by the Gestapo and forced to emigrate. Around twenty members were in exile in London during the war where they formed a loose group of intellectuals, well connected with parts of British academia and the media. On *Neu Beginnen* see Walter Loewenheim, *Geschichte der Org [Neu Beginnen] 1929–1935*, ed. Jan Foitzik (Berlin: Edition Hentrich, 1995); Eiber, *Die Sozialdemokratie in der Emigration*; Francis L. Carsten, 'From Revolutionary Socialism to German History', in Peter Alter (ed.), *Out of the Third Reich: Refugee Historians in Post-War Britain* (London and New York: I.B. Tauris, 1998); Mario Keßler, *Kommunismuskritik im westlichen Nachkriegsdeutschland: Franz Borkenau, Richard Löwenthal, Ossip Flechtheim* (Berlin: Verlag für Berlin-Brandenburg, 2011), pp. 76–77; Harold Hurwitz, *Demokratie und Antikommunismus in Berlin nach 1945: Vol. 4, Part 1, Die Anfänge des Widerstands* (Cologne: Verlag Wissenschaft und Politik, 1990), pp. 33–50; Richard Löwenthal, *Die Widerstandsgruppe Neu Beginnen* (Berlin: Gedenkstätte Deutscher Widerstand, 2001); Werner Röder, *Die deutschen sozialistischen Exilgruppen in Großbritannien 1940–1945* (Bonn-Bad Godesberg: Verlag Neue Gesellschaft GmbH, 1973).

5 On the ISK and Socialist Vanguard Group see Kelly, *Ethical Socialism and the Trade Unions*; Saran, *Never Give Up*; Geoff Spencer, *Beloved Alien: Walter Fliess 1901–1985* (Vancouver, British Columbia and Donhead St Andrew, Wiltshire: Privately printed, 1985); Christian Bailey, 'The European Discourse in Germany, 1939–1950: Three Case Studies', *German History*, Vol. 28, No. 4, December 2010, pp. 453–478; Minion, 'Left, Right or European?' pp. 229–248; R.M. Douglas, 'No Friend of Democracy: The Socialist Vanguard Group 1941–50', *Contemporary British History*, Vol. 16, No. 4, pp. 51–86; Lawrence Black, 'Social Democracy as a Way of Life: Fellowship and the Socialist Union, 1951–59', *Twentieth Century British History*, Vol. 10, No. 4, 1999, pp. 499–539; Eiber, *Die Sozialdemokratie in der Emigration*; Röder, *Die deutschen sozialistischen Exilgruppen in Großbritannien;* Hellmut Becker, Willi Eichler and Gustav Heckmann (eds), *Erziehung und Politik: Minna Specht zu ihrem 80. Geburtstag* (Frankfurt am Main: Verlag Öffentliches Leben, 1960); Werrner Link, *Die Geschichte des Internationalen Jugend-Bundes (IJD), und des Internationalen Sozialistischen Kampf-Bundes (ISK)* (Meisenheim am Glan: Verlag Anton Hain, 1964).

6 For Albu's political views see Albu, 'Back Bench Technocrat', and the Socialist Clarity Group's journal, *Labour Discussion Notes*, in AP14. For Flanders' views see Kelly, *Ethical Socialism and the Trade Unions*, material collected by Mary Saran on Allan Flanders' life and work, in Modern Records Centre, Flanders papers (henceforward FP), MSS.65/199, and editorials in the Socialist Vanguard Group's journal, *Socialist Commentary*, such as 'Liberated Britain', August 1945.

7 Editorial, 'Liberated Britain' in *Socialist Commentary*, August 1945, pp. 142–145. See also Wolfgang Rudzio, 'Großbritannien als sozialistische Besatzungsmacht in Deutschland – Aspekte des deutsch-britischen Verhältnisses 1945–1948', in Lothar

Kettenacker, Manfred Schlenke and Hullmut Seier (eds), *Studien zur Geschichte Englands und der deutsch-britischen Beziehungen: Festschrift für Paul Kluke* (Munich: Wilhelm Fink Verlag, 1981), p. 341.

8 Now part of Imperial College of Science and Technology, London.

9 Albu, 'Back Bench Technocrat', chapter I, p. 5.

10 Albu, 'Back Bench Technocrat'.

11 Ibid., chapter II, p. 11.

12 IWM Sound Archive, accession no. 4483, Francis Carsten.

13 Eiber, *Die Sozialdemokratie in der Emigration*, p. CLXII. During the war Gordon-Walker worked for the BBC on propaganda broadcasts to Germany, assisted by German exiles and *Neu Beginnen* members. See Patrick Gordon-Walker, *Political Diaries 1932–1971* (London: The Historians' Press, 1991).

14 Robert G.W. Kirk, 'Between the Clinic and the Laboratory: Ethology and Pharmacology in the Work of Michael Robin Alexander Chance, *c.*1946–1964', *Medical History*, October 2009, pp. 513–536. Available online: http://www.ncbi.nlm.nih.gov/pmc/articles/PMC2766138/ (accessed 8 March 2016).

15 Jon and David Kimche, *The Secret Roads: The 'Illegal' Migration of a People 1938–1948* (London: Secker and Warburg, 1954).

16 Albu, 'Back Bench Technocrat', chapter II, p. 11. Socialist Clarity Group papers (in AP 17/1 and 17/2), refer to *Neu Beginnen* members attending meetings or writing for the journal, including Paul and Evelyn Anderson and Richard (Rix) Löwenthal.

17 AP 7/1, 'Group Material' August 1939–August 1941, 'AA manifesto'.

18 AP 7/1, 'AA manifesto'. See also AP Box 14, 'Causes of German Aggression', in *Labour Discussion Notes,* 22 May 1941. A note in the file stated that the article had been written following discussions with 'Paul Sering, a member of the Neubeginnen group'. 'Paul Sering' was a pseudonym used by Richard Löwenthal.

19 Albu, 'Back Bench Technocrat', chapter II, pp. 27, 29.

20 Ibid., chapter II, p. 31; Jonathan Schneer, *Labour's Conscience: The Labour Left 1945–51* (Boston: Unwin Hyman, 1988), p. 166. Albu lost to Geoffrey Bing in Hornchurch and to Ian Mikardo in Reading.

21 Albu, 'Back Bench Technocrat', chapter II, p. 33. See also FO 1049/2113, 'Establishment of German Political and Intelligence branch', 22 February 1946.

22 Kelly, *Ethical Socialism and the Trade Unions*, p. 7; SVG MSS.173/17/4, Flanders' ISK membership application, 2 August 1930.

23 Kelly, *Ethical Socialism and the Trade Unions,* p. 16; Allan Flanders, 'Constant Adventure' and Hanna Bertholet, 'Gedanken über die Walkemühle', in Becker, Eichler and Heckmann (eds), *Erziehung und Politik*. For a history of the *Walkemühle* see Rudolf Gisselmann, *Geschichten von der Walkemühle*, available online: http://www.allerart.de/walkemuehle/index.shtml (accessed 8 March 2016).

24 SVG MSS.173/17/4, Flanders' ISK membership application, 2 August 1930.

25 Spencer, *Beloved Alien*, pp. 5–13; Kelly, *Ethical Socialism and the Trade Unions*, pp. 10–11; Black, 'Social Democracy as a Way of Life'; Link, *Die Geschichte des Internationalen Jugend-Bundes (IJD), und des Internationalen Sozialistischen Kampf-Bundes (ISK)*, pp. 3–38, 339–341.

26 Kelly, *Ethical Socialism and the Trade Unions*, p. 19.

27 Ibid., p. 20.

28 Ibid., pp. 20, 23; Black, 'Social Democracy as a Way of Life', p. 528; C.L. Herzenberg, 'Grete Hermann: An early contributor to quantum theory', 19 December 2008, available online: http://arxiv.org/pdf/0812.3986.pdf (accessed 8 March 2016).

29 Eiber, *Die Sozialdemokratie in der Emigration*, pp. CXXIX, 776.

30 FP MSS.65/199, material collected by Mary Saran on Allan Flanders' life and work, undated typescript by Flanders, 'The Future of British Socialism.'

31 Kelly, *Ethical Socialism and the Trade Unions*, pp. 57, 54.

32 Ibid., p. 57; Allan Flanders, 'Cartels – A Challenge', in *Socialist Commentary*, August 1945, pp. 145–149.

33 Eiber, *Die Sozialdemokratie in der Emigration*, pp. XXVIII–XXXIV.

34 SVG MSS.173/3/4, 'Minutes Agendas of Exec: 1943–48', executive meeting, November 1945.

35 FO 371/55612, 'Appointment of Regional Commissioners'.

36 FO 1049/2113, 'Establishment of German Political and Intelligence branch', 22 February 1946; AP 13/2, letter of appointment, 31 May 1946; Kelly, *Ethical Socialism and the Trade Unions*, p. 66; FP MSS.65/199, material collected by Mary Saran on Allan Flanders' life and work, letter from Albu, 21 January 1975.

37 AP 12/3, letter from Albu to his wife, 14 August 1946.

38 On the Fusion campaign see the monumental work by Hurwitz, *Demokratie und Antikommunismus in Berlin nach 1945*. See also a report by Noel Annan in AP 11/6 on 'The campaign for Fusion of the Social Democratic and Communist Parties in eastern Germany' and his later book Noel Annan, *Changing Enemies: The Defeat and Regeneration of Germany* (London: HarperCollins, 1995), pp. 187–197.

39 AP 11/6, Noel Annan, 'The campaign for Fusion of the Social Democratic and Communist Parties in eastern Germany', undated but marked in pencil '1946'.

40 Herf, *Divided Memory*, p. 15. At a party conference in October 1932, Ernst Thälmann, KPD party leader, quoted Stalin's view that fascism and 'social fascism' were 'twin brothers'.

41 Hurwitz, *Die Anfänge des Widerstands*, pp. 864, 1022ff.

42 AP 11/6, Noel Annan, 'The campaign for Fusion of the Social Democratic and Communist Parties'.

43 Annan, *Changing Enemies*, pp. 195, 198. See also Spencer Mawby, 'Revisiting Rapallo: Britain, Germany and the Cold War, 1945–1955', in Michael F. Hopkins, Michael D. Kandiah and Gillian Staerck (eds), *Cold War Britain, 1945–1964* (London: Palgrave Macmillan, 2003).

44 FO 1050/130, letter from Steel to Military Government detachment commanders, with a covering letter from Templer, 5 November 1945.
45 Hurwitz, *Die Anfänge des Widerstands*, pp. 33–50.
46 Keßler, *Kommunismuskritik im westlichen Nachkriegsdeutschland*, pp. 74ff; Eiber, *Die Sozialdemokratie in der Emigration*, pp. CVII, 646–649.
47 Annan, *Changing Enemies*, pp. 195, 198.
48 AP 13/2, diary entry for 3 February 1946.
49 Hurwitz, *Die Anfänge des Widerstands*, p. 873.
50 AP 13/2, diary entry for 25 February 1946; AP 12/3, letter to his wife, 20 February 1946.
51 Ibid., diary entry for 19 March 1946.
52 Albu, 'Back Bench Technocrat', chapter III, p. 17.
53 Ibid.
54 Ibid. See also Hurwitz, *Die Anfänge des Widerstands*, p. 1070; FO 371/55363, telegram from Bercomb (CCG Berlin) to FO, 31 March [1946] with the text of the statement issued by 'a senior member of the Control Commission in Berlin' [i.e. Albu].
55 Hurwitz, *Die Anfänge des Widerstands*, pp. 1194–1195.
56 Ibid., p. 1218. Around 19,526 Berlin SPD members voted against and 2,937 in favour of immediate Fusion; 14,763 voted for and 5,599 against collaboration. In total 23,775 members voted, out of 32,547 SPD members entitled to vote.
57 Ibid., pp. 1232, 1278.
58 FO 371/55363.
59 AP 13/2, diary entry for 25 March 1946.
60 AP 11/6, report by Annan on 'The campaign for Fusion of the Social Democratic and Communist Parties in eastern Germany'.
61 AP 28/3, memorandum, 14 March 1946.
62 AP 12/3, letter to his wife, 24 May 1946.
63 AP 28/3, memorandum, 19 June 1946.
64 E.g. Charles Wheeler, Foreword to *Germany 1944: The British Soldier's Pocketbook* (Kew, Richmond, Surrey: The National Archives, 2006), p. vi; Reinisch, *The Perils of Peace*, pp. 74ff; Marita Krauss, *Heimkehr in ein fremdes Land* (Munich: Verlag C. H. Beck, 2001), p. 65; Claus-Dieter Krohn and Axel Schildt (eds), *Zwischen den Stühlen: Remigranten und Remigration in der deutschen Medienöffentlichkeit der Nachkriegszeit* (Hamburg: Christians, 2002), p. 14; Gabriele Clemens, 'Remigranten in der Kultur- und Medienpolitick der britischen-Zone', in Krohn and Schildt, *Zwischen den Stühlen*, pp. 50–65; Kurt Kosyk, 'The Press in the British Zone of Germany', in Nicholas Pronay and Keith Wilson (eds), *The Political Re-education of Germany and Her Allies after World War II* (London and Sydney: Croom Helm, 1985), p. 113.
65 Isabelle Tombs, 'The Victory of Socialist "Vansittartism": Labour and the German Question, 1941–1945', *Twentieth Century British History*, Vol. 7, 1996, pp. 287–309.

66 On Vansittart and 'Vansittartism' see Jörg Später, *Vansittart: britische Debatten über Deutsche und Nazis 1902–1945* (Göttingen: Wallstein Verlag, 2003).

67 Philip Noel-Baker was appointed junior Minister of State for Foreign Affairs in 1945, Secretary of State for Air in 1946 and Secretary of State for Commonwealth Relations in 1947. Gordon-Walker was elected MP in 1945, appointed PPS to Herbert Morrison in October 1946 and a year later Under-Secretary of State for Commonwealth Affairs.

68 Später, *Vansittart*, p. 396.

69 Healey, *The Time of My Life*, p. 74.

70 Reusch, 'Die Londoner Institutionen der britischen Deutschlandpolitik 1943–48', p. 341. Similarly, in my research for this book I came across many examples of German refugees employed by Military Government or the Control Commission, including *inter alia* press officers George Clare, Michael Thomas, Robert Maxwell and Marion Bieber, the agricultural expert Werner Klatt, the education officer Werner Burmeister, Walter Fliess, economic adviser to the joint British and 'Bipartite Control Office, Francis Carsten, who wrote the Military Government handbook on Germany, and Harry Bohrer and Henry Ormond who helped create the news magazine *Der Spiegel*. Around 9,000 refugees volunteered to serve with the British army in the Pioneer Corps. Many ended the war in Germany and served as interpreters or in relatively junior positions in Military Government detachments. On the Pioneer Corps see Waltraud Strickhausen, 'Großbritannien', in Claus-Dieter Krohn, Patrik von zur Mühlen, Gerhard Paul and Lutz Winkler (eds), *Handbuch der deutschsprachigen Emigration 1933–1945* (Darmstadt: Wissenschaft Buchgesellshaft, 1998), p. 262.

71 Other leading SPD, ISK and *Neu Beginnen* members who spent the war in exile in Britain and later held important positions in post-war Germany in the SPD and trade unions include, *inter alia*, Fritz Heine, Werner Hansen, Fritz Eberhard, Waldemar von Knoeringen and Erwin Schoettle. Only around 3–4 per cent of the estimated 278,500 Jewish refugees who left Germany before 1939 returned after 1945. A higher proportion, of a much small initial number of non-Jewish refugees returned: 10–25 per cent of professionals such as academics and journalists, and around 50 per cent of political émigrés. Estimates vary, as no statistics were kept, refugees moved from one country to another both before and after the war, and many cannot be classified simply as 'Jews', 'socialists', 'trade unionists' or 'academics'. At the outbreak of war in 1939 there were around 40,000 German-Jewish refugees in Britain. In 1940 after the fall of France there were around 5,000 German political émigrés in Britain. Around 4,000 political émigrés returned to the western zones of Germany after the war from all exile countries. See the articles by Wolfgang Benz, 'Die jüdische Emigration', pp. 5–16, Werner Röder, 'Die politische Emigration', pp. 16–30, Waltraud Strickhausen, 'Großbritannien', pp. 253–254 and Marita Krauss, 'Westliche Besatzungszonen und Bundesrepublik

Deutschland', in the *Handbuch der deutschsprachigen Emigration 1933–1945*, pp. 1161–1171. See also the introduction and articles by Jan Foitzik, 'Remigranten in parlamentarischen Körperschaften Westdeutschlands', pp. 71–90, Hartmut Mehringer, 'Impulse socialdemokratischer Remigranten auf die Modernisierung der SPD', pp. 91–110 and Julia Angster, 'Wertewandel in den Gewerkschaften: Zur Rolle gewerkschaftlicher Remigranten in der Bundesrepublik der 1950er Jahre', in Klaus-Dieter Krohn and Patrik von zur Mühlen (eds), *Rückkehr und Aufbau nach 1945: Deutsche Remigranten im öffentlichen Leben Nachkriegsdeutschlands* (Marburg: Metropolis Verlag, 1997), pp. 111–138.

72 FO 1030/307, letter from Richards to Robertson, 18 April 1946.

73 Ibid., reply from Robertson to Richards, 25 April 1946.

74 AP 12/3, letter to his wife, 3 August 1946.

75 Ibid., letter to his wife, 9 June 1946.

76 Ibid., letter to his wife, 3 August 1946.

77 Albu, 'Back Bench Technocrat', chapter IV, p. 21.

78 AP 12/3, letter to his wife, 9 June 1946.

79 Albu, 'Back Bench Technocrat', chapter III, p. 8.

80 'The British Zone', *Socialist Commentary*, November 1946. All articles were unsigned, but this piece was very probably written by Flanders, as it was his area of expertise and he remained chairman of the editorial board throughout his time in Germany.

81 FP MSS.65/199, 'Personal Notes', October 1947.

82 AP 12/3, letter to his wife, 3 August 1946.

83 Ibid., undated letter to his wife, postmarked 11 February 1946.

84 Ibid., letter to his wife, 16 February 1946.

85 Ibid., diary entries for 12, 14 February 1946.

86 FO 1030/303, letter from Robertson to Street, 26 March 1946.

87 AP 12/3, letter to his wife, 22 March 1946.

88 Ibid., letter to his wife, 26 March 1946.

89 Ibid., letter of appointment, 31 May 1946; letter to his wife, 26 June 1946.

90 Ibid., letter to his wife, 14 April 1946.

91 Ibid., letter to his wife, 3 August 1946.

92 As Deputy Chairman of the Governmental Sub-Commission and, from July 1946, Chairman of SCOGAS, the Standing Committee on Governmental and Administrative Structure.

93 Reusch, 'Die Londoner Institutionen', p. 402.

94 Reusch, *Deutsches Berufsbeamtentum*, pp. 363–364.

95 Reusch, 'Die Londoner Institutionen', p. 402.

96 Albu, 'Back Bench Technocrat', chapter III, p. 27.

97 FO 1051/224; FO 1050/138.

98 Ibid.; FO 1030/148, 'The Evolution of Government in the British Zone', 3 December 1945.

99 FO 1051/224, FO 1030/148 and BLM 88/8, 'The Evolution of Government in the British Zone (II)', 25 March 1946.

100 FO 371/55612.

101 Ibid.

102 FO 371/55591, C10014, 'Future political structure of Germany'.

103 FO 371/55614, C6002, 'Development of Government in the British Zone', letter from Dean to Wilberforce, 1 July 1946.

104 FO 1051/224, memorandum on 'Germany: the Nature of Federal Government' with an attached note stating this had been prepared by the Deputy President, Governmental Sub-Commission (i.e. Albu). Undated, but probably written in June 1946, as Albu told his wife on 22 June 1946 (AP 12/3) that he was working on a paper on federalism.

105 Ibid.

106 Reusch, *Deutsches Berufsbeamtentum*, pp. 363–364.

107 FO 371/55593, C12323, 'Policy in Germany', letter from Sholto Douglas to The Permanent Secretary, COGA, 5 October 1946.

108 FO 371/55591, C10014, 'Future political structure of Germany'.

109 AP 12/3, letter from Albu to his wife, 14 August 1946.

110 FO 371/55591, C10670, 'Note on a short visit to Berlin by Mr Dean between the evening of Friday, August 16th and the morning of Monday 19th'.

111 CAB 129-12-40 Foreign Office Cabinet Paper on Germany 9 September 1946; HC Deb. vol. 427, c1510, in Beate Ruhm von Oppen (ed.), *Documents on Germany under Occupation 1945–1954* (London, New York and Toronto: Oxford University Press, 1955), p. 182.

112 CAB 129/12/40, 9 September 1946; FO 800/466; FO 371/55591.

113 Ruhm von Oppen (ed.), *Documents on Germany under Occupation*, pp. 192–195; 'This New Germany', *British Zone Review,* Vol. 1, No. 33, 21 December 1946, p. 1.

114 AP 12, 'Draft of a talk to German Press to be given by Mr. A.H. Albu', 8 February 1947.

115 AP 11/1, letter to C. O'Neill, 30 January 1947.

116 Ibid.

117 AP 11/1, Control Commission BFN broadcast, 13 March 1947, 'Reform of Government in the British Zone'.

118 FP MSS.65/199, 'Personal Notes' by Allan Flanders, October 1947.

119 AP 28/3, Memorandum, 11 September 1947.

120 AP 12/2, letter from Albu to Mayhew 1 November 1949 and reply 12 December 1949. Christopher Mayhew, Foreign Office Minister for Germany, told Albu that staff numbers were around 7,000, but would be reduced further to 3,000–3,500 by December 1950.

121 AP 11/1, letter from Albu to Hynd, 26 March 1947.

122 Albu, 'Back Bench Technocrat', pp. 7–8.

123 'The British Zone', *Socialist Commentary*, November 1946.
124 Ibid.
125 FP MSS.65/199, 'Personal Notes' by Allan Flanders, October 1947. Another copy is in AP 12/2.
126 FP MSS.65/199, 'Personal Notes'. See also Klaus Körner, 'Emigranten im kulturellen Wiederaufbau: Die Europäische Verlagsanstalt', in Krohn and von zur Mühlen (eds), *Rückkehr und Aufbau nach 1945*, pp. 139–156.
127 FP MSS.65/199, 'Personal Notes'.
128 Flanders was appointed Senior Lecturer in Industrial Relations at the University of Oxford in 1949 and elected Fellow of Nuffield College in 1964. He and Hugh Clegg were the two leading members of the Oxford School of Industrial Relations.
129 Kelly, *Ethical Socialism and the Trade Unions*, pp. 87, 57.
130 FP MSS.65/199, material collected by Mary Saran on Allan Flanders' life and work, letter from Albu, 21 January 1975. See also AP 122/3, letters to Albu from Marion Bieber, 26 February 1949, 21 August 1949, 25 October 1949.
131 AP 13/2, handwritten letter from Robertson to Albu, 20 December 1947.
132 SVG MSS.173/3/4, 'Minutes Agendas of Exec: 1943–48', personal message, unsigned but almost certainly by Flanders as the leader of Socialist Vanguard Group, advising members of the decision to dissolve the group: 'The hope of realising the Just State in our time is a receding dream. Its achievement will be the responsibility of those who follow us. But we can try and help to smooth the path.' The Socialist Vanguard Group was succeeded by a less formal association, the Socialist Union. The group's journal *Socialist Commentary* continued to appear until 1979. See Black, 'Social Democracy as a Way of Life: Fellowship and the Socialist Union, 1951–59'.

Chapter 7

1 Bath Record Office, Berry papers (henceforward BRO BP), telegram from Helmut Schmidt to Joan Berry, 3 March 1979.
2 Somerset Heritage Centre, Berry papers (henceforward SHC BP) A/BCU8, Monthly Reports for March 1947, December 1948.
3 Private family archive, letter from Berry to his great-niece, Kate Owen, December 1975.
4 Hilary Ann Balshaw, 'The British Occupation in Germany, 1945–1949, with special reference to Hamburg' (PhD Diss: Oxford, 1972), p. 53.
5 Ahrens, *Die Briten in Hamburg*, pp. 84–85.
6 Rosenfeld, 'The Anglo-German Encounter', p. 245.
7 Ahrens, *Die Briten in Hamburg*, p. 255; SHC BP A/BCU9, notebook with translated extracts from German newspapers.
8 FO 371/55612, 'Appointment of Regional Commissioners'.

9 The other three Regional Commissioners appointed in 1946 were William Asbury, a former leader of Sheffield City Council, Hugh de Crespigny, a former Air Vice-Marshal who resigned his position in 1944 to stand unsuccessfully for Parliament as a Labour Party candidate, and General Gordon Macready, chief of staff in Washington during the war. Montgomery and Robertson requested that one commissioner should be a senior army officer, as they believed this would be 'gratifying to the military element of the Control Commission'. Macready wrote later that it was thought desirable to have a general in his region, Lower Saxony, 'owing to the long common frontier with the Russian Zone and the likelihood of incidents requiring co-operation with the Army'. See Lt-General Sir Gordon Macready, *In the Wake of the Great* (London: William Clowes and Sons Ltd, 1965), p. 206.

10 The Union Discount Company of London was the leading player in the London money market, offering short-term loans to international trading organizations on the security of bills of exchange guaranteed by London merchant banks. Many German banks were customers of the Union Discount Company and were visited by Berry in the 1920s and 1930s.

11 Bath Record Office, 'The Life and Times of Sir Vaughan Berry', set of 45 discs (henceforward 'Berry Memoir'), discs 29–33; BRO BP, press cutting from *The Guardian,* 28 October 1964, 'London Letter' column (on the XYZ Club); SHC BP A/BCU4, '1927–1971: Papers relating to the XYZ Club'.

12 FO 371/55612, 'Appointment of Regional Commissioners'.

13 Montgomery was born in 1887, Douglas in 1893, Robertson in 1896, Bishop and Ingrams in 1897, Albu in 1903 and Flanders in 1910.

14 Berry Memoir, disc 25.

15 Berry Memoir, discs 1–3; BRO BP, press cutting of the obituary of 'The Late Mr. J.H. Berry', *Madras Mail,* 29 May 1895.

16 Berry Memoir, disc 4. Pupils were sponsored by members of the school trust and were charged no fees for education, food or accommodation, until they reached the age of 15, when they had to leave.

17 Ibid., disc 5.

18 Ibid., discs 5–8.

19 Private family archive, letter from Berry to his great-niece, Kate Owen, 10 June 1971.

20 Berry Memoir, discs 13–15.

21 Ibid., discs 15–16.

22 Berry Memoir, disc 16; Private family archive, letter from Berry to his great-niece, Kate Owen, 20 December 1973.

23 SHC BP A/BCU7, notes for speech on 'The Problem of Germany'.

24 BRO BP, letter to the historian Ulrich Reusch, undated, probably March 1978.

25 Berry Memoir, discs 40–41.

26 Ibid., disc 41.

27 Ibid.
28 Berry Memoir, disc 41.
29 FO 371/55612, 'Appointment of Regional Commissioners'; Berry Memoir, disc 42.
30 Ahrens, *Die Briten in Hamburg*, p. 366; *British Zone Review*, Vol. 1, No. 43, 10 May 1947, p. 6.
31 Berry Memoir, disc 43.
32 Ibid., discs 43–44; BRO, BP, 'Sir Vaughan Berry's speeches (Hamburg)'.
33 Berry Memoir, disc 43.
34 Ibid., disc 44.
35 Ibid., disc 45; SHC, BP ABCU8, Monthly Report for February 1947.
36 Wildt, *Der Traum vom Sattwerden*, p. 47.
37 Axel Schildt, 'Das "Hamburg project". Eine kritische Phase der britischen Besatzungspolitik in Hamburg 1945–47', in Frank Otto and Thilo Schulz (eds), *Großbritannien und Deutschland: gesellschaftliche, kulturelle und politische Beziehungen im 19. und 20. Jahrhundert* (Rheinfelden: Schäuble Verlag, 1999).
38 SHC BP A/BCU8, Monthly Report for February 1947.
39 Ibid.
40 Wildt, *Der Traum vom Sattwerden*, p. 121.
41 SHC BP A/BCU8, Monthly Reports for February and March 1947.
42 Ibid., Monthly Report for January 1947.
43 Wildt, *Der Traum vom Sattwerden*, p. 51.
44 SHC BP A/BCU8, Monthly Report for April 1947.
45 Ahrens, *Die Briten in Hamburg*, p. 366.
46 SHC BP A/BCU8, Monthly Report for January 1947.
47 SHC BP A/BCU7, speech dated 29 December 1947.
48 Ibid.
49 Ahrens, *Die Briten in Hamburg*, p. 369.
50 SHC BP A/BCU8, Monthly Report for January 1947.
51 Wildt, *Der Traum vom Sattwerden;* p. 56; Arnold Sywottek, 'Verständigung mit den "Engländern" nach dem Zweiten Weltkrieg. Zu einem noch ungeschriebenen Kapitel der "Vielvölkerstadt" Hamburg', in Frank Otto and Thilo Schulz (eds), *Großbritannien und Deutschland: gesellschaftliche, kulturelle und politische Beziehungen im 19. und 20. Jahrhundert* (Rheinfelden: Schäuble Verlag, 1999), p. 150.
52 SHC BP A/BCU8, Monthly Report for June 1947.
53 Ibid., Monthly Report for October 1947.
54 Rosenfeld, 'The Anglo-German Encounter', p. 151.
55 Ahrens, *Die Briten in Hamburg*, p. 142; Rosenfeld, 'The Anglo-German Encounter', pp. 136–137; Berry Memoir, disc 45.
56 Schildt, 'Das "Hamburg project"', pp. 137–139.
57 Ibid., pp. 140–143; FO 1014/890, 'Notes for the Commander' on progress to date', by L.G. Holmes, 27 June 1946.

58 Schildt, 'Das "Hamburg project"', pp. 143–145; FO 1014/48.
59 Ibid.
60 Ibid.
61 Berry Memoir, disc 43.
62 Ibid.
63 FO 1005/1354, minutes of Regional Commissioners' conference, 17 December 1946.
64 There is a brief reference to the decision to suspend the project in FO 1014/15, minutes of an informal conference of Regional Commissioners with the Chancellor (Hynd), 15 January 1947.
65 FO 1030/306, letter from Berry to Robertson, 28 December 1946.
66 FO 1030/306, letter from Robertson to Berry, 3 January 1947.
67 Rosenfeld, 'The Anglo-German Encounter', p. 144.
68 FO 1032/1272, memo from Armytage to Robertson, 'Dangerous Overcrowding at Hamburg', 24 July 1946, cited by Ahrens, *Die Briten in Hamburg*, p. 166.
69 Ibid.
70 Philip Ramsbotham, (Lord Soulbury), educated at Eton and Magdalen College Cambridge, later a British diplomat and ambassador to the United States, 1974–1977.
71 FO 1014/897, 'Brief for Deputy Regional Commissioner', 20 September 1946, cited by Schildt, 'Das "Hamburg project"', p. 146.
72 Ibid. Ramsbotham's recommendation foreshadowed the decision two years later, in 1949, to locate the capital of the Federal Republic in Bonn, a small town at the southern edge of the British Zone.
73 FO 1014/904, minutes of a meeting to discuss and 'examine the eventual implementation of the Hamburg Project', 3 January 1947.
74 FO 1014/15, informal conference of Regional Commissioners with the Chancellor, 15 January 1947.
75 FO 1014/890, letter from the *Bürgermeister* to the Regional Commissioner, 28 March 1947.
76 FO 1014/890, 'Minutes of a meeting of the Regional Commissioner's conference with the Burgomaster and members of the Building Administration', 1 April 1947.
77 FO 1014/890.
78 SHC BP A/BCU8, letter from Robertson to Berry, 18 February 1949.
79 'Grindel high-rise houses', after the name of the district in which they are situated.
80 'Renaissance der Grindelhochhäuser', *Die Welt*, 12 July 2006, available online: http://www.welt.de/print-welt/article228872/Renaissance-der-Grindelhochhaeuser.html (accessed 8 March 2016).
81 FO 936/693, 'Relations between CCG Personnel and Germans', letter from Pakenham to Robertson, 25 March 1948.

82 Rosenfeld, 'The Anglo-German Encounter'.
83 FO 1050/1312, 'Anglo-German Discussion Groups', cited in Rosenfeld, 'The Anglo-German Encounter', pp. 215–219.
84 FO 1050/1290, 'Education for Citizenship', cited in Rosenfeld, 'The Anglo-German Encounter', p. 236.
85 Robert Birley, 'Education for Democracy', *British Zone Review*, Vol. 2, No. 4, 27 September 1947, cited in Rosenfeld, 'The Anglo-German Encounter', pp. 220–230.
86 FO 1050/1312, memo by M.M. Simons, cited in Rosenfeld, 'The Anglo-German Encounter', p. 215. The 'British Way and Purpose' was the title of a series of booklets produced during the war by the Directorate of Army Education.
87 FO 1005/1354, minutes of the 3rd Regional Commissioners' conference, 11 September 1946.
88 *British Zone Review,* Vol. 1, No. 34, 4 January 1947, p. 16.
89 Ibid.
90 Rosenfeld, 'The Anglo-German Encounter', p. 245.
91 FO 1030/172, letter from General Philip Balfour to Regional Commissioners, 18 July 1946, cited in Ahrens, *Die Briten in Hamburg,* p. 361.
92 FO 936/693, 'Special Routine Order' No. 263, 'Relations between C.C.G. Personnel and Germans', 30 May 1947.
93 Ibid.
94 FO 936/693, draft order submitted to the 16th Regional Commissioners' conference, 18 May 1948.
95 SHC BP A/BCU7, speech to the Hamburg International Club, cited in Rosenfeld, 'The Anglo-German Encounter', p. 267 and Ahrens, *Die Briten in Hamburg,* p. 377.
96 Ibid.
97 Ahrens, *Die Briten in Hamburg,* pp. 420–422; Arnold Sywottek, 'Verständigung mit den "Engländern"', p. 154.
98 SHC BP A/BCU8, Monthly Report for December 1948.
99 Ahrens, *Die Briten in Hamburg,* p. 426; http://www.anglo-german-club.de/index.php (accessed 8 March 2016).
100 SHC BP A/BCU8, Monthly Report for March 1947.
101 Ibid., Monthly Report for February 1948.
102 Ibid., Monthly Report for August 1948.
103 Ibid., Monthly Report for October 1948.
104 Ibid., Monthly Report for March 1948.
105 Ibid., Monthly Report for June 1948.
106 Ibid., Monthly Report for July 1948.
107 Ibid.
108 Ibid., Monthly Report for April 1949.
109 '*Ein grossartiger Mann*', Balshaw, 'The British Occupation of Germany', p. 243.

110 SHC BP A/BCU8, letter from Robertson to Berry, 18 February 1949.
111 SHC BP A/BCU11, speech by Berry given during his return visit to Hamburg in 1959.
112 Schildt, 'Das "Hamburg project"', p. 131.
113 Sywottek, 'Verständigung mit den "Engländern"', pp. 150–151.
114 Ahrens, *Die Briten in Hamburg*, pp. 446–447.
115 Rosenfeld, 'The Anglo-German Encounter', pp. 346, 353.
116 Ibid., pp. 347–348.
117 Ibid., p. 18.
118 SHC BP A/BCU7, speech at a reception on leaving Hamburg, undated.

Chapter 8

1 Imperial War Museum Sound Archive (henceforward IWM SA), accession number 30895, interview with J.M.G. Thexton.
2 The twenty-one IWM SA oral history interviews were with Bernard Garrood, accession no. 16307; Ronald Mallabar, accession no. 11211; George Philip Henry James, accession no. 14837; Kenneth Taylor, accession no. 23230; Frank Arthur Bicknell, accession no. 23844; Samuel Falle, accession no. 25207; Alfred Leslie (Les) Lucas, accession no. 29446; Ralph Frederick Dye, accession no. 20064; John Isaac Godfrey Brown, accession no. 11035; Oliver Bland, accession no. 19606; Stephen Lewis Edmonstone Hastings, accession no. 27455; Bernard Fisher, accession no. 10653; Eric Gregg-Rowbury, accession no. 30418; Walter Greenhalgh, accession no. 11187; Annie (Nancie) Norman, accession no. 16705; Martin Cosmo Hastings, accession no. 20733; James Samuel Chambers, accession no. 11329; Arthur Norman Travett, accession no. 10462; James Robert Heppell, accession no. 16778; John Ashcombe, accession no. 23187; and Richard Harland, accession no. 12920. Michael Howard was also interviewed by the IWM sound archive, accession no. 31405, and my interview with Sir Michael Palliser has been lodged with the archive, accession no. 32236/4.
3 For a discussion of the use and relevance of the concept in modern German historiography see Ulrike Jureit and Michael Wildt (eds), *Generationen: Zur Relevanz eines wissenschaftlichen Grundbegriffs* (Hamburg: Hamburger Edition, 2005).
4 Karl Mannheim, 'Der Problem der Generationen', *Kölner Vierteljahrshefte fur Sociologie*, No. 7, 1928, pp. 157–185 and 309–330; Helmut Fogt, *Politische Generationen, Empirische Bedeutung und theoretisches Modell* (Opladen, 1982), cited in von Hodenberg, *Konsens und Krise*, p. 28.
5 Historians of modern Germany who have used the concept of 'generation' include: Dirk Moses, *German Intellectuals and the Nazi Past* (New York:

Cambridge University Press, 2007); von Hodenberg, *Konsens und Krise*; Herbert, 'Liberalisierung als Lernprozeß'; Fulbrook, *Dissonant Lives*.

6 Other generals who served under Montgomery in Germany were of a similar age: General Horrocks was born in 1895, General Templer in 1898.

7 IWM SA, Frank Arthur Bicknell.

8 IWM SA, Richard Harland.

9 IWM SA, Palliser.

10 John Chaloner, *Occupational Hazard* (Wallington, Surrey: Severn House Publishers, 1991), p. 402.

11 Only one IWM interviewee mentioned Montgomery and this was in relation to the war in North Africa, not Germany. He said that when Montgomery arrived, the whole atmosphere changed, adding 'incredible man' (IWM SA, Bernard Garrood).

12 Similar views were held by many other British soldiers facing demobilization at the end of the war, as described in Alan Allport, *Demobbed* (New Haven and London: Yale University Press, 2009).

13 Allport, *Demobbed*, pp. 19–49.

14 IWM SA, Thexton.

15 Ibid.

16 Ibid.

17 Articles 48 and 49 of the Hague Conventions of 1907 allow for an army of occupation to collect taxes to 'defray the expenses of the administration of the occupied territory' and raise other contributions and levies for the needs of the army and the administration of the territory. See Yale Law School, The Avalon Project, 'Laws of War'. Available online: http://avalon.law.yale.edu/20th_century/hague04.asp (accessed 8 March 2016).

18 IWM SA, Thexton.

19 Ibid.

20 IWM SA, Palliser.

21 A leading British public school, with a reputation for preparing pupils to follow a career as officers in the army.

22 IWM SA, Palliser.

23 John Chaloner Obituary, *The Times*, 16 February 2007.

24 Information provided by Joan Woodward, John Chaloner's sister, as written answers to questions, 10 April 2010.

25 Hildegard Feidel-Mertz, 'Integration and Formation of Identity: Exile Schools in Great Britain', *Shofar: An Interdisciplinary Journal of Jewish Studies*, Vol. 23, No. 1, 2004, pp. 71–84.

26 Douglas Martin, 'Ernst Bulova, 98, Founder of Camp with a Free Spirit', *The New York Times*, 28 January 2001.

27 Woodward, written answers to questions.

28 Brawand, *Der Spiegel – ein Besatzungskind*, p. 14.

29 Ibid., pp. 27–28.
30 One of the most prestigious British public schools.
31 IWM SA, Michael Howard.
32 Ibid.; Howard, *Otherwise Occupied*, pp. 22–23.
33 Sean Longden, *T-Force: The Race for Nazi War Secrets, 1945* (London: Constable, 2009).
34 Howard, *Otherwise Occupied.*
35 IWM SA, Richard Harland.
36 Ibid., Eric Gregg-Rowbury.
37 Ibid., Annie 'Nancy' Norman.
38 Ibid., George Philip Henry James; Kenneth Taylor.
39 Ibid., Thexton.
40 Ibid., Ronald Mallabar.
41 Ibid., Bernard Garrood.
42 Ibid., John Ashcombe.
43 Balfour and Mair, *Four Power Control*, p. 7.
44 Alice Förster and Birgit Beck, 'Post-Traumatic Stress Disorder and World War II: Can a Psychiatric Concept Help Us Understand Postwar Society?' in Richard Bessel and Dirk Schumann (eds), *Life after Death: Approaches to a Cultural and Social History of Europe during the 1940s and 1950s* (Cambridge: Cambridge University Press, 2003); Jordan (ed.), *Conditions of Surrender*, p. 149.
45 Jordan (ed.), *Conditions of Surrender*, p. 149, provides figures of an estimated 4.2 million civilians killed in Poland and 7 million in the Soviet Union.
46 IWM SA, Samuel Falle, James Samuel Chambers.
47 IWM SA, Chambers.
48 Ibid.
49 IWM SA, Howard.
50 Howard, *Otherwise Occupied*, pp. 14, 54.
51 IWM SA, Palliser.
52 Ibid.
53 E.g. Ursula Büttner, 'Not nach der Befreiung. Die Situation der Deutschen Juden in der britischen Besatzungszone 1945–1948', in *Das Unrechtsregime*, Vol. 2 (Hamburg: Christians, 1986); Frank Stern, 'The Historic Triangle: Occupiers, Germans and Jews in Postwar Germany', in Robert G. Moeller (ed.), *West Germany under Construction: Politics, Society and Culture in the Adenauer Era* (Ann Arbor: The University of Michigan Press, 1997).
54 Hagit Lavsky, 'A Community of Survivors: Bergen-Belsen as a Jewish Centre after 1945', in Jo Reilly, David Ceserani, Tony Kushner and Colin Richmond (eds), *Belsen in History & Memory* (London and Portland, OR: Frank Cass, 1997); Johannes-Dieter Steinert, *Nach Holocaust und Zwangsarbeit: Britische humanitäre Hilfe in*

Deutschland, Die Helfer, die Befreiten und die Deutschen (Osnabrück: secolo Verlag, 2000), pp. 104–105, 123.

55 Steinert, *Nach Holocaust und Zwangsarbeit*, p. 101.

56 Ibid., p. 100; Atina Grossmann, 'Trauma, Memory and Motherhood: Germans and Jewish Displaced Persons in Post-Nazi Germany, 1945–1949', in Bessel and Schumann (eds), *Life after Death*, pp. 97–98.

57 Wolfgang Jacobmeyer, *Vom Zwangsarbeiter zum Heimatlosen Ausländer* (Göttingen: Vandenhoeck & Ruprecht, 1985), pp. 41, 185.

58 Balfour and Mair, *Four Power Control*, p. 121; Matthew Frank, *Expelling the Germans: British Opinion and Post-1945 Population Transfer in Context* (Oxford: Oxford University Press, 2007); Francis Graham-Dixon, *The Allied Occupation of German: The Refugee Crisis, Denazification and the Path to Reconstruction* (London and New York: I.B. Tauris, 2013).

59 FO 1030/307, letter from Galloway to Robertson, 21 April 1946, enclosing a report by Major Murphy, 14 April 1946, and reply from Robertson to Galloway, 2 May 1946.

60 Ibid.

61 For the background and context to the dispute and some of the reasons for Jewish survivors' discontent at their treatment by the British, see Lavsky, 'A Community of Survivors'; Büttner, 'Not nach der Befreiung'.

62 On the *Exodus* affair, see Ruth Gruber, *Exodus 1947: The Ship that Launched a Nation* (New York: Union Square Press, 2007). First published in 1948 as *Destination Palestine: The Story of the Haganah Ship Exodus 1947*; Jon and David Kimche, *The Secret Roads*, pp. 175–192; David Holly, *Exodus 1947* (Annapolis, MD: Naval Institute Press, 1969), revised edition 1995; Aviva Halamish, *The Exodus Affair: Holocaust Survivors and the Struggle for Palestine* (London: Vallentine Mitchell, 1998), translated by Ora Cummings.

63 Jon and David Kimche, *The Secret Roads*, p. 175.

64 The accounts by Kimche, Gruber, Holly and Halamish broadly agree that there was relatively little resistance to the disembarkation from refugees on the first two ships. On the *Empire Rival* this was probably because the refugees knew that a bomb had been left on the ship and wished to leave before it exploded. On the third ship, the *Runnymede Park*, coshes and fire hoses were used by British troops to force refugees to disembark. Accounts differ as to how serious the injuries were. The most reliable account appears to be by Halamish (*The Exodus Affair*, p. 215) who states that fifteen men and seven women required medical attention.

65 Kimche, *The Secret Roads*, p. 192; Holly, *Exodus 1947*, p. 203; Gruber, *Exodus 1947*, pp. 187–188.

66 SHC BP A/BCU8, Monthly Report for September 1947.

67 Ibid.

68 AB1, Bishop, 'Look Back with Pleasure', pp. 100–101. Bishop joined a German audience in Hamburg, incognito in civilian clothes, to observe their reaction to the film, which was to watch it in complete silence and remain silent afterwards. 'Some of the women were in tears.' He concluded that a large number of those in the audience had not known of the 'terrible cruelties which had been perpetrated in these places', or 'perhaps they did not wish to know'. See also Stephan Dolezel, 'Welt im Film 1945 and the Re-education of Occupied Germany', in K.R.M. Short and Stephan Dolezel (eds), *Hitler's Fall: The Newsreel Witness* (London, New York and Sydney: Croom Helm, 1988) and Roger Smither, 'Welt im Film: Anglo-American Newsreel Policy', in Nicholas Pronay and Keith Wilson (eds), *The Political Re-education of Germany and Her Allies after World War II* (London and Sydney: Croom Helm, 1985). There was a clear break in content and style of the Anglo-American newsreel *Welt im Film* in August 1945, compulsorily shown in all German cinemas in the US and British Zones. For the first four months after its first release on 18 May 1945, the newsreel was produced by the Americans and emphasized subjects such as Allied unity and power and German guilt and atrocities. The fifth issue of the newsreel, released on 15 June 1945, was devoted entirely to material from the camps. After the British joined the newsreel production staff in September the tone softened, with Germans presenting their point of view in front of Allied cameras, on issues relating to post-war reconstruction.
69 Woodward, written answers to questions.
70 Chaloner, *Occupational Hazard*, p. 353.
71 Brawand, *Der Spiegel - ein Besatzungskind*, p. 196.
72 Woodward, written answers to questions.
73 IWM SA, Martin Cosmo Hastings.
74 Ibid., James Robert Heppell.
75 Ibid., Frank Arthur Bicknell.
76 Bessel, *Germany 1945*, p. 52.
77 Ibid., p. 164.
78 Ibid., p.165.
79 IWM SA, Ronald Mallabar.
80 Ibid.
81 L. Mosley, *Report from Germany* (London: Victor Gollancz Ltd, 1945), p. 93. The war correspondent Alan Moorhead, who was also present at the liberation of Belsen, responded similarly. See Ramsden, *Don't Mention the War*, pp. 226–227.
82 Patrick Gordon Walker, *The Lid Lifts* (London: Victor Gollancz Ltd, 1945).
83 WO32/15772, Lt. Col. J.H.A. Sparrow (later Warden of All Soul's College, Oxford), 'Report on Visit to 21 Army Group and Tour of Second Army 30th March to 5th May 1945'. Sparrow reported that all knew of the 'uncovering' of the camps but reactions were mixed. While there was some increase in hostility to Germans generally, most British soldiers made a distinction between the SS, who they believed were responsible for the camps, and the 'ordinary Germany citizen'.

84 IWM SA, Palliser.
85 IWM SA, Martin Cosmo Hastings.
86 Ibid.
87 IWM SA, Bicknell.
88 *British Zone Review*, Vol. 1, No. 2, 13 October 1945.

Chapter 9

1 'The Englishman who saved Hitler's Beetle', *BBC News*, 30 July 2003, available online: http://news.bbc.co.uk/1/hi/magazine/3104469.stm (accessed 8 March 2016).
2 Michael Howard, *Otherwise Occupied: Letters Home from the Ruins of Nazi Germany* (Tiverton, Devon: Old Street Publishing, 2010), p. 90.
3 IWM SA, Thexton.
4 William (later Lord) Barnetson, was chairman of United Newspapers. See Edward Pickering, 'Barnetson, William Denholm, Baron Barnetson (1917–1981)', rev. *Oxford Dictionary of National Biography* (Oxford University Press, 2004), available online: http://www.oxforddnb.com/view/article/30793 (accessed 15 March 2016). On Annan and Maxwell see Annan, *Changing Enemies*; Tom Bower, *Maxwell: The Outsider* (London: Mandarin Paperbacks, 1991), first published by Aurum Press Limited, 1988; Richard Davenport-Hines, 'Maxwell, (Ian) Robert (1923–1991)', in *Oxford Dictionary of National Biography* (Oxford University Press, 2004); online edition, January 2014, available online: http://www.oxforddnb.com/view/article/49894 (accessed 15 March 2016).
5 The number '30' referred to the army corps to which the information unit was attached. The British 21st Army Group comprised three corps. At the end of the war 30 Corps occupied most of Lower Saxony, 8 Corps occupied Schleswig Holstein and Hamburg, and 1 Corps occupied the Rhineland, Ruhr and Westphalia.
6 Brawand, *Der Spiegel – ein Besatzungskind*, pp. 27–28.
7 Ibid., pp. 31, 37–70.
8 Jessica Gienow-Hecht, 'Art Is Democracy and Democracy Is Art: Culture, Propaganda and the *Neue Zeitung* in Germany, 1944–1947', *Diplomatic History*, Vol. 23, No. 1, Winter 1999, pp. 21–43; Jessica Gienow-Hecht, *Transmission Impossible: American Journalism as Cultural Diplomacy in Postwar Germany 1945–1955*' (Baton Rouge: Louisiana State University Press, 1999), p. 167.
9 Hodenberg, *Konsens und Krise*, 2006, p. 90.
10 Ibid, pp. 219–225.
11 Peter Merseburger, *Rudolf Augstein* (Munich: Deutsche Verlags-Anstalt, 2007), p. 7; 'Einem Blatt des Widerspruchs und des Infragestellens, ohne die demokratische Diskurs nicht zu denken ist.'

12 Hodenberg, *Konsens und Krise,* pp. 225–227.
13 E.g. Ivone Kirkpatrick, a senior Foreign Office Official, was Controller of BBC European services from 1941 to 1944, then briefly Deputy Director of PWE and joint head of the embryonic Control Commission for Germany, before returning to the Foreign Office in 1945. He was appointed British High Commissioner in Germany in 1950 and Permanent Under-Secretary at the Foreign Office in 1953. See Yvone Kirkpatrick, *The Inner Circle* (London: Macmillan, 1959).
14 Balfour, 'In Retrospect'; Garnett, *The Secret History of PWE*; AB1, Bishop, 'Look Back with Pleasure', p. 86.
15 Garnett, *The Secret History of PWE*, pp. 41–42; Conrad Pütter, 'German Refugees and British Propaganda', in Gerhard Hirschfeld (ed.), *Exile in Great Britain: Refugees from Hitler's Germany* (Leamington Spa: Berg Publishers, 1984).
16 German refugees employed by the station included *Neu Beginnen* members Waldemar von Knoeringen, Richard Löwenthal and Werner Klatt, and former ISK member Fritz Eberhard.
17 Pütter, 'German refugees and British Propaganda'; Delmer, *Black Boomerang.*
18 Balfour, 'In Retrospect'.
19 Ibid.; Reusch, 'Die Londoner Institutionen', pp. 318–443.
20 FO 371/39054, Germany File no. 78, C6084, SHAEF PWD paper, 'Proposals for the establishment of a Tripartite Anglo-American Russia control over Information and Propaganda in Germany during the occupation period', 24 April 1944.
21 Koszyk, 'The Press in the British Zone of Germany'; FO 371/39078, Germany File no. 124 (Information control), C12035, note from McClure, 18 August 1944, requesting comments on the 'Talisman' plan prepared by PWD/SHAEF.
22 FO 371/39078, C12036, memo from Viscount Hood, 22 August 1944; FO 371/39054, C11900, memo from Kirkpatrick to Harvey, 6 September 1944.
23 Reusch, 'Die Londoner Institutionen', pp. 347–348; Koszyk, 'The Press in the British Zone of Germany', p. 118.
24 Hodenberg, *Konsens und Krise,* p. 94.
25 Kurt Koszyk, 'Presse unter alliierter Besatzung', in Jürgen Wilke (ed.), *Mediengeschichte der Bundesrepublik Deutschland* (Cologne, Weimar and Vienna: Böhlau Verlag, 1999).
26 Hans Habe, *Ich stelle mich* (Munich, Berlin: Herbig, 1986), revised edition, first edition published 1954, p. 479.
27 Koszyk, 'Presse unter alliierter Besatzung', pp. 39–41; Balfour and Mair, *Four Power Control*, p. 70. The first licensed paper in the US Zone was the *Frankfurter Rundschau,* which appeared on 31 July 1945.
28 Sian Nicholas, 'Keeping the News British: The BBC, British United Press and Reuters in the 1930s', in Joel H. Wiener and Mark Hampton (eds), *Anglo-American Media Interactions, 1850–2000* (Basingstoke and New York: Palgrave Macmillan, 2007), pp. 195–214.

29 Delmer, *Black Boomerang*, pp. 228–250; Peter J. Humphries, *Media and Media Policy in Germany: The Press and Broadcasting since 1945* (Oxford and Providence, USA: Berg, 1990), pp. 33, 62.
30 Delmer, *Black Boomerang*, p. 233.
31 Gienow-Hecht, 'Art Is Democracy and Democracy Is Art'; Gienow-Hecht, *Transmission Impossible*; Hans Habe, *Im Jahre Null* (Munich: Verlag Kurt Desch, 1966); Habe, *Ich stelle mich*.
32 Delmer, *Black Boomerang*, pp. 250–254. See also Balfour, 'In Retrospect', p. 146.
33 Koszyk, 'The Press in the British Zone of Germany', p. 120.
34 Delmer, *Black Boomerang*, pp. 235–237.
35 BLM 85/15, Montgomery's second 'Note on the present situation', 6 July 1945.
36 FO 898/401, memo from RHBL (Bruce Lockhart) to Harvey, 10 July 1945 and attached 'minute on our difficulties over our information services in Germany'.
37 Ibid.
38 Bishop, 'Look Back with Pleasure', p. 84.
39 Austen Albu and Harold Ingrams, for example, both reported to army generals as their immediate superiors; Albu to General Erskine, and Ingrams to General Philip Balfour.
40 Koszyk, 'The Press in the British Zone of Germany', p. 120; FO 946/22. Sprigge was replaced as Head of PR/ISC by Raymond Gauntlett with effect from 1 November 1947.
41 Lothar Kettenacker (ed.), *Das 'Andere Deutschland' im Zweiten Weltkrieg: Emigration und Widerstand in internationaler Perspektive* (Stuttgart: Ernst Klett Verlag, 1977), brief biography of Michael Balfour in the list of discussion participants.
42 Brawand, *Der Spiegel – ein Besatzungskind*, pp. 37–70.
43 Ibid., pp. 64–65; 'Political Activities (Hannover Region)', *British Zone Review*, Vol. 1, No. 31, 23 November 1946, p. 15. The original dummy is preserved in *Der Spiegel* archives.
44 FO 1056/27, 'Notes of a visit to No. 30 Information Control Unit', 3 April 1946.
45 'Political Activities (Hannover Region)'.
46 Brawand, *Der Spiegel – ein Besatzungskind*, pp. 95–96.
47 Ibid. pp. 79–80.
48 Leo Brawand, *The Spiegel Story* (Oxford: Pergamom Press, 1989). First published in German as *Der Spiegel-Story* by ECON Verlag GmbH, 1987, pp. 9–10.
49 Brawand, *Der Spiegel – ein Besatzungskind*, pp. 31, 98–99.
50 Harry Bohrer, 'Es wird grossen Spass machen', *Spiegel Almanach*, December 1948.
51 *Der Spiegel* archives (henceforward DSA), interview with John Chaloner, 2 November 2006.
52 Brawand, *Der Spiegel – ein Besatzungskind*, p. 223.
53 DSA 1381, letter from Chaloner to COGA, London, 9 October (1946).

54 FO 1056/29, letter from Chaloner to Balfour, October 1946; letter from Chaloner to Rinne, 15 October 1946.
55 DSA 1381, letter initialled 'O' to 'Press Chief', 21 October 1946. See also 'Political Activities (Hannover Region)', p. 15.
56 DSA 1381, letter from Chaloner to 'Publications Production Unit', 28 October 1946.
57 Ibid., letter initialled 'O' to 'Press Chief', 2 November 1946; report initialled 'O' to 'Press Chief', 14 December 1946.
58 Ibid., letter initialled 'O' to 'Press Chief', 8 November 1946.
59 Ibid., letter from Chaloner to Ormond, 31 October 1946.
60 DSA, interview with John Chaloner, 2 November 2006.
61 Ibid.
62 Brawand, *Der Spiegel – ein Besatzungskind,* p. 165.
63 Information provided by Joan Woodward, John Chaloner's sister, as written answers to questions, 10 April 2010.
64 'Hunger an der Ruhr', *Diese Woche,* No. 1, 16 November 1946, p. 1.
65 'Auch ein Ostflüchtling: Er wollte nicht nach Rußland', *Diese Woche,* No. 1, 16 November 1946, p. 4. (Another refugee from the East: he didn't want to go to Russia.)
66 '… und wohin mit den Polen?' *Diese Woche,* No. 1, 16 November 1946, p. 10.
67 FO 1005/386, 'Coordinating Committee agendas and minutes'; FO 1005/373, 'Control Council Agendas and Minutes'. The coordinating committee of Allied Deputy Military Governors discussed the issue of the deportation of scientists from Germany at its meetings on 29 October and 4 November 1946 (before the first issue of *Diese Woche* appeared on 16 November) in acrimonious discussions in which accusations and counter-accusations were exchanged between the British and Soviet representatives. The issue was escalated to the Allied Control Council meeting (of Military Governors) on 20 November at which the Soviet representative, Marshal Sokolovsky, claimed there was 'an anti-Soviet campaign in the German press'.
68 Brawand, *Der Spiegel – ein Besatzungskind,* pp. 131–132. Augstein used same argument, that he was repeating a story that had already appeared in newspapers in Britain, when criticized later, in June 1947, for publishing a cartoon of Stalin. The British censor considered this to be 'a serious affront to the head of an occupying power'. See DSA, 1381, letter from 'Censorship officer, for Senior PR/ISC officer, Land Niedersachsen' to 'The Editor, Der Spiegel', 30 June 1947 and reply from Augstein to Deneke, 30 June 1947. See also FO 1056/27. Augstein had good grounds for his defence, as a report by Sir Walter Layton on 'German Re-education', circulated by Bishop to his immediate subordinates, had recommended that the foreign press be made available to Germans as 'no German editor can be expected to do his job properly unless he can read the foreign press'.
69 Brawand, *Der Spiegel – ein Besatzungskind,* pp. 156–158.

70 FO 1056/16 folio 195, letter from Sprigge to Bayer, 29 November 1946 and folio 195A, letter from Sprigge to Gibson, 29 November 1946.

71 Ibid.

72 FO 1056/37, letter from Gibson to Bayer, 13 December 1946.

73 Brawand, *Der Spiegel – ein Besatzungskind*, p. 163.

74 FO 1056/37, letter from Gibson to Bayer, 13 December 1946.

75 Ibid.

76 A full set of copies of *Diese Woche*, including Chaloner's dummy, dated 29 March, and the two pre-production issues dated 25 October and 1 November, are held in Der Spiegel Archive (DSA).

77 E.g. 'Geistiger Export Deutschlands', *Diese Woche*, No. 5, 21 December 1946. The article criticized the work done by Michael Howard and his colleagues in T-Force (without mentioning the unit by name).

78 DSA 1381.

79 DSA 1381, report initialled 'O' to 'Press Chief', 31 December 1946.

80 Brawand, *The Spiegel Story*, p. 47.

81 DSA 1381, Licence no. 123, July 1947. After 12 July 1947, the 'Impressum' (Imprint) at the back of the magazine changed from 'Herausgegeben von Rudolf Augstein, (mit vorläufiger PR/ISC Genehmigung 600/PR vom 1 Januar 1947)' to 'Veröffentlicht unter Zulassung Nr. 123 der Militär-Regierung'.

82 Brawand, *Der Spiegel – ein Besatzungskind*, pp. 188–189.

83 DSA, letter from Balfour to Brawand, 18 January 1987.

84 DSA 1381, Letter from 'Deputy Press Chief 30 Information Control Unit' to 'Publications Production Unit', 23 October 1946.

85 DSA 1381, Report initialled 'O' to Press Chief, 9 December 1946.

86 Ibid., 14 December 1946.

87 See TNA FO 1056/37, lists of licensed newspapers and periodicals in the British Zone, 9 January 1946 and 9 February 1946. The circulation figure for *Der Spiegel* is given as 15,000 in the 9 January list and as 50,000 in the 9 February list. See also DSA 1381. In October 1947 *Der Spiegel* requested permission to increase circulation to 100,000, stating that although the permitted circulation was 50,000, in practice only 30,000 copies were produced.

88 DSA 1381, Memo initialled 'O' to 'Press Chief', 25 January 1947: 'Die Amerikaner schienen ziemlich verblüfft zu sein, daß die Briten sie nun ein einziges Mal in der Zeitungswelt in den Schatten gestellt haben!'

89 DSA 1381, Report initialled 'O' to Press Chief, 9 December 1946.

90 New York University, The Tamiment Library, Guide to Heinz Norden papers, available online: http://dlib.nyu.edu/findingaids/html/tamwag/tam_122/bioghist .html (accessed 8 March 2016).

91 DSA 1381, Letter from Heinz Norden, 'US Civilian and Chefredakteur HEUTE' to 'die Redaktion 'Diese Woche', 4 December 1946.

92 John Chaloner Obituary, *The Times*, 16 February 2007. It is not clear exactly when Chaloner left Hanover. According to one file he was due to leave the Control Commission at the end of 1946, which is when he would have been due for demobilization. See FO 1056/16, letter from Sprigge to Gibson, 19 November 1946.

93 DSA 1382. Bohrer and Ormond, but not Chaloner, attended a party on 11 July 1947, organized by *Der Spiegel*, to celebrate the grant of a full licence. Bohrer was appointed London representative of *Der Spiegel* when he left Germany in July 1947.

94 FO 1056/30, memo from Acting Chief PR/ISC, 9 September 1947, headed 'Press liaison'; Thomas, *Deutschland, England über alles*, pp. 234–236, 246.

95 Hodenberg, *Konsens und Krise*, pp. 219–225.

96 Koszyk, 'Presse unter alliierter Besatzung'. Allowing for the larger population in the British Zone, around 22 million in 1946, compared to 17 million in the US Zone, newspaper circulation per head of population was still higher in the British Zone at approximately 435 per 1,000, compared to 373 per 1,000 in the US Zone.

97 Humphries, *Media and Media Policy in Germany*, p. 62.

98 Alan Bance (ed.), *The Cultural Legacy of the British Occupation in Germany* (Stuttgart: Verlag Hans-Dieter Heinz, Akademischer Verlag Stuttgart, 1997), p. 140.

99 FO 1056/195, memo from A.L. Pope, Director, Press Branch 24 November 1948, and reply from Senior Press Officer for Niedersachsen.

100 FO 1056/318, 'Suppression of newspapers and other publications', minute dated 9 August 1950, headed 'Communist activity in Western Germany'.

101 Ibid., brief initialed W.L.G. (Gibson) for A.H.C. (Allied High Commission) recommending a temporary ban on *Der Spiegel*.

102 FO 1023/322, verbatim notes of the 39th meeting of the Allied High Commission.

103 Martin Doerry and Hauke Janssen (eds), *Die Spiegel- Affäre: Ein Skandal und seine Folgen* (Munich: Deutsche Verlags-Anstalt, 2013).

104 DSA, Interview with John Chaloner, 2 November 2006.

105 Doerry and Janssen (eds), *Die Spiegel- Affäre*; Herbert, 'Liberalisierung als Lernprozeß', p. 29; Moses, *German Intellectuals and the Nazi Past*, p. 172.

106 Woodward, written answers to questions.

107 Ibid.

108 Brawand, *Der Spiegel – ein Besatzungskind*, p. 201.

109 Ibid., p. 191.

110 Brawand, *The Spiegel Story*, p. 79.

111 Brawand, *Der Spiegel – ein Besatzungskind*, pp. 192–194.

112 Ibid., p. 204.

113 Ibid.

114 Information received from Heinz Egleder, Archivist at Der Spiegel, 22 February 2010.

Chapter 10

1 Robert Vansittart, *Black Record* (London: Hamish Hamilton, 1941), p. 18.
2 IWM SA, J.M.G. Thexton, accession number 30895.
3 The debate continued in the letters pages for five issues of the *British Zone Review*, from 13 October to 8 December 1945. It was started by a letter from Subaltern Lucia Lawson, who wrote:

> It is hard to believe when we have just been through six years of a war which was not of our asking that anyone can feel sorry for the people who caused it, but I challenge any average English man or woman to spend one week in Berlin and not feel some small measure of pity for some Berliners… Well, it is open to discussion, but think before you write, or get someone who has been to Berlin to tell you what conditions are like. Maybe I am too sensitive and soft hearted, but I still say I am sorry for some of them.

4 Or even an ability to speak Latin. J.M. Cobban, who worked with Ingrams in the Administration and Local Government branch of the Control Commission, recalled working with a German civil servant, a 'very cultivated man', adding 'When my German and his English failed we fell back on Latin.' See James Cobban, *One Small Head* (Charlottesville, VA: Privately published, 1998), p. 55.
5 FO 1056/30, circular from Chief Administrative Officer, 10 January 1947, which summarized the current orders on fraternization. Regulations were relaxed further in May 1947 and abolished in May 1948 at the instigation of Frank Pakenham, Minister for Germany. See FO 936/693, 'Special Routine Order' No. 263, 'Relations between C.C.G. Personnel and Germans', 30 May 1947 and FO 936/693, draft order submitted to the 16th Regional Commissioners' conference, 18 May 1948.
6 Imperial War Museum Sound Archive (IWM SA), George Henry Phillip James.
7 IWM SA, Thexton.
8 Ibid., Frank Arthur Bicknell.
9 Ibid., Richard Harland.
10 Ibid., Palliser.
11 Ibid.
12 IWM SA, Ronald Mallabar, Frank Arthur Bicknell, Samuel Falle, Martin Cosmo Hastings.
13 Ibid., Alfred Leslie (Les) Lucas.
14 Ibid., Ralph Frederick Dye.
15 Ibid., Ronald Mallabar.
16 Ibid.
17 IWM SA, Annie (Nancy) Norman.
18 Ibid.

19 Atina Grossmann, *Jews, Germans and Allies: Close Encounters in Occupied Germany* (Princeton and Oxford: Princeton University Press, 2007), chapter 2 'Gendered defeat'; Raingard Esser, '"Language No Obstacle": War Brides in the German Press, 1945–1949', *Women's History Review*, Vol. 12, No. 4, 2003, pp. 577–603; Inge Weber-Newth, 'Bilateral Relations: British Soldiers and German Women', in Louise Ryan and Wendy Webster (eds), *Gendering Migration: Masculinity, Femininity and Ethnicity in Post-War Britain* (Aldershot: Ashgate, 2008).

20 E.g. Harry Furness, the first serving British soldier in Germany to marry a German woman, first saw his future wife hanging washing on a line, as his troop entered a small German town on the last day of the war. They were married nearly two years later, on 22 March 1947. See my blog post on 'Marriage with ex-enemy nationals', available online: http://howitreallywas.typepad.com/how_it_really_was/2013/05/marriage-with-ex-enemy-nationals-continued.html (accessed 8 March 2016).

21 Ahrens, *Die Briten in Hamburg*, pp. 81–82; Goedde, *GIs and Germans*, p. 84; Naimark, *The Russians in Germany*, chapter 2, 'Soviet Soldiers, German Women and the Problem of Rape'; Atina Grossmann, 'A Question of Silence: The Rape of German Women by Occupation Soldiers' in Robert G. Moeller (ed.), *West Germany under Construction: Politics, Society and Culture in the Adenauer Era* (Ann Arbor: The University of Michigan Press, 1997).

22 Chaloner described a relationship with a German woman he called 'Heidi' in his semi-autobiographical novel *Occupational Hazard.* Howard's and Thexton's relationships are discussed in this chapter.

23 E.g. IWM SA, James Samuel Chambers.

24 IWM SA, Thexton.

25 Ibid., Arthur Norman Travett.

26 Ibid., Walter Greenhalgh.

27 Ibid., Thexton.

28 Ibid., Howard.

29 Howard, *Otherwise Occupied.*

30 Ibid., p. 133.

31 Ibid., p. 148.

32 Ibid., p. 147.

33 Ibid., p. 211.

34 Ibid., pp. 229–230.

35 Ibid.

36 Ibid., p. 262.

37 Ibid., p. 268.

38 Ibid., pp. 286–287.

39 Ibid., pp. 317–318.

40 Inge Weber-Newth, 'Bilateral Relations: British Soldiers and German Women', p. 53; Steinert and Weber-Newth, *Labour and Love*, p. 7.

41 Goedde estimated, based on exit applications to travel to the United States, that 14,175 German wives, six husbands and 750 children entered the United States between 1947 and June 1950, plus another 1,862 entering the United States as fiancés. Esser gives similar figures, stating that: 'According to US statistics, 15,028 German brides, bridegrooms, fiancées and fiancés entered the USA between 1946 and 1949.' Comparable figures for GI brides and grooms emigrating from Britain to the United States were 34,944 wives, 53 husbands and 472 children, and from Japan, 758 wives. See Goedde, *GIs and Germans*, pp. 100–101; Esser, 'Language No Obstacle', p. 381.

42 Notably Gerda Erika Baker, *Shadow of War* (Oxford, Batavia and Sydney: Lion Publishing Ltd, 1990) and Renate Greenshields, *Lucky Girl Goodbye and Its Sequel A Bit of Time* (Hawkchurch, Devon: Renate Greenshields, 2006).

43 Steinert and Weber-Newth, *Labour and Love.*

44 Weber-Newth, 'Bilateral Relations: British Soldiers and German Women', pp. 61, 63.

45 Ibid., pp. 55–57.

46 Ibid., p. 62.

47 In 1946 there were 7,279,400 more women than men in Germany. In the age group between 20 and 45 there were 1,482 women for every 1,000 men. Out of every 100 Germans born in 1924, 25, mostly male, were dead or missing and a further 31 severely mutilated. See Balfour and Mair, *Four Power Control in Germany and Austria 1945–1946*, p. 10.

48 Isabel Schropper, 'Austrian female migration to Britain, 1945 to 1960' (PhD Diss: London, 2010).

49 E.g. Steinert and Weber-Newth, *Labour and Love.*

50 FO 371/70845. In 1948 the Foreign Office, with the support of the Minister for Germany, Frank Pakenham, considered proposals from the Society for the Unmarried Mother and her Child to allow civil claims, for paternity, maintenance and support for illegitimate children, to be pursued by German mothers in Control Commission courts in Germany. The proposals were dropped following objections from service chiefs.

51 Weber-Newth, 'Bilateral Relations: British Soldiers and German Women', p. 59.

52 FO 1030/174, copy of Hansard Vol. 142, No. 126, 31 July 1946. The situation was slightly different in the US Zone. Marriage was not explicitly prohibited, but American servicemen who married Germans were forbidden to enter their wives' homes, and wives were excluded from US premises in Germany. Until the end of 1946, Germans were also excluded from the American War Brides Act, which enabled spouses and children of servicemen to enter the United States. In January and June 1947, US regulations were revised to offer certain limited privileges to German wives of US servicemen, while the couple were in Germany, and to enable marriage permits and US entry visas for spouses, subject to various conditions similar to those applying in the British Zone. See Esser, 'Language No Obstacle', pp. 582–583.

53 FO 1030/174, 'The conditions under which British Service men may marry German women in the British Zone of Germany'.
54 FO 1020/683, cited in Schropper, 'Austrian female migration to Britain', section 2.1.2.3, 'Marriage requirements'. Similar regulations applied in Germany.
55 FO 1030/174, 'The conditions under which British Service men may marry German women in the British Zone of Germany'.
56 Ibid.
57 IWM SA, Thexton.
58 Weber-Newth, 'Bilateral Relations: British Soldiers and German Women', p. 56.
59 IWM SA, Martin Cosmo Hastings.
60 E.g. Report by Noel Annan on Displaced Persons in Pelly & Yasamee, *Documents on British Policy Overseas, Series 1,* pp. 43–47; FO 1056/1040, Goronwy Rees' tour diary; Dickens *Lübeck Diary*, pp. 21, 43, 84, 86; Mosley, *Report from Germany,* pp. 58, 78–79.
61 IWM SA, Palliser.
62 Longden, *T-Force*, pp. 139–140. See also 'Honour for major who led capture of German port in WWII', BBC News, available online: http://www.bbc.co.uk/news/10356336 (accessed 8 March 2016).
63 Longden, *T-Force*, p. 145.
64 IWM SA, Palliser.
65 Ibid.
66 IWM SA, Howard, John Isaac Godfrey Brown, Oliver Bland, Bernard Fisher, Martin Cosmo Hastings, James Samuel Chambers, Frank Arthur Bicknell.
67 IWM SA, Ronald Mallabar, Martin Cosmo Hastings, James Samuel Chambers, Arthur Norman Travett.
68 IWM SA, Martin Cosmo Hastings.
69 Ibid.
70 IWM SA, James Samuel Chambers.
71 Jacobmeyer, *Vom Zwangsarbeiter zum Heimatlosen Ausländer*, p. 41.
72 Ibid., pp. 41, 60.
73 Ibid., p. 83.
74 Steinert, *Nach Holocaust und Zwangsarbeit*, p. 130.
75 Ibid.
76 Jacobmeyer, *Vom Zwangsarbeiter zum Heimatlosen Ausländer,* pp. 185, 224.
77 Ibid., p. 25.
78 Steinert, *Nach Holocaust und Zwangsarbeit*, p. 130.
79 Ibid., pp. 100–101; Grossmann, 'Trauma, Memory and Motherhood', pp. 97–98.
80 Jacobmeyer, *Vom Zwangsarbeiter zum Heimatlosen Ausländer,* p. 15.
81 Ibid., pp. 48–49.
82 FO 1060/2793, Register of Military Government Court, High Court in Hamburg.
83 Kirkpatrick, *The Inner Circle*, p. 190.
84 IWM SA, Palliser.

85 Howard, *Otherwise Occupied*, pp. 119–120.

86 Ibid., pp. 118–119.

87 Quoted in Steinert, *Nach Holocaust und Zwangsarbeit*, p. 42. Padover left Germany soon after VE Day and was referring to the period before the end of the war (when Goebbels was still alive).

88 Jacobmeyer, *Vom Zwangsarbeiter zum Heimatlosen Ausländer*, p. 50, 'Criminality by DPs appeared, in the judgement of the Allies, not only as pure disobedience but, worse still, as malicious ingratitude.'

89 'The Early Days', *British Zone Review*, Vol. 1, No. 4, November 1945, p. 1.

90 E.g. Donnison, *Civil Affairs and Military Government*, p. 357. See also FO 1056/540, Goronwy Rees' Tour Diary for 1 July 1945, in which he wrote that: 'Displaced persons, especially Russians and Poles, are able to roam the country at will, raiding isolated farms or houses for food, valuables or women.'

91 Jacobmeyer, *Vom Zwangsarbeiter zum Heimatlosen Ausländer*, p. 52.

92 E.g. IWM SA, Eric Gregg-Rowbury.

93 Jacobmeyer, *Vom Zwangsarbeiter zum Heimatlosen Ausländer*, pp. 185, 224.

Chapter 11

1 Fulbrook, *Dissonant Lives*, p. 477.

2 Rosenfeld, 'The Anglo-German Encounter in Occupied Hamburg, 1945–50', pp. 346, 353.

3 Turner, *Reconstruction in Post-War Germany*, pp. 4–5; Tony Judt, *Postwar: A History of Europe since 1945* (London: William Heinemann, 2005), p. 100.

4 E.g. Cairncross, *The Price of War*, p. 75; Balfour and Mair, *Four Power Control in Germany and Austria 1945–1946*, p. 29.

5 Margaret Kertesz, 'The Enemy – British Images of the German People during the Second World War' (PhD Diss: University of Sussex, 1993), p. 178.

6 FO 1030/329, 'Verbatim notes of speech by Deputy Military Governor to Staff on 31 7 47'.

7 Noel Annan, *Our Age: Portrait of a Generation* (London: Weidenfeld and Nicolson, 1990), pp. 37ff.

8 The exceptions were Chaloner and Thexton. Chaloner would have been exposed to similar ideas at Sandhurst.

9 With the possible exception of Flanders. The Socialist Vanguard Group supported independence for India and were opposed to Empire, on the basis that they believed in self-determination and objected to exploitation in any form.

10 AP15, Austen Albu, 'Back Bench Technocrat', unpublished autobiography chapter I, p. 2; chapter II, p. 1. Albu wrote that he was given the name Austen after Austen Chamberlain, the brother of the liberal imperialist politician Joseph Chamberlain.

Select Bibliography

Michael Ahrens, *Die Briten in Hamburg: Besatzerleben 1945–1958* (Munich and Hamburg: Dölling und Gallitz Verlag, 2011).

Alan Allport, *Demobbed* (New Haven and London: Yale University Press, 2009).

Peter Alter, *Out of the Third Reich: Refugee Historians in Post-War Britain* (London and New York: I.B. Tauris, 1998).

Noel Annan, *Changing Enemies: The Defeat and Regeneration of Germany* (London: HarperCollins, 1995).

Michael Balfour and John Mair, *Four Power Control in Germany and Austria 1945–1946* (Oxford: Survey of International Affairs 1939–1946, Oxford University Press, 1956).

Hilary Ann Balshaw, 'The British Occupation in Germany, 1945–1949 with special reference to Hamburg' (PhD Diss: Oxford, 1972).

Alan Bance (ed.), *The Cultural Legacy of the British Occupation in Germany* (Stuttgart: Verlag Hans-Dieter Heinz, Akademischer Verlag Stuttgart, 1997).

John Bayley, *In Another Country* (Oxford: Oxford University Press, 1955).

Stefan Berger, 'British Socialism as Perceived in Twentieth-Century Germany', in A. Bauerkämper and C. Eisenberg (eds), *Great Britain as a Model of Modern Society? German Views* (Augsburg: Wissner, 2006), pp. 184–202.

Volker R. Berghahn and Simone Lässig (eds), *Biography between Structure and Agency: Central European Lives in International Historiography* (New York and Oxford: Berghahn Books, 2008).

Richard Bessel, *Germany 1945: From War to Peace* (London, New York, Sydney and Toronto: Simon & Schuster, 2009).

Richard Bessel and Dirk Schumann (eds), *Life after Death: Approaches to a Cultural and Social History of Europe during the 1940s and 1950s* (Cambridge: Cambridge University Press, 2003).

Frank Biess and Robert G. Moeller (eds), *Histories of the Aftermath: The Legacies of the Second World War on Europe* (New York and Oxford: Berghahn Books, 2010).

Adolf Birke and Eva Mayring (eds), *Britische Besatzing in Deutschland: Aktienerschliessung und Forschungsfelder* (London: German Historical Institute, 1992).

Lawrence Black, 'Social Democracy as a Way of Life: Fellowship and the Socialist Union, 1951–59', *Twentieth Century British History*, Vol. 10, No. 4 (1999), pp. 499–539.

Rebecca Boehling, *A Question of Priorities* (Providence and Oxford: Berghahn Books, 1996).

Rebecca Boehling, 'The Role of Culture in American Relations with Europe: The Case of the United States's Occupation of Germany', *Diplomatic History*, Vol. 23, No. 1 (Winter 1999), pp. 57–69.

Douglas Botting, *In the Ruins of the Reich* (London: George Allen & Unwin, 1985).

Leo Brawand, *Der Spiegel – ein Besatzungskind: Wie die Pressefreiheit nach Deutschland kam* (Hamburg: EVA Europäische Verlagsanstalt, 2007).

Jon Bridgman, *The End of the Holocaust: The Liberation of the Camps* (London: B.T. Batsford Ltd, 1990).

Fenner Brockway, *German Diary* (London: Victor Gollancz Ltd, 1946).

Martin Broszat, Klaus-Dietmar Henke and Hans Woller (eds), *Von Stalingrad zur Währungsreform: Zur Sozialgeschichte des Umbruchs in Deutschland* (Munich: R. Oldenbourg Verlag, 1988).

Amy Buller, *Darkness over Germany* (London, New York and Toronto: Longmans, Green and Co, 1943).

Ursula Büttner, 'Not nach der Befreiung. Die Situation der Deutschen Juden in der britischen Besatzungszone 1945–1948', in *Das Unrechtsregime*, Vol. 2 (Hamburg: Christians, 1986).

W. Byford-Jones, *Berlin Twilight* (London: Hutchinson, 1947).

Alec Cairncross, *A Country to Play with: Level of Industry Negotiations in Berlin 1945–46* (Gerrards Cross: Colin Smythe Limited, 1987).

Alec Cairncross, *The Price of War: British Policy on German Reparations 1941–49* (Oxford: Basil Blackwell, 1986).

Antone Capet, '"The Creeds of the Devil" Churchill between the Two Totalitarianisms, 1917–1945', *Finest Hour Online,* 31 August 2009, available online: http://www.winstonchurchill.org/support/the-churchill-centre/publications/finest-hour-online/725-the-creeds-of-the-devil-churchill-between-the-two-totalitarianisms-1917-1945 (accessed 3 March 2016).

John Chaloner, *Occupational Hazard* (Wallington, Surrey: Severn House Publishers, 1991).

John Chaloner, *To Europe with Love* (London: Severn House Publishers, 1984). First published 1969 by Dobson Books Ltd as *Family Hold Back.*

Paul Chambers, 'Post-War German Finances', *International Affairs*, Vol. 24, No. 3 (July 1948), pp. 364–377.

George Clare, *Berlin Days* (London: Macmillan, 1989).

Lucius D. Clay, *Decision in Germany* (London: William Heinemann Ltd, 1950).

Henry E. Collins, *Mining Memories and Musings: Autobiography of a Mining Engineer* (Ashire Publishing Ltd, 1985).

Krista Cowman, 'Collective Biography', in Simon Gunn and Lucy Faire (eds), *Research Methods for History* (Edinburgh: Edinburgh University Press, 2012), pp. 83–100.

Hugh Dalton, *High Tide and After* (London: Frederick Muller Ltd, 1962).

John Darwin, *Unfinished Empire: The Global Expansion of Britain* (London: Allen Lane, 2012).

Anne Deighton, *The Impossible Peace: Britain, the Division of Germany and the Origins of the Cold War* (Oxford: Clarendon Press, 1990).

Sefton Delmer, *Black Boomerang: An Autobiography,* Vol. 2 (London: Secker and Warburg, 1962).

Arthur Geoffrey Dickens, *Lübeck Diary* (London: Victor Gollancz Ltd, 1947).

Martin Doerry and Hauke Janssen (eds), *Die Spiegel- Affäre: Ein Skandal und seine Folgen* (Munich: Deutsche Verlags-Anstalt, 2013).

Frank Donnison, *Civil Affairs and Military Government. Central Organisation and Planning* (London: HMSO, 1966).

Frank Donnison, *Civil Affairs and Military Government. North-West Europe 1944–1946* (London: HMSO, 1961).

Sholto Douglas, *Years of Combat: The First Volume of the Autobiography of Sholto Douglas, Marshal of the Royal Air Force Lord Douglas of Kirtleside G.C.B. M.C. D.F.S.* (London: Collins, 1963).

Sholto Douglas with Robert Wright, *Years of Command: The Second Volume of the Autobiography of Sholto Douglas, Marshal of the Royal Air Force Lord Douglas of Kirtleside G.C.B. M.C. D.F.S.* (London: Collins, 1966).

Ruth Easingwood, 'British Women in Occupied Germany: Lived Experiences in the British Zone 1945–1949' (PhD Diss: University of Newcastle Upon Tyne, 2009).

Raymond Ebsworth, *Restoring Democracy in Germany: The British Contribution* (London: Stevens & Sons Limited, 1960).

Ludwig Eiber, *Die Sozialdemokratie in der Emigration* (Bonn: J H W Dietz Nachfolger, 1998).

Raingard Esser, '"Language No Obstacle": War Brides in the German Press, 1945–1949', *Women's History Review*, Vol. 12, No. 4 (2003), pp. 577–603.

John E. Farquharson, 'The British Occupation of Germany, 1945–1946: A Badly Managed Disaster Area?' *German History*, Vol. 11, No. 3 (1993), pp. 316–338.

John E. Farquharson, 'Emotional but Influential: Victor Gollancz, Richard Stokes and the British Zone in Germany: 1945–1949', *Journal of Contemporary History*, Vol. 22 (1987), pp. 501–519.

John E. Farquharson, 'From Unity to Division: What Prompted Britain to Change Its Policy in Germany in 1946', *European History Quarterly*, Vol. 26 (1996), pp. 81–123.

John E. Farquharson, 'Governed or Exploited? The British Acquisition of German Technology, 1945–48', *Journal of Contemporary History*, Vol. 32, No. 1 (1997), pp. 23–42.

John E. Farquharson, *The Western Allies and the Politics of Food, Agrarian Management in Postwar Germany* (Oxford: Berg Publishers Ltd, 1985).

Henry Faulk, *Group Captives: The Re-education of German Prisoners of War in Britain 1945–1948* (London: Chatto & Windus, 1977).

Josef Foschepoth and Rolf Steininger (eds), *Britische Deutschland- und Besatzungspolitik* (Paderborn: Ferdinand Schöningh, 1985).

Matthew Frank, *Expelling the Germans: British Opinion and Post-1945 Population Transfer in Context* (Oxford: Oxford University Press, 2007).

Matthew Frank, 'The New Morality – Victor Gollancz, "Save Europe Now" and the German Refugee Crisis, 1945–46', *Twentieth Century British History*, Vol. 17, No. 2 (2006), pp. 230–256.

W.G. Friedmann, *The Allied Military Government of Germany* (London: Stevens & Sons Limited, 1947).

Mary Fulbrook, *Dissonant Lives: Generations and Violence through the German Dictatorships* (Oxford: Oxford University Press, 2011).

David Garnett, *The Secret History of PWE: The Political Warfare Executive 1939–1945* (London: St Ermin's Press, 2002).

G.E.R. Gedye, *The Revolver Republic: France's Bid for the Rhine* (London: J.W. Arrowsmith Limited, 1930).

Jessica Gienow-Hecht, 'Art Is Democracy and Democracy Is Art: Culture, Propaganda and the *Neue Zeitung* in Germany, 1944–1947', *Diplomatic History*, Vol. 23, No. 1 (Winter 1999), pp. 21–43.

Jessica Gienow-Hecht, *Transmission Impossible* (Baton Rouge: Louisiana State University Press, 1999).

A. Glees, *Exile Politics during the Second World War: The German Social Democrats in Britain* (Oxford: Oxford University Press, 1982).

Petra Goedde, 'From Villains to Victims, Fraternization and the Feminization of Germany, 1945–1947', *Diplomatic History*, Vol. 23, No. 1 (Winter 1999), pp. 3–20.

Petra Goedde, *GIs and Germans: Culture, Gender and Foreign Relations 1945–49* (New Haven and London: Yale University Press, 2003).

Victor Gollancz, *In Darkest Germany* (London: Victor Gollancz Ltd, 1947).

Victor Gollancz, *Shall Our Children Live or Die? A Reply to Lord Vansittart on the German Problem* (London: Victor Gollancz Ltd, 1942).

Patrick Gordon Walker, *The Lid Lifts* (London: Victor Gollancz Ltd, 1945).

Francis Graham-Dixon, *The Allied Occupation of German: The Refugee Crisis, Denazification and the Path to Reconstruction* (London and New York: I.B. Tauris, 2013).

Renate Greenshields, *Lucky Girl Goodbye and Its Sequel A Bit of Time* (Hawkchurch, Devon: Renate Greenshields, 2006).

Atina Grossmann, *Jews, Germans and Allies: Close Encounters in Occupied Germany* (Princeton and Oxford: Princeton University Press, 2007).

Ruth Gruber, *Exodus 1947: The Ship that Launched a Nation* (New York: Union Square Press, 2007). First published 1948 as *Destination Palestine: The Story of the Haganah Ship Exodus 1947*, by Current Books, Inc.

Christian Haase, 'Democratic Citizenship in the Industrial Age: The British Sociologist T.H. Marshall and the Democratisation of Germany', in A. Bauerkämper and C. Eisenberg (eds), *Great Britain as a Model of Modern Society? German Views* (Augsburg: Wissner, 2006), pp. 89–110.

Christian Haase, 'In Search of a European Settlement: Chatham House and British German Relations, 1920–1955', *European History Quarterly*, Vol. 37, No. 3 (2007), pp. 371–397.

Hans Habe, *Im Jahre Null* (Munich: Verlag Kurt Desch, 1966).
Aviva Halamish, *The Exodus Affair: Holocaust Survivors and the Struggle for Palestine* (London: Vallentine Mitchell, 1998). Translated by Ora Cummings.
Nigel Hamilton, *Monty: The Field-Marshal 1944–1976* (London: Hamish Hamilton, 1986).
Jose Harris (ed.), *Civil Society in British History: Ideas, Identities, Institutions* (Oxford: Oxford University Press, 2003).
Arthur Hearnden, *The British in Germany* (London: Hamish Hamilton, 1978).
Ulrich Herbert, 'Liberalisierung als Lernprozeß. Die Bundesrepublik in der deutschen Geschichte – eine Skizze', in Ulrich Herbert (ed.), *Wandlungsprozesse in Westdeutschland: Belastung, Integration, Liberalisierung 1945–1980* (Göttingen: Wallstein Verlag, 2002), pp. 7–49.
Gerhard Hirschfeld (ed.), *Exile in Great Britain: Refugees from Hitler's Germany* (Leamington Spa: Berg Publishers, 1984).
Eric Hobsbawm, *Age of Extremes* (London: Abacus, 1995). First published by Michael Joseph, 1994.
Christina von Hodenberg, *Konsens und Krise: Eine Geschichte der westdeutschen Medienöffentlichkeit 1945–1973* (Göttingen: Wallstein Verlag, 2006).
Lieutenant General Sir Brian Horrocks, *A Full Life* (London: Leo Cooper, 1974). Revised and extended edition. First published by William Collins, 1960.
Michael Howard, *Otherwise Occupied: Letters Home from the Ruins of Nazi Germany* (Tiverton: Old Street Publishing, 2010).
Harold Hurwitz, *Demokratie und Antikommunismus in Berlin nach 1945: Vol. 4, Die Anfänge des Widerstands* (Cologne: Verlag Wissenschaft und Politik, 1990).
Harold Hurwitz, *Die Stunde Null der deutschen Presse. Die amerikanische Pressepolitik in Deutschland 1945–1949* (Cologne: Verlag Wissenschaft und Politik, 1972).
Harold Ingrams, 'Building Democracy in Germany', *The Quarterly Review*, No. 572 (April 1947), pp. 208–222.
Harold Ingrams, *Seven across the Sahara* (London: John Murray, 1949).
Wolfgang Jacobmeyer, *Vom Zwangsarbeiter zum Heimatlosen Ausländer* (Göttingen: Vandenhoeck & Ruprecht, 1985).
Konrad H. Jarausch, *After Hitler: Recivilizing Germans, 1945–1995* (New York: Oxford University Press, 2006).
Jill Jones, 'Eradicating Nazism from the British Zone of Germany: Early Policy and Practice', *German History*, Vol. 8, No. 2 (1990), pp. 145–162.
Ulrike Jordan (ed.), *Conditions of Surrender, Britons and Germans Witness the End of the War* (London and New York: I.B. Tauris Publishers, 1997).
Tony Judt, *Postwar: A History of Europe since 1945* (London: William Heinemann, 2005).
Ulrike Jureit and Michael Wildt (eds), *Generationen: Zur Relevanz eines wissenschaftlichen Grundbegriffs* (Hamburg: Hamburger Edition, 2005).
John Kelly, *Ethical Socialism and the Trade Unions: Allan Flanders and the British Industrial Relations Reform* (New York and Abingdon: Routledge, 2010).

Margaret Kertesz, 'The Enemy – British Images of the German People during the Second World War' (PhD Diss: University of Sussex, 1993).
Lothar Kettenacker (ed.), *Das 'Andere Deutschland' im Zweiten Weltkrieg: Emigration und Widerstand in internationaler Perspektive* (Stuttgart: Ernst Klett Verlag, 1977).
Lothar Kettenacker (ed.), *Ein Volk von Opfern? Die neue Debatte um den Bombenkrieg 1940–45* (Berlin: Rowohlt, 2003).
Lothar Kettenacker (ed.), *Krieg zur Friedenssicherung: Die Deutschlandplanung der britischen Regierung während des zweiten Weltkrieges* (Gottingen: Vandenhoeck & Ruprecht, 1989).
Yvone Kirkpatrick, *The Inner Circle* (London: Macmillan, 1959).
Kurt Koszyk, 'Presse unter alliierte Besatzung', in Jürgen Wilke, *Mediengeschichte der Bundesrepublik Deutschland* (Cologne, Weimar and Vienna: Böhlau Verlag, 1999), pp. 31–58.
Alan Kramer, *The West German Economy, 1945–1955* (Oxford: Berg Publishers Ltd, 1991).
Claus-Dieter Krohn and Patrik von zur Mühlen (eds), *Rückkehr und Aufbau nach 1945: Deutsche Remigranten im öffentlichen Leben Nachkriegsdeutschlands* (Marburg: Metropolis Verlag, 1997).
Claus-Dieter Krohn, Patrik von zur Mühlen, Gerhard Paul and Lutz Winkler (eds), *Handbuch der deutschsprachigen Emigration 1933–1945* (Darmstadt: Wissenschaft Buchgesellschaft, 1998).
Hagit Lavsky, 'A Community of Survivors: Bergen-Belsen as a Jewish Centre after 1945', in Jo Reilly, David Cesarani, Tony Kushner and Colin Richmond (eds), *Belsen in History and Memory* (London and Portland, OR: Frank Cass, 1997), pp. 162–177.
Walter Loewenheim, *Geschichte der Org [Neu Beginnen] 1929–1935*, edited by Jan Foitzik (Berlin: Edition Hentrich, 1995).
Sean Longden, *T-Force: The Race for Nazi War Secrets, 1945* (London: Constable, 2009).
Richard Löwenthal, *Die Widerstandsgruppe Neu Beginnen* (Berlin: Gedenkstätte Deutscher Widerstand, 2001).
Alf Lüdtke and Bernd Weisbrod (eds), *No Man's Land of Violence: Extreme Wars in the 20th Century* (Göttingen: Wallstein Verlag, 2006).
Giles MacDonagh, *After the Reich: From the Liberation of Vienna to the Berlin Airlift* (London: John Murray (Publishers), 2007).
Colin MacInnes, *To the Victors the Spoils* (London: Alison and Busby, 1986). First published in 1950.
Patrick Major, 'Britain and Germany: A Love-Hate Relationship', *German History*, Vol. 26, No. 4 (2008), pp. 457–468.
Ethel Mannin, *German Journey* (London: Jarrolds Publishers (London) Ltd, 1948).
Violet Markham, *Return Passage* (London: Oxford University Press, 1953).
Violet Markham, *A Woman's Watch on the Rhine* (London: Hodder and Stoughton, 1921).
Barbara Marshall, 'German Attitudes to British Military Government 1945–1947', *Journal of Contemporary History*, Vol. 15 (1980), pp. 655–684.

Barbara Marshall, *The Origins of Post-War German Politics* (London, New York and Sydney: Croom Helm, 1988).

Patricia Meehan, *A Strange Enemy People* (London: Peter Owen Publishers, 2001).

Peter Merseburger, *Rudolf Augstein* (Munich: Deutsche Verlags-Anstalt, 2007).

Drew Middleton, *The Struggle for Germany* (London and New York: Allan Wingate, 1949).

Mark Minion, 'Left, Right or European? Labour and Europe in the 1940s: The Case of the Socialist Vanguard Group', *European Review of History: Revue européenne d'histoire*, Vol. 7, No. 2 (July 2010), pp. 229–248.

Robert G. Moeller, *War Stories: The Search for a Usable Past in the Federal Republic of Germany* (Berkeley, Los Angeles and London: University of California Press, 2001).

Robert G. Moeller (ed.), *West Germany under Construction: Politics, Society and Culture in the Adenauer Era* (Ann Arbor: The University of Michigan Press, 1997).

Bernard Montgomery, *The Memoirs of Field-Marshal the Viscount Montgomery of Alamein, K.G.* (London: Collins, 1958).

Dirk Moses, *German Intellectuals and the Nazi Past* (New York: Cambridge University Press, 2007).

L. Mosley, *Report from Germany* (London: Victor Gollancz Ltd, 1945).

Norman Naimark, *The Russians in Germany: A History of the Soviet Zone of Occupation, 1945–1949* (Cambridge, MA and London,: The Belknap Press of Harvard University Press, 1995).

Anthony J. Nichols, *Always Good Neighbours – Never Good Friends? Anglo-German Relations 1949–2001* (London: German Historical Institute London, 2005).

Lord Pakenham, *Born to Believe* (London: Jonathan Cape, 1953).

Sarah Paterson, '"Operation Union": British Families in Germany, 1946', *Imperial War Museum Review*, Vol. 10 (1997), pp. 74–83.

M.E. Pelly and H.J. Yasamee (eds), assisted by G. Bennett, *Documents on British Policy Overseas, Series 1, Volume 5, Germany and Western Europe, 11 August–31 December 1945* (London: Her Majesty's Stationary Office, 1990).

Dietmar Petzina and Walter Euchner (eds), *Wirtschaftspolitik im britischen Besatzungsgebiet: 1945–1949* (Düsseldorf: Schwann, 1984).

Uta G. Poiger, 'Beyond "Modernization" and "Colonization"', *Diplomatic History*, Vol. 23, No. 1 (Winter 1999), pp. 45–57.

Gareth Pritchard, 'Schwarzenberg 1945: Antifascists and the "Third Way" in German Politics', *European History Quarterly*, Vol. 35, No. 4 (2005), pp. 499–522.

Nicholas Pronay, 'Defeated Germany in German Newsreels 1944–5', in K.R.M. Short and Stephen Dolezel (eds), *Hitlers Fall, the Newsreel Witness* (London, New York and Sydney: Croom Helm, 1990).

Nicholas Pronay and Keith Wilson (eds), *The Political Re-education of Germany and Her Allies after World War II* (London and Sydney: Croom Helm, 1985).

Nicholas Pronay and D.W. Spring (eds), *Propaganda Politics and Film 1918–1945* (London and Basingstoke: Macmillan Press Ltd, 1982).

John Ramsden, *Don't Mention the War: The British and the Germans since 1890* (London: Little Brown, 2006).

B.U. Ratchford and Wm. D. Ross, *Berlin Reparations Assignment: Round One of the Berlin Peace Settlement* (Chapel Hill: The University of North Carolina Press, 1947).

Goronwy Rees, *Sketches in Autobiography: 'A Bundle of Sensations' and 'A Chapter of Accidents' with 'A Winter in Berlin', a Further Autobiographical Essay*, edited with introduction and notes by John Harris (Cardiff: University of Wales Press, 2001).

Jessica Reinisch, *The Perils of Peace: The Public Health Crisis in Occupied Germany* (Oxford: Oxford University Press, 2013).

Ulrich Reusch, *Deutsches Berufsbeamtentum und Britische Besatzung 1943–1947* (Stuttgart: Klett-Cotta, 1985).

Ulrich Reusch, 'Die Londoner Institutionen der britischen Deutschlandpolitik 1943–48. Eine behördengeschichtliche Untersuchung', *Historisches Jahrbuch* 100 (1980), pp. 318–443.

David Reynolds, *In Command of History: Churchill Fighting and Writing the Second World War* (London: Allen Lane, 2004).

Brian Robertson, Lord Robertson of Oakridge, 'A Miracle? Potsdam 1945 – Western Germany 1965', *International Affairs*, Vol. 41, No. 3 (1965), pp. 401–410.

Werner Röder, *Die deutschen sozialistischen Exilgruppen in Großbritannien 1940–1945* (Bonn-Bad Godesberg: Verlag Neue Gesellschaft GmbH, 1973).

Frances Rosenfeld, 'The Anglo-German Encounter in Occupied Hamburg, 1945–50' (PhD Diss: Columbia University, 2006).

Wolfgang Rudzio, *Die Neuordnung des Kommunalwesens in der Britischen Zone* (Stuttgart: Deutsche Verlags-Anstalt, 1968).

Beate Ruhm von Oppen (ed.), *Documents on Germany under Occupation 1945–1954* (London, New York and Toronto: Oxford University Press, 1955).

Mary Saran, *Never Give Up* (London: Oswald Wolff, 1976).

Claus Scharf, and Hans-Jürgen Schröder (eds), *Die Deutschlandpolitik Grossbritanniens und die Britische Zone 1945–1949* (Wiesbaden: Franz Steiner Verlag, 1979).

Axel Schildt, 'Das "Hamburg project". Eine kritische Phase der britischen Besatzungspolitik in Hamburg 1945–47', in Frank Otto and Thilo Schulz (eds), *Großbritannien und Deutschland: gesellschaftliche, kulturelle und politische Beziehungen im 19. und 20. Jahrhundert* (Rheinfelden: Schäuble Verlag, 1999), pp. 131–147.

Axel Schildt, 'The Long Shadows of the Second World War: The Impact of Experiences and Memories of War on West German Society', *German Historical Institute London Bulletin*, Vol. XXIX, No. 1 (May 2007), pp. 28–49.

Isabel Schropper, 'Austrian Female Migration to Britain, 1945 to 1960' (PhD Diss: London, 2010).

Michael Sissons and Philip French (eds), *Age of Austerity* (London: Hodder & Stoughton, 1963).

Jörg Später, *Vansittart: britische Debatten über Deutsche und Nazis 1902–1945* (Göttingen: Wallstein Verlag, 2003).

Stephen Spender, *European Witness* (London: Hamish Hamilton, 1946).

Johannes-Dieter Steinert, *Nach Holocaust und Zwangsarbeit: Britische humanitäre Hilfe in Deutschland, Die Helfer, die Befreiten und die Deutschen* (Osnabrück: secolo Verlag, 2007).

Johannes-Dieter Steinert and Inge Weber-Newth, *European Immigrants in Britain 1933–1950* (Munich: K.G. Saur, 2003).

Johannes-Dieter Steinert and Inge Weber-Newth, *Labour and Love. Deutsche in Grossbritannien nach dem Zweiten Weltkrieg* (Osnabrück: secolo Verlag, 2000).

Peter Stirk, *The Politics of Military Occupation* (Edinburgh: Edinburgh University Press, 2009).

Arnold Sywottek, 'Verständigung mit den "Engländern" nach dem Zweiten Weltkrieg. Zu einem noch ungeschriebenen Kapitel der "Vielvölkerstadt" Hamburg', in Frank Otto and Thilo Schulz (eds), *Großbritannien und Deutschland: gesellschaftliche, kulturelle und politische Beziehungen im 19. und 20. Jahrhundert* (Rheinfelden: Schäuble Verlag, 1999), pp. 149–159.

Frederick Taylor, *Exorcising Hitler: The Occupation and Denazification of Germany* (London: Bloomsbury, 2011).

Jochen Thies, '"What Is Going on in Germany?" Britische Militärverwaltung in Deutschland 1945–6', in Claus Scharf and Hans-Jürgen Schröder (eds), *Die Deutschlandpolitik Grossbritanniens und die Britische Zone* (Wiesbaden: Franz Steiner Verlag, 1979), pp. 29–50.

Michael Thomas, *Deutschland, England über alles, Rückkehr als britische Besatzungsoffizier* (Berlin: Siedler Verlag, 1984).

Isabelle Tombs, 'The Victory of Socialist "Vansittartism": Labour and the German Question, 1941–1945', *Twentieth Century British History*, Vol. 7 (1996), pp. 287–309.

Günter J. Trittel, *Hunger und Politik: Die Ernährungskrise in der Bizone (1945–1949)*, (Frankfurt and New York: Campus Verlag, 1990).

Ian D. Turner (ed.), *Reconstruction in Post-War Germany: British Occupation Policy and the Western Zones 1945–1955* (Oxford: Berg Publishers Ltd, 1989).

Robert Vansittart, *Black Record* (London: Hamish Hamilton, 1941).

D.C. Watt, *Britain Looks to Germany: A Study of British Opinion and Policy towards Germany since 1945* (London: Oswald Wolff, 1965).

Inge Weber-Newth, 'Bilateral Relations: British Soldiers and German Women', in Louise Ryan and Wendy Webster (eds), *Gendering Migration: Masculinity, Femininity and Ethnicity in Post-War Britain* (Aldershot: Ashgate, 2008), pp. 53–70.

Cecil Weir, *Civilian Assignment* (London: Methuen & Co, 1953).

Bernd Weisbrod, 'Eine ganz unamerikanische Tante: Die BBC und der nationale Medienstil in der Nachkriegszeit', in Belinda Davis, Thomas Lindenburger and Michael Wildt (eds), *Alltag, Erfahrung, Eigensinn* (Frankfurt and New York: Campus Verlag, 2008).

Michael Wildt, *Der Traum vom Sattwerden: Hunger und Protest, Schwarzmarkt und Selbsthilfe in Hamburg 1945–1948* (Hamburg: VSA Verlag, 1986).

David Williamson, *A Most Diplomatic General: The Life of General Lord Robertson of Oakridge* (London and Washington: Brasseys, 1996).

David Williamson, *The British in Germany 1918–1930: The Reluctant Occupiers* (New York and Oxford: Berg, 1991).

F. Roy Willis, *The French in Germany: 1945–1949* (Stanford, CA: Stanford University Press, 1962).

Index

Note: Page references with the letters 'f' and 'n' refer to figures and notes, respectively.

Printed in Great Britain
by Amazon

62496275R00165